RETREAT FROM GLORY

by R·H·Bruce Lockhart

GARDEN CITY PUBLISHING CO., INC.
New York   1938

COPYRIGHT, 1934, BY R. H. BRUCE LOCKHART

All rights reserved. This book, or parts thereof, must
not be reproduced in any form without permission.

MANUFACTURED IN THE UNITED STATES OF AMERICA
CL

BOOK ONE

HEROES' HOMECOMING

"And when the storm of war is gone,
Enjoy the peace your valour won."
—AMERICAN PATRIOTIC SONG.

CHAPTER ONE

IT was under grey clouds that our train steamed out of Russian territory on that October afternoon of 1918. It was a sky more attuned to mourning than to rejoicing. And after the first emotional relief as we passed from the shadow of death into safety my own thoughts were sober and overshadowed with regret. Retrospection rather than anticipation was my mood.

For fifty-six hours our little train-load of British and French officials and refugees from Moscow was held up at Bieloostroff, the Russian frontier-station of the Finnish boundary. My mind went back to our last phase in Russia. Most of us had been arrested immediately after the attempt on Lenin's life on August 31st, when the Social-revolutionary woman called "Dora" Kaplan had fired two shots at him point-blank as he was leaving the Michelson factory. Most of us had spent a month or more in prison. I, as Head of the Special British Mission to the Bolsheviks, had been singled out as the ring-leader in an alleged plot to murder the chief Bolsheviks and had been honoured with solitary confinement in the Kremlin. For some days my fate had hung in the balance, while the Allied and neutral governments worked feverishly for my release. Finally, under an agreement negotiated by the Scandinavian Governments, we had been released in exchange for Litvinoff and other Russian Bolsheviks in England. We had left Moscow on October 1st under a guard of Lettish soldiers.

Now had come this trying delay at Bieloostroff, where the Bolsheviks had refused to let us go until they were certain that Litvinoff had left England. We had tried to appear unconcerned, but the plain truth is that this last-minute hold-up with freedom actually in sight had been a greater strain than even the long weeks of imprisonment. Our nerves were as taut as an overstretched violin string. Tempers were frayed.

Then, after innumerable telephone calls to Moscow, the Station Commandant came forward and told us that our train would leave immediately. We were free—free to go home, free from further fighting. The war in the West was as good as over. To the majority of our party it meant the end of all their troubles. Their emotional reaction expressed itself in a desire for decent food. At Riihimäki the Finns had prepared a sumptuous meal for us with white bread and butter and lager beer and a hundred other delicacies which we had not tasted for months. I do not know what I ate. I am not sure that I ate at all. All I remember is the smell of oranges—oranges which our party had bought up at the station restaurant and the pungent odour of which pervaded the whole train.

Now that the tension was past, I did not share the exultation of my colleagues. Regret at leaving Russia and remorse for my own failure dominated my thoughts, and I was not even certain that I wished to go home.

I was thirty-one. I had gone at the end of 1911 as Vice-Consul to Moscow, where fortune had favoured me marvellously. At the end of 1914 my Consul-General had been forced to return to England on sick leave, and for three years I had been left in charge of a post which because of the war had acquired more importance than many Legations. I had worked with all my energy. I had been in close touch with the Liberal and revolutionary leaders. Then, soon after the Bolshevik revolution and the withdrawal of the British Ambassador, I had been appointed unofficial British representative to the Bolshevik Government. For six hectic months I had lived cheek by jowl with the Bolshevik leaders. For weeks on end I had negotiated with Lenin, Trotsky, Chicherin, Radek, Karachan, and other important members of the Party. As a realist I had striven hard for an understanding with the new rulers of Russia. I had made myself very unpopular at home. I had been labelled as a pro-Bolshevik.

When the Allies had decided to intervene with armed force against the Soviet Government, I had made an unconvincing volte face and had done my best to assist the intervention. The Allies had landed troops at Archangel without giving me sufficient time to ensure the safe departure of the British officials. We had been caught like rats in a trap. Then had come the ridiculous charge of complicity in the plot to murder Lenin. It had been followed by my arrest, release, re-arrest, and, finally, imprisonment. Politically, I had fallen between the stools of recognition and intervention, and on my return home I knew that I could not avoid the charge of inconsistency. The interventionists would never forgive me for my advocacy of an understanding with the Bolsheviks. To those British Radicals who believed in the blessings of the glorious Russian revolution, I should always be suspect.

There was a more serious cloud over my chances of happiness. There was Moura. During those eight feverish months, when, shut off from all contact with the outside world, I had tried to obtain an advantage for my country from an impossible situation, she had been everything to me. These were exceptional times, when life was the cheapest of all commodities, and when no one could see twenty-four hours ahead. We had flouted all conventions. We had gone everywhere together, sharing our dangers and our pleasures during a period in which months were equivalent to years. On the occasion of my first arrest, Moura had been arrested with me. I had been allowed to go immediately, but Moura had been kept. I had secured her release at the cost of my own re-arrest. During my imprisonment she had visited me as often as she could obtain permission, had brought me books and clothes and tobacco, had written me every day brave, hopeful letters, which, although they had to pass the vigilant eyes of the Cheka censors, had saved me from despair. Had this cataclysm of our arrest not intervened, I think I would have stayed in Russia for ever. Now we had been forcibly torn apart. I had been sent out of Russia under an armed escort. I had left Moura behind. For all I knew I might never see her again.

As I thought of the future, there was a leaden feeling in my heart. The story of our unofficial romance had already been recorded in the archives of the Foreign Office. Soon my enemies at home would see that it was known to wider circles. There would be unpleasant explanations to make to my parents, to my wife, and to my relations. My grandmother, who was the prop of my financial existence, would cross-examine me. She would be more formidable and more successful than the professional investigators of the Cheka. There would be a lecture, richly illustrated with Biblical metaphors, on the inevitable consequences of sowing in the flesh. On the whole, I could expect little joy from my homecoming and no hope of advancement from the Foreign Office.

I had a foretaste of the kind of attack which I should have to face in England in the attitude of certain British refugees on the train. In Moscow, where I had been the sole link between the British Government and the Bolsheviks, the richer members of our colony, who had not previously left Moscow, had bombarded me with requests for the protection of their property and even of their lives. I had done my ineffectual best to help them. In most cases their attitude had been ingratiating and suppliant. Now all this had changed. With personal liberty had come carping criticism, and in me they found the scapegoat for their personal misfortunes. There was one elderly man, who had leant heavily on my support and who owed to me the retention of his luxurious flat and such other minor amenities as are sometimes obtainable even in the most violent of revolutions. No sooner had we crossed the Finnish frontier than his previous timidity was replaced by an arrogant self-confidence. His chest swelled. In the corridor I heard stray tags of vehement conversation in which he announced loudly what the Allies would do with these Bolshevik bandits and expressed his hope that the British Government would deal sternly with those officials who had coquetted with the enemies of capitalism. His only greeting to me was: "Well, you've made a nice mess of things." At a later stage of my journey a Foreign Office messenger denounced me violently as a Bolshevik. I understood their attitude. They were convinced that the intervention would be a success and that within a few weeks the Allied and White Russian troops would be in Moscow. From the beginning I had realised that from the manner in which it had been launched the intervention was doomed to failure. I bore no malice, then. I bear no malice to-day. But at the time their attitude did nothing to alleviate the protracted monotony of the journey home or to relieve my mental anguish.

For once the birches and firs, the hills and streams, of Northern Sweden, which on previous occasions had reminded me so vividly of Scotland, of my own care-free youth, and of all that I liked best in life, brought neither peace nor consolation. In Scotland each tree, each pool, was like a personal friend, unchanging and unchangeable. Here they were as cold and distant as a stranger. By a curious psychological perversion I felt more like an exile leaving home than a returning prodigal. Through my mind ran persistently the lines of the old Scottish song said to have been quoted later by Prince Charles Edward on leaving Scotland forever:

> *"O this is my departing time,*
> *For here no longer maun I stay.*
> *There's not a friend or foe o' mine*
> *But wishes that I were away.*
> *What I hae done frae want o' wit*
> *I never never can recall.*
> *I hope ye're all my friends as yit,*
> *Good-bye and joy be wi' you all."*

Ten years before, almost to a day, I had used them with effect in a farewell speech made on the eve of my departure from England for Malaya. Then the sentiment had been slightly artificial. Youth with adventure in its blood and the East before it has only momentary regrets. To-day, I reflected rather sadly that the war and my own perversity had played havoc with all my friendships. For the first time I was experiencing the bitterness of adverse fortune, and in an excess of self-pity I suffered.

Nevertheless, relief at my escape from death by the bullet of a Bolshevik firing-squad was not without its reaction. It took the form of sleep. During our long and tedious journey home I must have averaged sixteen hours a day. And from the time that we left Moscow it was sixteen days before we reached Aberdeen. On my first visit to Russia in 1912 the voyage had taken exactly sixty hours.

There were, of course, other diversions, and with Hicks, Hill, Lingner and Tamplin, the four surviving members of my mission, I spent hours in discussing our prison experiences and in trying to piece together a connected narrative of what had happened. Ever since that fatal night of August 31st, when the Kaplan girl had so nearly ended Lenin's life with her automatic pistol, we had been separated. The Bolshevik reaction to this attack had been an immediate raid on the various quarters of the Allied missions in St. Petersburg and Moscow. In St. Petersburg the raid had been attended by a terrible tragedy. When the Red Guards burst into the Embassy building, Cromie, our naval attaché, who had remained in St. Petersburg in order to prevent the Baltic Fleet from falling into the hands of the Germans, had tried to resist this illegal entrance. The Bolshevik Guards had shot him down and had trampled his body under their feet. During my own confinement in the Kremlin I had heard the briefest outline of this poignant drama. It was only when we all met in the train that I learnt for the first time the story of Oudendijk's courage.

Oudendijk was the Netherlands Minister to Russia. He was a little man and, like many men of small stature, he had a lion's heart. He was also one of the few diplomatists who spoke Russian. When the Bolsheviks arrested all the British officials in Moscow and St. Petersburg, he had been entrusted by the British Government with the protection of our interests. No man could have carried out his task with greater bravery or energy. As our Moscow group of prisoners was entirely separate from the St. Petersburg group, he had to spend most of his nights travelling backwards and forwards between the two capitals. Moreover, since Holland was not in a position to threaten the Bolsheviks with force, he had to rely on his own persuasiveness to secure our release. As he is a modest, retiring little man and as there was no one else at the time to tell it, his story has never been given to the world.

It was Oudendijk who obtained for Cromie an official funeral and a Christian burial. The Red Terror was then at its apogee, and at the conference of the ministers of the neutral powers, who were in charge of Allied interests, the proposal was put forward that, in order to avoid a possible scandal in the streets, the British naval attaché should be buried by night. Oudendijk, trembling with indignation, pointed out that in civilised countries only criminals were buried in this manner. He insisted on an official funeral. He carried his point both with his colleagues and with the St. Petersburg Cheka. He suffered every kind of humiliation and was kept waiting for hours like a peasant before he could gain access to the Cheka chiefs. But, by keeping his temper and by an exemplary display of firmness, he succeeded in persuading the Bolshevik officials to agree to all his demands. He arranged every detail of the funeral. He found a Scottish minister (Mr. Lombard, the official British chaplain, was in prison with the rest of us) to conduct the funeral service. He found a Union Jack to drape the coffin. He arranged a wonderful display of wreaths and, bareheaded and in uniform, himself headed the funeral procession to the cemetery.

It was an imposing procession attended by numerous residents of the British colony who had been assured of Oudendijk's protection. And there was one curious incident which throws a revealing light on the superstitious nature of the Russian peasant's mind. As the cortège filed along the Neva quay, it passed a group of dirty, ill-kept Russian destroyers tied up at the river's edge. The sailors had provided the worst elements in the Bolshevik revolution. They had murdered their officers with the most revolting cruelty. The guns of the destroyers were still trained on the streets to mow down any possible attempt at counter-revolution. Yet, in spite of the presence of Cheka agents in the procession, the Russian sailors stood to the salute, as the body of the British naval captain was being carried to its last resting-place.

In the end Oudendijk, who, incidentally, is married to an Englishwoman, secured the release of all the imprisoned British, and it was mainly due to his courage that we were at that moment able to discuss him in the comfort of a Finnish train. After my release I was never able to thank him personally for all that he did for us at great risk to his own safety, and I am glad to have this opportunity of paying my tribute to a very gallant gentleman.

I must return to our journey home. Naturally, there were many delays, and at Stockholm, where I had to face my first fusillade from the cameras of the press-photographers, I was held up for several days. The Swedes, who were in charge of the negotiations for the exchange of prisoners, would not let me leave until Litvinoff had landed in Norway.

In Stockholm, too, I was received by the late Crown Princess of Sweden, the elder daughter of the Duke of Connaught. Like other members of the British Royal family, she was interested in the fate of the Tsar and her other relations in Russia. Finally, after a formal visit to the Swedish Foreign Minister to thank him for the part his Government had played in obtaining our release, I was allowed to proceed.

Before reaching Aberdeen, I had one more adventure. In Christiania, where I arrived at the same time as Litvinoff, I received a message from him saying that he would like to see me. In spite of all that had happened, I should have gone without hesitation. Unfortunately, I received the note too late, just as my train was leaving for Bergen. We were not to meet again until fourteen years later when by a clever piece of stage management on the part of Chance we walked up the stairs of Londonderry House together with powdered flunkeys in knee-breeches lining the balustrades. The occasion was Lord Londonderry's reception for the delegates of the World Economic Conference. In a sea of diplomatic and court uniforms, Litvinoff and I were among the few present who wore ordinary evening dress.

Every British subject who gets himself embroiled in an official quarrel with a foreign government is sure of a hallelujah welcome from one section or another of the Press. Mine was fortunately tempered by the fact that the censorship was still in force, and the sleuth-hounds of Fleet Street had very little knowledge of my deeds and misdeeds. Still, the publicity was embarrassing enough. The Senior Naval Officer at Aberdeen met me as I stepped off the ship and delivered me safely into the hands of the station-master. At King's Cross reporters invaded my compartment and demanded to see the revolver with which I or some one else had shot Lenin. Photographers followed me to the Foreign Office and "snapped" me on the third floor corridor where seven years before I had played slip-catches with a tennis-ball with Guy Locock. Sir George Clerk and Don Gregory disputed the right to be my first host on English soil. The lion-hunters of Mayfair, hearing that a young man who had done something dreadfully interesting in Rustchuk, or Rostoff, or some other outlandish spot beginning with "R," bombarded me with invitations. I was "in the news" and had to be inspected. It all seemed very unreal.

Even the Foreign Office, still in the dark about what had actually happened in Moscow and quite ready to believe the worst, was anxious to know what I had done and was going to do. In Stockholm, Hicks had sounded Clive, our Chargé d'Affaires, about the reception I was likely to be given by my official chiefs. Clive's reply was soothing. "Lockhart," he said, "has nothing to fear. That young man is capable of looking after himself in any circumstances." The young man, however, had no ambition to look after himself. His one wish was to hide his head. Certainly, the high officials of the Foreign Office, who received me, were disarmingly kind and listened to my account of my adventures with polite attention. I lunched with Sir Ronald Graham, who was then acting as Permanent Under-Secretary in place of Lord Hardinge, who had broken his leg. I had tea with the gentle and rather tired-looking Sir Eric Drummond. Mr. Balfour, to whom and to Rex Leeper I owed my escape and perhaps my life, gave me two hours of his time.

Quite unwittingly I had aroused Mr. Balfour's interest. During the hectic months of my Moscow escapade he had drafted most of the telegrams to me in his own hand. When at one period there had been some question of my recall, he had minuted the suggestion with a laconic "Certainly not. This young man amuses me." While I was in my Kremlin prison, he had sent a daily message to my wife at Oxford and had written to her in his own handwriting saying that my safety was his chief pre-occupation of the moment. He was the best type of Scot, cold, courteous, but, like the trees in that magnificent avenue which faces his Whittingham home, splendidly steadfast in the fiercest storm.

How far he can be said to have succeeded as a Foreign Secretary is another matter. My interview with him was entertaining but curious. Although I had brought back a mass of new material from Russia, he showed little interest in the actual situation. Such matters as the relative strength of the Bolshevik and White armies were not mentioned. It was as one philosopher to another that Lenin appealed to him, and, seated with crossed legs and with the fingers of his two hands making an arch, he questioned me at great length, and with considerable knowledge, on the ideology of Bolshevism. Fortunately, I knew something of the subject, and I was able to keep my end up in a searching cross-examination. Although very gentle and not at all awe-inspiring, he was difficult to talk to, if only because there were long intervals during which he sat in silent reflection, with the sun shining on his white locks, before he quietly delivered another: "Very interesting, Mr. Lockhart, but..." Then would follow a further development of the question which I had just answered. When, after a further prolonged silence, I realised that the interview was ended, I rose from my chair and tried to thank him for the part he had played in securing my release.

"I'm more grateful to you than I can say, sir," I stammered emotionally. "I'm afraid I've given you a tremendous lot of trouble."

For a moment he seemed a little embarrassed and a far-away look came into his eyes. Then he smiled very pleasantly.

"Trouble," he said. "I'm used to trouble. I'm very glad to see you alive."

We shook hands, and I walked away. When I was at the door, he called me back.

"You will, of course, write a report on the present situation in Russia. I should like to read it. It should be very interesting."

I saw him only once again. Exactly a year later I passed him, a tall, handsome figure, with slightly drooping shoulders and his hands holding the lapels of his coat, as he was walking up the Haymarket. I raised my hat. By some miracle he recognised me and stopped. "Mr. Lockhart," he said, "I am disappointed in your Bolshevik friends. They have gone back on all their principles." While I was trying to evolve a wise-crack answer, he had passed on.

There were, however, others, who were not so magnanimous as Mr. Balfour. I had been the playboy of Mr. Lloyd George and Lord Milner, and with the end of the war the permanent officials were reasserting their authority. In the Foreign Office there were several who held strong views about the impropriety of raising junior vice-consuls to positions of even semi-official responsibility. I had committed the unforgivable sin. I was a bumptious schoolboy who had intrigued with the Prime Minister behind the Foreign Office's back. The charge was devoid of all truth, but the label stuck, and I confess that this attitude hurt me.

If the fact that my special mission to Russia in 1918 had been decided by the War Cabinet and not by the Foreign Office had made me certain enemies, there was a more serious bar to my official prospects. The plain truth was that Russia was now out of the picture. All eyes and all ambitions were fixed on Paris, and in every Government department the scramble for places at the Peace Conference had already begun. My own little star of glory had risen in Russia. Ten days in London convinced me very quickly that it had set and that I should have some difficulty in finding another job. Generals were already reverting to captains. It was quite clear that I had little to look forward to except a return to my pre-war humdrum existence as a junior Consular officer.

Fortified by this knowledge, I should have put Russia out of my mind and enjoyed the long leave to which I was entitled. Instead, I continued to hang about London. From a window in the Foreign Office I watched the Armistice Day celebrations on November 11th and at 11 o'clock saw Mr. Lloyd George emerge from 10 Downing Street to announce the final triumph of the Allied arms. Soon Mr. Balfour arrived at the Foreign Office and made a little speech which was appropriately cheered by the lady typists. Downing Street was dignified and decorous. It was different when I passed into Whitehall. Here the Juggernaut of

Victory had already started, and the crowd, good-humoured but riotously intoxicated, had taken command of every available vehicle from the fleet of the London General Omnibus Company to the smallest hawker's barrow. As I drifted with the tide of sweating humanity into Trafalgar Square, there was renewed cheering. To-day, the one impression which remains in my mind of that emotional scene is of a man's collar. It was a very low collar round the largest neck in England. It looked very far off and slightly ridiculous. Like a thin white circle it crowned the torso of Sir Eric Geddes suitably perched opposite Lord Nelson on a lofty Admiralty scaffolding, from which he received the nation's tribute to the Navy.

In the evening I went to the Russian ballet at the Coliseum. It was a psychological mistake. The music, faintly punctuated by the raucous cheering from Trafalgar Square, and the dancers themselves took my thoughts back to Moscow. Russia had no place in the Allied triumph. The part she had played in the first months of the war had been forgotten. She was now almost as unpopular as the hated Teutons whose Kaiser was being burnt in effigy. Irritated and alone, I went back into the streets to adjust my melancholy to the national jubilation. I found the task beyond my powers. I had spent most of my life outside of England. There were half-a-dozen European capitals that I knew much better than London. In a very real sense I was a stranger in my own country. I, too, had no part in the national celebrations. By the bonfire in Trafalgar Square I made an examination of my conscience in the approved fashion of the moment. "What did you do in the Great War?" I could find no satisfactory answer. The joy-riding and the flag-waving around me reminded me very forcibly of a similar undirected energy in the streets of Moscow in the first hours of the first Russian revolution. It was a perplexing evening.

My melancholy vanished with the morning. Before I could retreat from Whitehall, there was a deal of work to be done. I had to wind up the financial accounts of my mission—a task complicated by the fact that before my arrest I had been forced to destroy all my archives. I had, too, my report to write for Mr.

Balfour. I produced an eight-page memorandum with a map which was printed and circulated to the Cabinet. To-day, I should not like to publish my conclusions. They were a rather feeble attempt to adapt my views to those which I believed were popular in Whitehall. But as regards the actual situation in Russia itself the report stands the test of fifteen years remarkably well. I stressed the strength of the Bolshevik movement and the weakness of all the opposition Parties. Above all, I pointed out the futility and inevitable failure of an intervention which relied merely on White Russian bayonets and Allied money and which was not supported by strong Allied forces. I was shown the official comments on my masterpiece. Lord Hardinge's was an H. Lord Robert Cecil, preoccupied with Welsh Disestablishment and his forthcoming resignation, found it "very interesting." Mr. Balfour's neat handwriting summed it up as "a very able document whatever one may think of the conclusions." Like most official reports my memorandum altered no opinions. Mr. Lloyd George was already playing with the idea of meeting the Bolsheviks face to face at Prinkipo. Already Mr. Winston Churchill saw himself riding into Moscow on a White Russian horse. This conflict of views was reflected in every section and family of the community.

My report, however, brought me one compensation. One day soon after its publication I was stopped on the stairs of the Foreign Office by a young man with a wandering tie, rather baggy trousers, and a magnificent head. His whole face lit up most attractively, as he introduced himself. "You're Lockhart, aren't you?" he said in a pleasant well-modulated voice. "I want to tell you how much I enjoyed your report. It's one of the best official documents I've ever read." It was my first meeting with Harold Nicolson. At that time he was the admiration and the envy of every young man connected with the Foreign Office. Brilliant, self-reliant, clear-headed, he was a glutton for work, and his equanimity, his good temper, and his amazing quickness provided in times of storm a rock behind which even Lord Curzon was not too proud to shelter. Even in a service in which safety first is the golden path to promotion, he seemed marked out for a dazzling career.

Since then we have become friends. Day in, day out, we have worked together in conditions which would try the patience of a Gandhi, and in an atmosphere which might easily engender feelings of envy and mistrust. Yet never once have I seen even a frown of irritation disturb his serenity. In his "Essays in Biography," Mr. J. Maynard Keynes ascribes to us a common literary ancestor as a minor illustration of the theory of hereditary ability. In reality we are the complete opposite of each other. Harold is intellectually the most honest man I know. My mental cowardice causes him real pain. I am an egotist. He is supremely unselfish with a capacity for friendship that is rare in the world to-day. I would sooner go to him in trouble—or in triumph, which is a more difficult test—than to almost any man.

Yet he lies heavy on my conscience. It was I who first suggested his descent from diplomacy into Fleet Street. It was I who travelled to Berlin to bear him Lord Beaverbrook's invitation to join the *Evening Standard*. Harold is strong enough to accept the full responsibility for his own decision. But at a time when government in England has sunk to the lowest ebb of mediocrity I feel a genuine regret in the reflection that, indirectly, I have been responsible for depriving the Foreign Office of its ideal Permanent Secretary.

CHAPTER TWO

THERE were other exaltations to which the notoriety of my escape raised me. I was invited to Kensington Palace to take tea with Princess Beatrice and to tell her the details of the murder of the Imperial family. It was a rather trying ordeal. I had to answer a large number of questions and, as I was weak in my knowledge of the inter-relationship of European royalties, I floundered badly. Perhaps it was the Victorian background of chintz and tea-cake which unnerved me. At any rate, I retired in some confusion, determined that in future the Almanach de Gotha should have an honoured place among my desk-books.

My hour's audience with the King at Buckingham Palace was a much less trying affair. As, piloted by Lord Cromer, I made my way along the corridor, a sudden realisation of the awful pungency of mothball made me break into a cold sweat. The odour came from my morning-coat, which had been in store for a year. His Majesty, however, soon made me feel at ease. At Kensington Palace I had to give explanations and to tell the story of my Russian adventure. In the King's study King George himself helped me out. He had read every telegram and despatch on the Russian situation and showed a remarkable understanding both of the causes and of the effects of the revolution. His questions were put in the form of statements—recapitulations of his own views—which required a simple confirmation or contradiction. His memory was excellent. With the possible exception of Lord Milner he was better informed and better documented about Russia than any of his Ministers.

Lord Milner, who had been mainly responsible for the despatch of my mission to Russia, I saw frequently. Doubtless, I had let him down badly, but my failure in no way altered the friendliness of his attitude towards me. Although overwhelmed with work, he invited me frequently to his house in Little College Street, listened to my troubles with unfailing good-humour and an occasional chuckle, gave me the best of advice, and did much to restore my shaken confidence by asking me to write various memoranda on Russia for his personal use. His interest in my career lasted until his death in 1925, and, whenever I came to England, I never failed to receive an invitation to lunch or dine alone with him and talk things over. His capacity for sympathy with youthful ambitions and youthful foibles was infinite. Of all the great figures in public life whom I have ever met he was the most completely free from any thought of self.

On the other hand, he was very far from being an out-and-out capitalist. Service to the state and to the Empire was his highest ideal, and individual pursuit of purely selfish ends, whether capitalist or demagogic, never failed to provoke his condemnation. I remember very vividly dining with him at Brooks's Club just before the Victory election, which was to give to Mr. Lloyd George the majority he wanted and at the same time to undermine the foundations of his political power. Lord Milner had no use for the slogans with which that election was won. Ephemeral triumphs had no place in his scheme of things, and he expressed himself very forcibly on the folly of driving Germany to desperation. The "Hang the Kaiser" and "Squeezing the lemon till the pips squeaked" talk was repugnant to his common-sense. "How can we expect the Germans to pay anything," he said, "if we take away with one stroke all their means of payment?" He was looking ten years ahead, and he predicted with remarkable accuracy what would be the inevitable consequences of Mr. Lloyd George's surrender to the hysteria of victory. I have always believed that, as in the case of President Wilson, Mr. Lloyd George's position would have been very much stronger if he had never gone to Paris and had been content to leave the leadership of the British Delegation in the hands of Lord Milner. Certainly, we should have had a better peace. Lord Milner was a statesman detached from the trammels of Party. Mr. Lloyd George, who, admittedly, saw more clearly and did better at Versailles than any other politician might have done, was bound to the chariot of vote-catching. And, whatever Labour may say to-day in favour of universal suffrage, the terms of the Peace Treaty were dictated by the ignorant and victory-mad electors who voted for the "Hang the Kaiser" and the impossible Reparations policy in December, 1918.

Right over Christmas and well into January I continued to be in demand among the politically-minded as a kind of star turn on Russia. I sang for my supper, which means that I drank too much champagne, told the story of my arrest and imprisonment, and gave first-hand descriptions of the Bolshevik leaders. This interest seems strange to-day, but at that time I was almost the only Englishman and certainly the only English official who had ever seen the Bolshevik leaders face to face. True, my glory soon wore thin. But I lunched and dined with Sir Samuel and Lady Maud Hoare and in a moment of expansive exuberance presented them with possibly the only extant letter written by Lenin in his own handwriting in English. I sipped the excellent claret of the Reform Club and listened with appropriate gravity to the views of Mr. H. A. L. Fisher on intervention. They were sound views. He was opposed to intervention on principle and illustrated his principle by examples from history. I was asked to stay at Cliveden to address Lady Astor's wounded soldiers on Bolshevism, and went. It was an amusing week-end for every one except the soldiers. The guests were heterogeneous enough to remind me of a Russian country-house. They came and went with a bewildering rapidity. There was Alfred Zimmern, then a temporary clerk in the Foreign Office and an Oxford Don. Later, when the disillusionment of victory had set in, Mr. Harold Begbie ran him as a stunt. In the *News Chronicle* and the *Daily Express* and, I think, even the *Times* a photograph used to appear in the advertisement columns with the caption: "The Man Who Should Be England's Prime Minister. Do You Know Him?" I did. It took me some time to believe my eyes. The portrait was undoubtedly that of the brilliant but meek and gentle Zimmern. Then he was busily trying to circumvent the dangers of a peace of revenge.

Finance was represented by Major Rex Benson. There were

pram-loads of children. Lastly, there were Mr. and Mrs. J. H. Thomas, who were then living in a small house on the Astor estate.

Since that day I have come into contact with Mr. Thomas's political meteor on several occasions. I have seen him in his triumphs and in his defeats. I have seen him in sorrow and in anger. And always I have admired his courage and his self-righteousness. He could be a minister in no other country but England or an English dominion. This stricture, which applies to two-thirds of every Conservative and Labour cabinet in this country, is no reflection on Mr. Thomas's merits. It is merely an illustration of the fact that common sense and a shrewd judgment of human nature will take a man farther in English politics than all the brains in the world. And like every Celt Mr. Thomas knows his Englishman.

On that Sunday afternoon I went for a long walk with him and, while I admired the statuary on the terrace, he expressed himself forcibly about Russia and about things at home. He was in a pessimistic mood, prophesied trouble within two months, and was obviously afraid of Bolshevism in England. His apprehensions in no way affected his courage, and in the evening, when I gave my address to the soldiers, he presided and at the end delivered a fiery anti-Bolshevik attack in which he declared that "bad as was the old régime in Russia the new one was infinitely worse." He repeated the statement six weeks later in the House of Commons.

I had other flirtations with Labour. Soon after my return I lunched with those gentle Crusaders of Socialism, Mr. and Mrs. Sidney Webb, at their house in Grosvenor Road. I liked them and admired their enthusiasm, their erudition, and their ordered minds. The conversation, entirely confined to Russia, reminded me of a scene outside the excess luggage office of a railway station. I put my various bundles of knowledge on the scales. Mr. Webb weighed them, and from a vast cabinet of labels Mrs. Webb attached the appropriate one to each package. I give my diary account of that luncheon exactly as I wrote it at the time. "Lunched with the Webbs. With his straggling beard and unkempt hair he is marvellously like one of Chehoff's professors. She is very charming, but a little dogmatic. Talked much about Bolshevism. Webb is convinced Bolshevism must fail economically and thinks Lenin can know nothing of economics. I wish I could feel as sure about it as he does."

To-day, the Webbs are still crusading, still labelling. True, the labels have changed. Mr. Webb has become Lord Passfield, lives in Hampshire, and accepts Stalin as an economist. Mrs. Webb is still Mrs. Webb, lives in Hampshire, and is an even stronger believer in Stalin than is her husband. But their hearts have not changed. They are still the same kindly, generous devoted couple that they have always been.

I worshipped, too, for a short time at the feet of Mr. Cole, then labelled as a revolutionary, but in reality the most pacifist of Mensheviks, and renewed my acquaintance with Mr. Arthur Henderson, whom I had piloted round Moscow during his famous Russian visit of 1917. I had several talks with him at the Labour Party headquarters at 33, Eccleston Square. It is difficult for any one to dislike Mr. Henderson. In spite of a pontifical manner, he is essentially a man of peace and goodwill. He is, too, or was, no mean propagandist for his Party. Adroitly he cast a Labour fly before my hungry mouth. Labour wanted young men who knew something about foreign affairs. There was a great work to do for peace in Europe. A constituency could be found. I nearly rose. I asked for time to consider my position, and during the interval fate intervened. Somewhat foolishly I had accepted an invitation to give a public lecture on the Russian situation. The Foreign Office saw no objection and even thought that my eloquence might do some good. Even more foolishly I agreed to their perhaps natural condition that no questions should be permitted or answered at the lecture.

I took immense pains over the preparation of that lecture. I had a vast amount of material that was quite new to an English audience. When I had completed my notes, I was smugly satisfied and set out with something of my old confidence for King's College where I was to deliver my lecture. When I arrived, I found a packed hall. Lord Carnock, Harold Nicolson's father, was to have taken the chair. Fortunately for his peace of mind, indisposition prevented him from being present, and his place was taken by Sir Bernard Mallet. During my lecture I had no trouble. Indeed, there was no cause. My theme was the rise to power of the Bolsheviks with some account of their early history and a series of strictly accurate and unsensational pen-portraits of the leaders. I could have delivered the lecture in Moscow without undue dissent. The fireworks began after I had finished. A suspiciously polite young man at the back at once rose and asked if he might put a question. In gentle tones Sir Bernard Mallet explained that, as I was still an official, I could answer no questions. Then the organised Communist band at the back opened its bombardment. They knew nothing about their Russian masters. In my lecture they had found little into which they could put their teeth. But they had come to raise hell. Here was their opportunity. Insulting questions were hurled at me in a volley. The dominant one was a hoarse chant repeated *ad nauseam:* "Did you or did you not plot the murder of Lenin?"

The questions were idiotic. I could have answered them without difficulty. But in my inexperience I felt bound to observe my instructions, and, as I sat silent, the storm grew in violence. One of the rowdiest of my interrupters was a burly curate who before the war had been a tutor in Moscow. He had been in trouble, and more than once I had rescued him from an awkward predicament. He, too, was the ringleader in the mild scrapping which began between Communist and anti-Communist. This brought my ordeal to a close. As the rumpus swelled, the dowagers and respectable old gentlemen in front scuttled to the main exit, and in the confusion I was piloted safely out of the hall by a side-door.

Curiously enough, I delivered exactly the same lecture three months later to a Glasgow audience composed mainly of Clydesiders. On that occasion I was allowed to answer questions. They were intelligent questions, and I answered them frankly. I had an excellent reception.

The stupidity of the King's College performance filled me with disgust. It had, however, two beneficial results. It was followed by an attack of tonsilitis and by my first visit for several years from an English doctor, who gave a bad report of my general health. The strain of my Russian experiences was now beginning to make itself felt. As always in such cases the Foreign Office was suitably sympathetic, and I retired to the country on indefinite leave. My departure disturbed the development of my negotiations with Mr. Henderson and killed the germs of my Parliamentary ambitions. They have never troubled me since.

CHAPTER THREE

MY vegetation in the country lasted nearly a year. It can be divided into two periods: one of acute mental and physical discomfort and the other of pleasant relaxation and gradual return to health. A throat and nasal operation, which I underwent at this time, had left me depressed and a victim of nerves, and my doctor had ordered me complete rest. I went with my wife to Bexhill to recuperate and stayed there four months. It was an unsatisfactory choice. But there was no alternative. I had been home to my parents' house at Sandhurst for Christmas, but the place was full of ghosts. My favourite brother had been killed at Loos. Another brother, now Military Attaché at Kabul, was still in hospital suffering agonies from a suppurating wound received in Mesopotamia. My mother, whom war and illness had aged, had never got over the shock of my brother's death. She had become an ardent pacifist, bitter against the generals, the politicians and the war-mongers in the Press. She had lost much of her interest in life, and, although she was as kind to me and as indulgent to my failings as ever, I fancied I could always see in her eyes a non-existent look of reproach, a reflection of my own consciousness that the best had been taken and the worst left behind. In my father the change was more physical. As the headmaster of a once successful preparatory school he always had one fault: a foolish persistence to live up to the maxim "If you want a thing well done, do it yourself." The war had exaggerated this tendency. In normal circumstances he would have retired with a competence in 1918. During and after the war he "carried on," keeping his fees at pre-war level when other schools were raising theirs. Under the strain his once powerful frame had shrunk. The broad shoulders drooped. The hair was greyer. But the mind was as vigorous and as tolerant as ever. Neither war nor any other calamity could undermine that fortress of understanding or unbalance the character of a man whose whole life has been a model of self-denial and self-discipline.

My grandmother I had not seen. She was in Scotland. But she had heard of my failure, and I had received one of her famous epistles to the Ephesians. I did my best to be gay. I made light of my grandmother's condemnation by staging an elaborate Christmas charade, in which she was featured cutting me out of her will. It was a false frivolity, as false as my own presence in that home, where every one had borne his or her burden without flinching and without hope of reward.

My wife treated me as a nerve-shattered invalid who had escaped from the mad-house of Russia. She did her best to protect me from the reporters who wished to make a stunt out of my prison experiences and from the busybodies who sought to enlist my services for their schemes for the regeneration of Russia. For her, too, my homecoming brought its full measure of bitterness. With my fatal habit of postponing trouble I had told her nothing of my private life during that last year in Russia. She had met me on my arrival in London. She asked no questions. I gave no explanations. But her feminine instinct told her everything, and what she did not know in the way of detail kind friends were soon to tell her. Assuredly, it is the cowards who cause the greatest unhappiness in life.

Bexhill was little better. I had very little money, and we lived in furnished rooms. The place was full of retired officers and civilians, all intent on forgetting the war. To-day, economic duress and the world slump have forced the English to take some interest in foreign affairs. Then nobody cared what was happening at Versailles. "Make the blighters pay," said the ex-colonels and majors. Then they went off to play golf or to dance with the "flappers" at the Sackville. I golfed with them. What I wanted most was to put the past out of my mind. In the end I succeeded, but there was one period at this time when, if any one mentioned

Russia, I used to tremble as with ague and tears would well up in my eyes.

True, I dabbled a little in journalism—mainly in order to pay my rent. I wrote a long article for the Round Table on Bolshevik aims and ideals, and I sold to the *Times* for a ridiculously low sum a series of four articles entitled "Bolshevik Portraits" which contained the first English record of the lives and characteristics of the new Russian leaders. This apart, I abandoned practically every form of intellectual life, turned down a profitable proposition of a lecture tour in America, and left most of my letters unanswered. My only form of work at this period was an attempt to learn Italian. I have a certain gift for languages and have more or less mastered seven. I have learnt them through contact with the natives and not from books. I have never lived in Italy, but, whenever I am bored in my life, I take up an Italian grammar. Obviously my boredom cannot last very long. My knowledge of Italian has never progressed beyond the stage: "Dov' è la ritirata?"

If my mind rusted, my golf and my health improved. I reduced my handicap from thirteen to three, won the Bexhill Town Cup, and spent most of my money on endeavouring to take on Fred Robson, then the professional at Cooden Beach and one of the best fellows in the world, on my official handicap.

From time to time, too, I saw my friends who had been connected with me in Russian affairs. Will Hicks and his charming Russian wife were occasional visitors. In March my old friend, Rex Leeper, of the Foreign Office, came to spend a week-end. He brought me news of Russia and a first-rate story of Litvinoff. When Litvinoff had been bundled out of the country in exchange for me, he had left his English wife, a niece of the late Sir Sidney Low, in England. She was to follow later with her child. Litvinoff, already raised to the dignity of Assistant Commissar of Foreign Affairs in Moscow, was showing a natural interest in the safe transport of his family to Russia and had been telegraphing to Mrs. Litvinoff a whole series of domestic instructions about the journey. His telegrams contained frequent reference to an English perambulator. This was, of course, jam to the wise men of our intelligence service whose duty it is to seek the improbable in the obvious. Here was a very simple case. The Bolsheviks were as yet inexperienced in the art of ciphering. Obviously, these frequent references to a perambulator contained some cryptic message threatening the safety and existence of the British Empire. The intercepted telegrams with the word "pram" neatly encircled with a blue pencil line were brought to Leeper for further elucidation. When he suggested that the simplest interpretation might be the literal one, the wise men smiled indulgently. In the end, however, Mrs. Litvinoff was allowed to depart unmolested and to take her perambulator with her. Perhaps I malign our professional intelligence experts. In those days they were recruited mainly from the ranks of the successful novelists!

I made occasional deviations from my rule not to leave my bourgeois fastness in Bexhill. One day I returned from golf to luncheon to find my buxom landlady in a state of exasperation. The telephone had rung seven times in the last hour. "Would I ring Leatherhead 324? Lord Beaverbrook's secretary wanted to speak to me." I have an instinctive dread of the telephone. But my curiosity was aroused. No one had ever wanted me so insistently before. I rang Leatherhead 324. "This is Lockhart," I said. "I understand that Lord Beaverbrook's secretary wished to speak to me." "Is that Mr. Lockhart speaking?" I had already said so, but I confirmed my identity with a gentle "yes." "One minute, sir." This time another voice took up the refrain: "Is that Mr. Lockhart speaking?" It was. Would I lunch with Lord Beaverbrook at Cherkley the next day? Perhaps it was my innate craving for adventure or perhaps that strange influence which radiates from the Cherkley telephone and which makes it almost impossible for any one to say "no" even to Lord Beaverbrook's secretary. At any rate, before I had time to reflect, I had accepted.

The next day, as Lord Beaverbrook's car carried me down the long Cherkley drive, I felt completely at my ease. I had left London in a fog. Here the sun was shining. I rang the bell and waited. A footman came, took my name, and left me. This time I waited longer. Then the footman returned accompanied by the butler. His eyebrows arched politely. "Mr. Lockhart?" he asked. This time I nodded, and, the nod being approved, I was piloted through a front hall, through a central hall, through a large living-room with a piano at one end, out on to a terrace. There, facing the most beautiful view in the South of England and huddled up in a chair with a rug around his knees, sat a little man in an old blue suit. At first sight he seemed all head. His hair was touzled, and a long wisp hung across his forehead. He looked very pale. He was, in fact, desperately ill, suffering from a peculiar affection of the throat. A tall, bearded man with rather fierce magnetic eyes stood by his side. As I was announced, the heavily lined face of the little man in the chair lit up with a pleasing smile. He jerked himself slightly forward.

"You're Lockhart," he said. "I'm glad to see you. I read your telegrams while you were in Russia. I liked the way you stuck to your guns in Moscow."

I hadn't, but I felt flattered. The man had charm. He relapsed into silence, cocking his head on one side and taking me in with a series of rapid glances. He gave another jerk. "You know John, of course?" I didn't.

During luncheon I discovered from the questions which were asked him about his Peace Conference portraits that the bearded man was Augustus John. The rest of luncheon was a machine-gun fusillade of questions directed by my Lord Beaverbrook against myself. He was opposed to intervention. The questions were forceful and direct. I suppose my answers must have satisfied him, for as I was leaving he took me aside.

"What are you going to do? Government service won't offer you much now. Ever thought of journalism?"

I shook my head. That night I made the following entry in my diary: "Met Beaverbrook: a Rolls-Royce brain in a Ford body." There was no reference to journalism. Had any one suggested to me that within ten years I should be working for Lord Beaverbrook in Shoe Lane I should have laughed.

The truth is that, although my prospects were uncertain, I was not worrying very much about my future. I have one asset which has helped me in the various crises of my life. I never anticipate trouble. There was, too, Lord Milner. Just about this time he wrote me this letter.

Private.

Colonial Office,
Downing Street, S.W.1.
15th March, 1919.

My Dear Lockhart,

I am sorry to have been so long in answering your letter of the 3rd March. Thanks for sending me the article on Bolshevik Aims and Ideals.

Seeing in your letter that you would return to London about the 20th March, I was very much looking forward to seeing you soon. Unfortunately I am compelled to return to Paris again immediately. I very much dislike this. I hate being there and am quite out of sympathy with the line which the peace negotiations are taking, but once I get back there it is always uncertain how soon I may be able to get away again. However, I greatly hope to be back at any rate before the end of March and, if you will let my Secretary have your London address, I will see you as soon as I get back.

I quite understand your anxiety about your future, although I don't share it. My only anxiety is about your health. If that is once completely re-established, I feel sure that, with your capacity and experience, you will not long be left at a loose end. Personally I should be very sorry if you left the Government service, as I think it would be a public loss, but I quite understand that your relations with the Foreign Office are at present not comfortable. I have several ideas as to the direction in which you might be useful, but I prefer not to discuss them in a letter, especially as I still hope that we may meet before long.

Yours sincerely,
Milner.

That was good enough for me, and with a lofty indifference I turned down an offer from my old chief, Sir Arthur Steel-Maitland, of the post of 1st Commercial Secretary to our Legation in Warsaw. The salary and allowances amounted to over £2,000 a year, but I had no great liking for the Poles, and, in any case, Warsaw was too close to Russia. There was, however, a stronger reason for my refusal than my curious complex about Russia. It was spring, and both Scotland and Ireland called me. I wanted my share of that good time which every one coveted after the war. Above all things, I wanted to fish.

CHAPTER FOUR

AS a good Scot I chose Scotland. In East Lothian I had a rich uncle, who offered to put my wife and me up for a month or two. His hospitality would enable us to save our scanty income. We could afford even a month's fishing in Sutherlandshire on our own.

Before we set out, I made one last appearance in Whitehall. In Bexhill I had met Sir Reginald Brade, then Secretary of the War Office and an official of great experience and shrewd judgment. Sir Reginald had misgivings about our commitments in South Russia. We had discussed the situation frequently; more particularly, the prospects of General Denikin, who, supported by British arms and money, carried the hopes of Mr. Winston Churchill and the interventionists in England. Sir Reginald did not believe in the anti-Bolshevik intervention, and, thinking that my local knowledge might serve to curb Mr. Churchill's enthusiasm for the White armies, he asked me to come to London to see the great man. Our meeting took place at a luncheon in a private room at the Carlton Hotel. There were three other guests: Lord Peel, Sir James Stevenson, and Mr. R. D. Blumenfeld, but the conversation was confined to a duel of words between Mr. Churchill and myself. Sir Reginald Brade was mistaken if he thought that my expert knowledge could shake Mr. Churchill's views. Moreover, the occasion—June, 1919—was unpropitious. At that moment Denikin, having made a spectacular advance, was at the height of his success, and Mr. Churchill was in high fettle. He produced a map to show the extent and rapidity of Denikin's progress. I expressed my scepticism, suggesting that more important than the number of miles advanced was the foolish political programme of the Whites and the improbability of their consolidating their position in the territory they had captured. Mr. Churchill flouted my objections. In the end he became good-naturedly impatient and finished the argument with a blunt "I admire your courage, Mr. Lockhart, but dislike your politics."

Having been defeated by Mr. Churchill, I turned my back on London and took the train for Scotland. I never regretted my decision. That summer of 1919 gave me back my health. It restored my confidence and my high spirits. The Sutherland venture was a complete success ending up with ten salmon in one week, six of which were caught on a trout rod with a 3x cast.

I like to believe Romilly Fedden's adage that no man who appreciates trout-fishing can be wholly bad. Honesty, however, compels me to admit that as a fisherman I have come more than once within the reach of the law. During that same summer Sutherland provided the scene of my most discreditable and dangerous poaching adventure. Actually, the Scottish Sabbath and an African big-game hunter, who shall be nameless, were most to blame. The hunter had a car, and, as Sundays in our hotel were days of gloom rendered even more sabbatarian by the presence of the Bishop of London, we spent them making long tours of the country-side. On the first Sunday we discovered a loch at the end of a lonely country track miles from my home or cottage. It was full of trout. It belonged to Mr. Andrew Carnegie, the famous Scottish-American millionaire. Our first thoughts were strictly honest. Other proprietors had granted us a day's fishing on their lochs. Mr. McCorquodale had given us the free run of Tigh-na-craig. We would write to Mr. Carnegie. The reply was a curt refusal.

This was the first step in our descent. The next Sunday we set out in a car in which the night before we had concealed our rods. Had we received our deserts, we should have caught no fish, we should have been captured by the millionaire's keeper and exposed to the double ignominy of poaching and of fishing on the Sabbath. Instead, everything was for the best in the best of possible worlds. We found a crazy, leaking boat and a rise of trout which provided one of those golden days in the angler's calendar. They were game, well-fed fish. For two hours they came with a rush that brought its reward to almost every cast. Then the wooden leg of the big-game hunter stove in a plank of our boat and, wet but triumphant, we retreated. Our iniquity was never disclosed. Wisely, perhaps, we never repeated it.

My money exhausted, I went back to my uncle's place near Edinburgh and spent a glorious August shooting grouse on the Lammermoors and the Pentlands. My time was not devoted entirely to slaughter. I combined my high living with a certain amount of high thinking. I explored Edinburgh with all the enthusiasm of an American tourist. I wandered for hours alone over the country-side, tracing the steps of David Balfour and Alan Breck and Catriona. I read voraciously and seriously. Stevenson, who with Loti had always appealed to my romantic soul, was my constant companion. But my reading-list was wide and comprehensive. During that August I re-read, with the aid of a Loeb translation, the dramas of Sophocles and Æschylus. Rousseau's Social Contract provided the necessary antidote to the plutocratic existence I was now leading, and I began my first notes on Burton, whose life I have an ambition to write and in whose career, with characteristic modesty, I found certain parallels to my own.

In September we travelled back to the Highlands to stay with my father and mother, who were spending their usual summer holiday in Speyside, and to pay my respects to my grandmother.

My first encounter with the old lady was not entirely happy. I motored North with my uncle and a friend whose name is a household word in the annals of Scottish science. We lunched at Perth, and, although it was a Sunday, we lunched well off roast grouse and claret. At the end there were two bottles of Cockburn 1908. Afterwards, I sat with my uncle in the back, my eyes glued to the country-side as I tried to pick out Killiecrankie, the Tummel, the Garry, and all the old historical landmarks which I had known so well as a boy. It was not the Rob Roy country. But no matter. Centuries before these hills and glens had resounded to the tramp of the armed marauders, whose blood flowed in my veins. I plied my uncle with questions. The man of science slept soundly beside the driver from the moment we left the hotel until we drew up before my grandmother's house in Speyside. Exhausted by the emotional experience which I had undergone, I entered the drawing-room. My grandmother was seated in a high arm-chair with her feet resting on a hassock. A white cap covered her grey hair. Her beautiful hands were correctly folded on her lap. Her poise was regal—eighty years of plump Victorian dignity. I kissed her affectionately on both cheeks. Tears welled up in her eyes. Then she waved me back and fixed me with a stern eye. Had she noticed anything? She had a nose which would have done credit to a prize blood-hound. Like a flash my mind went back twenty years, as I remembered how she had repelled me after a similar embrace. "Boy, you've been smoking!" My conscience was not quite clear. The man of science came to my rescue. He was standing with his hands clasped, his fine head thrown back and his eyes fixed on the Grampians, a granite statue of Scottish rectitude.

"Mrs. Macgregor-r-r," he said solemnly. "Every time I motor-r through your glor-rious Highlands I am reminded of the wor-ds of our beautiful Scottish psalm: 'I to the hills will lift mine eyes.'"

Mr. Ramsay MacDonald could not have done it better. My grandmother's face was transfigured. The effort, however, was too much for my uncle. He roared with laughter.

"Mother," he said, "don't believe a word the old humbug says. He drank a whole bottle of port to himself and has been snoring all the way from Perth to Speyside."

The moral reprimand which this blasphemy evoked from the indignant old lady successfully diverted her thoughts from my own shortcomings. I was spared my lecture. Indeed, I never received it. The war, which had diminished my grandmother's fortune, had softened her and had smoothed the edges of her Presbyterianism. If her purse strings were now of necessity drawn tighter, she was as generous to me as ever. She died in 1922 at the age of eighty-four, courageous to the last and with all her faculties unimpaired.

The Highlands, too, gave me a new interest in my own country which I had known only as a boy. Scotland's war record thrilled my pride of race, and I became an ardent nationalist. I read my Highland history in the gravestones of the rural cemeteries. More poignantly than any book they told me the whole story of Scotland's glory and of Scotland's decline. In the little parish cemetery of Kirkmichael nearly every gravestone bore the names of Gordons, Grants, Macgregors—crofters' sons, who had died in every outpost of the Empire. My nationalism took the form of a sense of burning injustice. Scotland had been "bled white" in the war. But here before my eyes was a more terrible bleeding. Farms, which in my boyhood had been flourishing, were without tenants. The life's blood of the Highlands was being drained away, because for years successive British governments had disregarded the first and soundest instinct of race preservation—the maintenance of a healthy peasant stock. Saddest of all was the indifference of the richer Scot—the Scot who was making his money out of England—to the extermination of his race. Had Scots sunk so low that they were content to-day to play the rôle of Swiss hotel-keepers to English and American tourists? The guide-books, presumably written by Scots, goaded me to fury when they described places like Crieff as "the Scottish Montpelier," Pitlochry as the "Scottish Switzerland." Why in the name of Alpin this comparison with some French or Swiss "midden" to which, indeed, our own Highland resorts bear no resemblance? Even more irritating were the apologies for the Stuarts. "Bonnie Prince Charlie" is a great "draw" both with the English and the American tourist. In the guide-books he is invariably introduced as an advertisement for Highland loyalty. "Nothing is more wonderful in Scottish history than the devotion of the Highlander to an unworthy cause." So write our modern Scottish professors. Why this unworthiness? Why this belittling of our own royal line? The Scots have served the present royal line as loyally as any subject of the throne. Now that the Stuarts have passed into the shade of history, Scotland has no need to be ashamed of her own race of Kings.

Nobody likes the boastful Scot. But Scottish patriotism to-day is more boastful than deep-rooted. It needs a "Highland spate" to clean its bed. With too many of my compatriots it is confined to a raucous shouting of "Feet, Scotland, Feet" at Twickenham and Murrayfield.

That summer, too, I indulged in a little ancestor hunting. On my mother's side I am a Macgregor. The wild Macgregor blood, tempered by a thin flow of Lockhart caution, is the dominant in my veins. Every Macgregor claims his descent from Rob Roy, if not from Alpin, King of Scotland. It is a sinister descent in more senses than one. In the case of my mother's family there is no trace of any direct connection. As far as the records show, my branch of the Macgregors springs from a band of clansmen whom Rob Roy sent to the Caringorms to levy tribute from the local clans. After various feuds with Cummings, Grants, and Shaws they settled down in Glenmore. When one of the Dukes of Richmond wished to turn this wild tract of country into a deer forest, he had to move the local Macgregors and to find them farms on another part of his estates. He transferred them, including my forbears, to Tomintoul, the highest village in Scotland.

It was from Tomintoul that my great-grandfather crossed the Haughs of Cromdale to start the once famous Balmenach distillery. Whisky has made and lost fortunes for some of us. It has exacted its revenge from at least one member of every generation. If none of Rob Roy's blood flows in our veins, we have at least many of his characteristics: the same gambling spirit, the same recklessness, the same love of music, some of the same cunning and some of the same lawlessness.

In my researches into the turbulent history of my ancestors I did find one forbear whose refusal to submit to discipline has been inherited down to the present generation. This is his story. A Grant chieftain, who held the lands of Tulloch in wadset, had a beautiful daughter called Iseabel. With the first awakening of youth she fell in love with a Macgregor called Ian. Her choice was tragic, for both Grants and Macgregors refused to allow the marriage. Both lovers were tenacious and continued to meet, until one day they were surprised by a mixed party of Grants and Macgregors, who were determined to end Ian's life rather than permit the union. The odds were twenty to one, and to all appearances Ian was doomed. Like Alan Breck, however, he was a bonny fighter, and, taking refuge in a barn, he kept his assailants at bay with his sword, while Iseabel, loading and reloading her musket, fired lead into the legs of her kinsmen. There was one moment when Ian faltered. He was being attacked by Iseabel's own brother. He was about to lower his sword, when Iseabel intervened. " 'Tis his life or yours," she said firmly. "Kill." Ian killed and continued to kill, until the barn door was a shambles. When the last of his opponents lay dead, Ian called to Iseabel and there and then, alone at last with his betrothed, he sat down and composed a dance of triumph. The tune he wrote has made history. It was the famous Reel of Tulloch. I am bound to add that in this case the course of true love ended violently. Soon afterwards Ian was ambushed and slain by his enemies. When his head was brought to Iseabel, she died of grief and shock. So much for the romantic spirit of the Macgregors and for their love of women and song.

My long and care-free holiday came to an end in October when I returned to London. I was now on the half-pay of a Vice-Consul. I could not continue living indefinitely on my uncle. Financial duress made it essential for me to seek a job. The new commercial diplomatic service seemed to offer more scope and, above all, better pay than any other government post that I was likely to obtain. I therefore wrote to the Foreign Office, saying that I was fit for work again and would be glad to know what was to be done for me. I was referred to Sir William Clark, the new Comptroller of the Commercial Diplomatic Service, and received an invitation to lunch with him at Brooks's Club. The upshot of that luncheon was an offer to go on a special mission to Denikin in South Russia. My heart sank. I had no faith in Denikin or the White Russian movement. I refused firmly but with all the anxiety of a man who knows that he is risking his bread and butter. The alternative was the post of Commercial Diplomatic Secretary at our Prague or Belgrade Legations. I could have my choice. Both posts were definitely inferior to the appointment I had refused six months before. This time, however, my poverty dictated an acceptance.

I settled the question of Prague or Belgrade in characteristic manner. Sir George Clerk, whom I had met in Russia and liked, was to be our new Minister at Prague. Sir Alban Young, our Minister in Belgrade, was an unknown quantity. Here was one chip of fate on the Prague number. On the other hand, I had heard tales of wondrous trout fishing in Bosnia, and at that moment I was more interested in trout than in ministers. I could come to no decision. I referred again to the encyclopædia of my personal knowledge. I had met both the Czech and Serbian political and diplomatic leaders in Russia. I had formed no preference. I was prepared to decide my choice by the spin of my lucky Singapore dollar. Then fate intervened in the form of a chance encounter with an old schoolfellow whom I had not seen since before the war. We had been in the same house at Fettes, that admirable Scottish institution, which, alone among British public schools to-day, continues to turn out "rugger" Blues and scholars with monotonous regularity. We talked of old times: of a terrific "pi-jaw" by the Head for an awful oath which had proceeded from a scrum during a lull in the cheering in the match against Loretto; of mothers, who had come to see a house-match before sending their boy to school and who, having seen, had promptly decided in favour of some less Spartan institution; of the five hundred Fettesians, who had fallen in the war; of "Skinny" Anderson and his three brothers, all of whom had died for Scotland, taking with them to their unknown grave a V.C., a D.S.O., and two M.C.'s.

"Do you remember when 'Young Darkie' tried to blow up B. K.?" asked my friend. I did, and with the memory a great wave of sympathy swelled over my heart. "B. K." had been our drawing master. His real name was Bohuslav Kroupa, which, rendered into English, means Mr. "Praise-God Barleycorn." He was a grotesque figure—a plump little man with a drooping beer-stained moustache, a large purple nose, and an amazingly shaped bald head which we imagined had been scalped by a Red Indian. It had been, but by a Prussian sabre at Koeniggraetz in the Austro-Prussian war of 1866.

Each generation of Fettesians had its own story of him. The best, doubtless embellished by Time, concerned young "Darkie"

Sivright, the most fearsome of all Scottish "rugger" international forwards, who, intent on staging a Koeniggraetz of his own, had put a hermetically sealed ink bottle in "B. K.'s" class-room fire. These were the days when "B. K." was "ragged" unmercifully, and on that particular morning the Head had chosen to pay one of his rare visits to the drawing school. For ten awful minutes he had elected to stand before the fire warming his august coat-tails in front of the loaded ink bottle. For the first and only time in his life "Young Darkie" sweated blood. Just as he was summoning up courage to stand up and confess his crime, the Head left the room. There was a death-like silence broken only by the sound of his steps receding down the stone corridor. Then Hell gave up its own. There was a terrific explosion, and windows, walls, and plaster casts were drenched with a rain of ink and splintered glass. Sixty seconds sooner, and the Head would have received this murky lyddite in the seat of his pants.

For two years I had been one of "B. K.'s" chief tormentors. Then one day, after a particularly successful "booby" trap, the old man had ordered me to come to him after work. Instead of sending me up to my housemaster or to the Head he tried sweet reasonableness. The effect was shattering and after our interview I felt the limpest of cads. We then became firm friends, and, although I never learnt to draw, I never ragged him again. Instead, I used to encourage him to talk about his own life and I discovered unknown virtues in the old man. He was a Bohemian in both senses of the word, an artist and a political exile, who had travelled the whole world. He had served drinks behind a bar in Mexico. He hated the Habsburgs and the Hohenzollerns with the perfervid fanaticism of the Slav. He was one of the pioneers of Bohemian independence. He died six years before his country achieved its freedom.

On that post-war evening, when my Fettes friend jogged my memory so pleasantly, suddenly it flashed through my mind that "B. K." was a Czech—the first Czech I had ever known. A latent sentimentality welled up in my soul. My love of the exotic, my passion for travel, my interest in small nations—all were due to these early schoolday talks with "B. K." "Praise-God Barleycorn" had done the trick. Prague was his Mecca. I would go to Prague.

The next week I had to appear before the special Selection Committee which had to confirm my appointment. When I had first passed into the Consular Service, I had bounced the examiners and the Foreign Office committee with complete success. On this occasion I cut an inglorious figure. I had had some personal experience of the Czechs. I had conducted the negotiations with Trotsky which were supposed to guarantee to the Czech army an unhampered passage out of Russia. The outbreak of the hostilities between the Czechs and the Bolsheviks had been directly responsible for all my Moscow misfortunes. True, I had only the haziest idea of the commercial riches of Czechoslovakia. In the circumstances it might have been wiser to read one of the official handbooks on the new Republic. Secure in my personal knowledge of the Czech leaders, I neglected this precaution and set out to the Foreign Office with an easy confidence. All might have been well had the Committee been composed solely of officials. Unfortunately for my peace of mind, it included one outside member, a hard-boiled businessman, who was a human encyclopædia on Czech imports and exports and who bombarded me with impossible questions about kaolin and calcium. I made the best of a bad job. I confessed my complete ignorance of the new country and, like Scipio, put my fate to the test of my past victories. I gave a succinct résumé of my views on the duties of a commercial secretary. The services which an official could render to British businessmen had nothing to do with the ingredients of china or of glass. He must be a good "mixer." He must have his ear to the wind. He must know the language of the country to which he was accredited. He must be on terms of intimacy with the local ministers, bankers and businessmen and in a position to approach them at any moment. These services I could render. I had employed them with success in Russia. I knew the Slavs. I could learn Czech in six weeks. All this talk of business knowledge and experience was superfluous. It was the businessman's job to know the details of his own business. All that the government official could do was to oil the wheels of the businessman's approach and to warn him of the local pitfalls.

Let not the reader think that my views, expressed with the requisite mixture of modesty and cocksureness, were mere bluff. They were full of the meat of common sense. The experience of the past fifteen years has proved that the paragons of the conglomerate virtues, which I had extolled, make the best commercial secretaries. At any rate my effort extracted me from an awkward hole. Within a few days I received the official confirmation of my appointment. A private letter from Sir Arthur Steel-Maitland informed me that I had been selected on my past reputation. I was to proceed to Prague at the end of the year.

My fate was settled for me, and, with a mind charged with good resolutions, I began my preparations for my departure. My new job was poorly paid. It was, too, a big bump down after the responsible post I had filled in Moscow. Still, it was activity again, and I was full of energy. The new Europe offered a wonderful field for youthful ambitions. I was only thirty-two. I would work like a beaver and make myself the greatest Slav expert in the Foreign Office. I had had some hard knocks, but I was still resilient as a tennis-ball. I was going on my travels again. Russia was behind me, and I was learning to store it away in a back recess of my mind where it no longer worried me. For months now I had been cut off from all communication with Moura. At first, we had corresponded regularly through the good offices of the various foreign governments who still maintained embassies and legations in Russia. For weeks her letters had been the mainstay of my existence. Then gradually, as Russia became more and more shut off from the rest of the world, communication became increasingly difficult. When the last foreign mission was withdrawn her letters ceased. Even her fate was unknown to me. And as I tried to put Russia out of my mind, so, too, I tried to forget Moura.

She had left a wound in my heart, but it was healing. How was it possible to recapture a past which was no longer mine? I should live for the present. Prague was a new world to conquer. I had the necessary armour and weapons—letters of recommendation from such stalwart pro-Czech champions as Wickham Steed and Seton Watson, the gratitude of all new nations to any one who has assisted them in however minor a way, and my own irrepressible high spirits. I should assault it with hope and courage. The gods, I reflected, as I packed my rods and guns, looked with favour on those who faced adversity with a smile. They should smile back on me. They should make me a minister in five years.

BOOK TWO

☆

CASTLES IN BOHEMIA

"Chetifs mortels, qui péchez sans plaisir."
—VOLTAIRE.

CHAPTER ONE

MY first impressions of Prague were mixed. Looking back to-day after a residence there of nearly seven years, I find the same curious difficulty in forming a definite opinion. There are moments when its beauty haunts me to the exclusion of all other beautiful cities. There are other occasions when some baleful curse seems to emanate from its cobbled alleys and when its rococo gargoyles gibber and mock. The fault is perhaps my own. In Prague lies the wreckage of the last years of my youth.

I arrived, if not as a conqueror, at least in some of the reflected glory of the victorious Allies. I came, too, alone, and my wife did not join me until seven months later. In that winter of 1919-1920 conditions of life in Central Europe were still uncomfortable and unsettled. The railway system had not yet begun to function, and I travelled from Paris in a special military train. The journey took the best part of three days, and our route lay through Switzerland and Austria. I was, I think, the only civilian. My companions were French officers. We travelled in isolated luxury. At Feldkirchen on the Austrian frontier we stopped, and I had time to inspect an Austrian train which was standing alongside our own. In the grey, cold dusk of that January afternoon the contrast between the luxury of our own overheated train and the long row of dilapidated Austrian carriages made me feel uncomfortable. Starved faces peered through the broken window-panes. There was no heating. Candle stumps stuck in bottles supplied the only light—and the only warmth. Austria delenda est. For years this had been the motto of the Slavs and of the champions of the oppressed minorities in the old Austria-Hungary. The deletion had already begun.

I arrived at Prague late in the evening and was met on the platform by John Latter, a nephew of General Sir Nevil Macready and then Third Secretary at our Legation. Here all was bustle and efficiency. The station, re-christened by the Czechs in gratitude for their newly-won independence the Wilson station, was crowded with Czech porters, Czech legionaries, Czech Jans, Antons and Karels, which are the Czech equivalents for our Tom, Dick and Harry. The station was now their station. The trains were their trains. The fruits of independence and of possession had not yet lost their savour.

I collected my luggage and drove off with Latter to my hotel. At break-neck speed we passed through the Hoover Gardens, past the Historical Museum and the huge statue of St. Wenceslaus, down the wide Wenceslaus Place into the Poric. The street lamps revealed buildings, mostly shops and offices. The pavements were thronged with men and women. They looked happy, well-fed, but undistinguished. My first impression was of a Belgian provincial town. I was in the business quarter. It did not attract me then. I do not like it to-day.

In a few minutes we drew up before a cold, barrack-looking building with the sign "Hotel Imperial" surmounting its circular swinging door. My heart sank. In apologetic tones Latter explained that Prague was filled to overflowing. There were as yet no new hotels. Those that existed offered merely a choice of evils. To-morrow, we should see about a house or a flat. The Government would help. There was a big reception that night at the Municipal House. If I liked to change, he would wait for me and introduce me to the Corps Diplomatique and to the various Czech ministers. I pleaded tiredness, unpacked my belongings, and retired to bed. The blinds did not work. The light of the street lamps and the noise of the street-cars below my window kept me awake for hours. I spent a restless and unhappy night.

The next morning the sky was blue, and, as I waited for the car which was to take me to our Legation, the keen winter air stirred me to a new energy. That drive was a memorable one. In a few seconds I had passed from the modern materialism of the business quarter into a new world. Its gate was the old Powder Tower. Its streets—narrow cobbled alleys, flanked with the baroque palaces of the aristocrats—were full of mystery. They twined and twisted, ending sometimes in ridiculous culs-de-sac with a postern and a grinning gargoyle barring further progress. On our way we passed through the Old Town Square with its great statue of Jan Hus and its old Town Hall with its clock and performing apostles, who make their round as every hour strikes, past the University, where Hus was rector, past the colossal statue of Charles IV,* down on to the glorious Charles Bridge with its stone buttresses and its statues of the saints. There, glittering in the winter sun, was the Prague which I had imagined in my dreams. Below my feet was the Vltava, its slow waters studded with picturesque islands, and behind the river rising up from the water's edge to the summit of high hills, Old Prague with its castle, its palaces, its churches, its ridiculous staircase streets, and its hanging gardens. As I crossed the bridge, I felt as if I were entering fairyland. Gone was all the twentieth century shoddiness. Here was the home of romance—that romance which has inspired "The Witch of Prague," "The Winter Queen," "Golem," and a score of other histories and novels of the Middle Ages. Here, too, hidden somewhere between the base, formed by the river and the Wallenstein Palace, and the apex of St. Vitus's Cathedral, with its quaint Alchemists' Alley behind it, lay the Thun Palace, now the home of the British Legation and my new headquarters. Here in this fairy-city, more beautiful than any city I have ever seen, was the soul of Prague.

Here, every house had its history,—a history written in the blood of religious wars. Here, too, were landmarks in the life-story of England. Here was the birthplace of Anne of Bohemia, the ill-fated consort of our own ill-fated Richard II. Here that dashing cavalry leader, Prince Rupert, had made his entry into the world. Here was unloosed the Thirty Years War between Catholic and Protestant, between Slav and German. Here the works of Wycliffe,

* Greatest of all Czech kings and son of that John of Luxembourg who fell at Crecy and from whose shield the Prince of Wales gets his three feathers and his motto, "Ich Dien."

the inspirer of Hus, had been publicly burnt in front of the Archbishop's palace. Here Žižka, the Czech Cromwell, had listened to the fiery counsels of Peter Payne, the English Taborite, who because of his origin was known as "Magister Engliš" and whose part in the history of Czech Protestantism is commemorated in the Catholic song:

"The devil sent us Engliš;
He creeps through Prague in stealth,
And whispers English doctrines,
Unwholesome for our health."

Here, too, at the Battle of the White Mountain in 1620 a Stuart Queen lost her throne. In that battle the Czech nation was deprived of its independence. Its lands were given to the Catholic invader. Its nobility disappeared. Its spirit had been enchained. But it had never been conquered. It still lived in the stone walls of the old city. Here was the Prague of Masaryk and of the countless Czech patriots who during three hundred years of subjection had never ceased to lift their eyes to these silent sentinels of the past glory of their race. As a schoolboy I had been taught to sneer at Shakespeare's ignorance of geography in giving a seaport to Bohemia. But Shakespeare had been more erudite than my professors. In the Middle Ages the kingdom of Bohemia, under the Premyslides, had stretched from the Baltic to the Adriatic. Here in the soughing of the wind round the castle walls and in the lapping waters of the Vltava were the plaintive notes of the song which through the years of tribulation had kept alive the national spirit of the Czechs. The song of liberty is deathless. If there is no other merit in the Peace Treaties, they have, at least, restored to a sturdy, cultured race its birthright and its freedom.

The old and the new Prague represent that queer mixture of Slav mysticism and Teutonic materialism which form the basis of the Czech character. To me they were a stone and stucco symbol of the eternal struggle between the spirit and the flesh. In the secluded shelter of the old city I was happy and at peace. Across the river, calling more and more insistently, were the Nachtlokals of a materialist modern city drunk with the wine of its newly-won liberty. During my stay in Prague this struggle overshadowed my daily life, and in the process my character was to be weighed in the balance and found wanting.

My entry into the Legation was a new thrill. My car spluttered and almost fell back as it strove to mount the steepest of short streets. It turned sharply at right angles, and there before my eyes was a huge portcullis surmounted by a towering wall. My chauffeur rang the bell, and a porter, old as Franz Josef himself, turned back the studded gate with loving care. Dear old Plachy. He has long since gone to his last rest. But for the last year or two of his life I must have plagued him sorely. For later, when I stayed at the Legation as Sir George Clerk's guest, it was sometimes sunrise before I rang his bell. Yet he never complained. "Jesus Maria!" he would mutter. Then he would shake his head. "So late home, Pan Lókart, so late home."

The promise of the entrance was more than fulfilled by the palace itself. Built halfway up the slope of the Hradčany hill, it rose sheer from the cobbled courtyard to its full height of five storeys. On the west side one walked straight from the ballroom on the third floor out into the most secluded of gardens. Once the palace of the Statthalter of Bohemia, it was as much a fortress as a home. No British ambassador or minister is housed with greater dignity abroad than in this imposing residence, which is, thanks to Sir George Clerk's persistence, now the property of the British Government. It has of course its ghost: a mournful gentleman with a plaintive voice still searching for his lost wife. I met neither the wife nor the sleepless husband.

Still in a daydream I went upstairs to pay my respects to our Chargé d'Affaires, Cecil Gosling, a vigorous and good-looking man with a fine presence. During the short time we were together in Prague, I experienced nothing but kindness from him. But I soon discovered that he was a disappointed man, for he had already been a minister in South America and had probably had hopes of further promotion. And to feel that he was only a glorified "locum tenens" must have been galling. In any case it was clear that his sympathies were with the "Blacks," the name we gave to the old feudal aristocrats, who, Habsburg in sympathy and now shorn of their former glory, were to a man contemptuous of the Czechs, and it is not surprising that the Czechs were up in arms against him—not altogether without reason. His chief ally in the Legation was Basil Coulson, the military attaché. Coulson was a Scot, a Catholic, and a man of parts. He, too, had chosen the easier and the more comfortable path. He had made his friends among the aristocrats and, far more than Gosling, had exceeded the bounds of diplomatic discretion in his comments on the Czechs. He was housed even more magnificently than the Legation staff in the Lobkowitz Palace. The most capable member of the staff was John Latter, the Third Secretary, who, although new to the job, was a glutton for work and ran his Chancery with exemplary efficiency. Like a good soldier, he kept his political opinions to himself. The rest of the English staff was completed by Cynthia Seymour (now Lady Cheetham) and Irene Boyle, the two secretaries whom Sir George Clerk had engaged at the Peace Conference and who had arrived in advance of their chief. I found them unhappy and uncomfortable. They had no palace. They were living in a couple of shoddy rooms in the Hotel de Saxe, where during the war the Czech "Maffia," which plotted the downfall of Austria, held its meetings, and Prague, not yet emerged from three hundred years of provincialism and unaccustomed to the idea of lady secretaries, was unable to fit them into its new microcosm and was disagreeably curious in its efforts to do so. The position, when I arrived, was that the French, who were represented not only by a Legation but by a posse of generals and an army of 400 officers, were hand in glove with the Czechs, while Britain was regarded in government circles with suspicion and even with dislike. Sadly I realised that for the time being there was nothing to do but to await the arrival of Sir George.

My first day in Prague, however, was not to pass without adventure. On my way back from the Legation to my hotel my car ran over a boy in the Celetna Street. The fault was the boy's. He had been playing in the street and had run right into the bonnet. We had been travelling very slowly. But in a moment my car was surrounded by an angry crowd headed by an officious policeman.

The boy's mother was wrangling with the chauffeur. The boy himself was lying motionless on the cobbles. The crowd glowered at me with hatred in its eyes. My beaver-collared Russian fur coat was too plutocratic for the time and place in which I lived. If I were not to be hauled ignominiously to the police station, I must act at once. Knowing that German was unpopular, I unloosed my Russian. It produced nothing but a vacant stare from the crowd and a splutter of Czech from the policeman. With exemplary patience I switched into German. Babel broke loose. All I could understand was the policeman's reiterated demand for my passport. It was in my despatch case at the hotel. The situation looked more serious than ever. It was relieved by a grunt from the boy, who rose to his feet, rubbed himself, grinned, and then ran to his mother. I examined him carefully. He was more frightened than hurt. The radiator had pushed him down flat and the car had run over him without touching him. I gave him twenty crowns, and the crowd, which a moment before had been demanding my arrest, went away laughing.

That same evening I took our two lady secretaries out to dinner. In those early days Prague had only one tolerable restaurant —the Chapeau Rouge. Later, it was to descend from the respectable to the dissolute, but at that moment it was the haunt of the diplomatic corps, the foreign military missions, and the younger members of the aristocracy who had not as yet realised the full significance of their own fate.

We were, I admit, rather over-dressed for the occasion. Prague had not yet begun to wear "smokings" nor was it accustomed to the sight of two young English girls, hatless and in the full glory of low-cut evening dresses, in a public restaurant. Our entry provoked a general stare. The stare was kept up all through dinner by a young man, who had obviously a high opinion of his own charms. In the end his leers and smirks became so objectionable that I sent him a polite note by the maître d'hôtel suggesting that he might change his seat or fix his eyes on another part of the room. Back came the waiter with another note begging me to step outside in order to explain my message. The young man had already left the room. I followed and found him waiting in the hall outside.

"You wish to insult me?" he stammered. "Then I suppose you will give me satisfaction. If you will give me your name and address, I shall send my friends to call on you."

I bowed.

"Sir," I said, "I have no card. I am the new Secretary at the British Legation. These two ladies are Sir George Clerk's secretaries. We have just arrived in Prague. We were told that this was a respectable restaurant. Obviously, it is not, or you, presumably, would not behave as you have done. If you want to pursue the matter further, I suggest that we step into the street, and I'll give you all the satisfaction you want."

I was firm, not to say aggressive. The young man, a member of the minor nobility, was a good two stone lighter than I was. At the same time I was apprehensive of the consequences into which my boldness might lead me. After Russia my Foreign Office copybook would not stand another blot. Fortunately, the young man giggled.

"Good God," he said, "I'm most terribly sorry. I thought that you were all from Vienna and that your companions were..." He giggled again and stammered out more apologies. "Please accept my sincere apologies and please, please, say nothing about this at the Legation. I would not have had this happen for worlds."

I tried to be dignified.

"Sir," I said, "I accept your apology. At the same time I should like to point out that I should have been just as annoyed by your conduct even if the two ladies had been—Viennese."

This puzzled him for a moment. He had, however, a saving sense of humour. "Even with two?" he asked politely. "Yes," I said. "Even with six, if they are in my company."

In the end I had to laugh. His distress was so genuine. He introduced himself formally and we shook hands. Afterwards, we became good friends.

This was my nearest approach to a duel in all my twenty-five years abroad, and, although it ended happily, the experience pulled me up with a jerk. My Scottish caution reasserted itself. Prague, I decided, was a place for serious study and not for social distractions. I had had a disturbed day. I should find myself a house. I should work. I should read history and economics. I should learn the Czech language. Above all, I should eschew restaurants. I kept my good resolutions for exactly six months.

CHAPTER TWO

FROM the point of view of my official career Prague was worth a good resolution. The geographical centre of Europe, it was an admirable political observatory from which to watch the storm-clouds which the Peace Treaty had left over the Danubian plain. The old Austro-Hungarian Empire, with its mosaic of different races, had been complex enough. The new Central Europe gave to the world a whole list of new names which for years to come were to present a problem in pronunciation to the average Englishman. During my four years at our Prague Legation we continued to receive letters, even from official departments, with such strange addresses as Prague, Czechoslavia; Prague, Yugoslovakia; Prague, Czechoslovenia; Prague, Vienna; and even The Prague, Poland. These mistakes were understandable. Englishmen take less interest in foreign affairs than any other nation in the world. Even to this day nine members out of ten of the House of Commons confuse Budapest with Bucharest, and it is a safe bet that not one-half of the British Cabinet could place the present capitals of Europe in their proper states.

In those five years of peace no Englishman at home cared a continental damn about the new map of Europe. His one ambition was to make up the enjoyment which he had lost during four-and-a-half years in the trenches. The diplomatists shared this not unnatural reaction. But, as the problem was before their noses, they had to study it. If the new map of Central Europe was an improvement in that it had removed the most glaring racial injustices, it had nevertheless repeated many of the old mistakes. The new Czechoslovak Republic was, in fact, in many respects a miniature of the former Austro-Hungarian Monarchy. Its population of under 14,000,000 was made up of 9,000,000 Czechs and Slovaks, 3,000,000 Germans, 750,000 Magyars, 450,000 Roumanians and other oddments including Poles and Jews. The same anomalies were to be observed in Roumania and in Yugoslavia, which with Czechoslovakia formed the three states which had reaped the greatest benefit from the dismemberment of Austro-Hungary. The Peace Treaties, it is true, had given political liberty to 21,000,000 Slavs and Rumanians. In the process, however, they had separated some 5,000,000 Germans and some 2,000,000 Hungarians from their co-nationals. Moreover, they had cut off from its economic Hinterland a city which was once the capital of an Empire of 50,000,000 inhabitants, and had confined it in a tiny Republic of 6,000,000 people. Vienna had been left to starve.

The Peace Treaties were admittedly far from perfect. Yet even the fairest ethnographic division could not have appeased immediately the racial animosities which had been unchained by the collapse of the monarchy. To the impartial observer it was clear from the first that, while the Czechs, the Rumanians, the Croats and the Slovenes, were fully entitled to their political liberty, some form of economic co-operation between the various Succession States was essential if Central Europe was to be saved from chaos and starvation. Unfortunately, this rock of economic common sense was submerged by the waves of chauvinism. Soon after the war I remember Mr. Winston Churchill being asked to define the proper attitude of a country towards its enemies. Without a moment's hesitation he threw out this brilliant epigram: "In war—resolution, in defeat—defiance, in victory—magnanimity, in peace —goodwill." In post-war Europe there was to be neither magnanimity nor goodwill.

As far as the Czechs were concerned, there was some excuse for this attitude. For centuries the wealth of Bohemia had been exploited for the benefit of Vienna and of the feudal landowners. Their instinctive dread of a return to the old order was magnified by the attitude of the monarchists in their midst.

When I arrived in the Czech capital, Prague society was divided into four distinctive groups. Most numerous, of course, were the Czechs, thrifty, hard-working, ambitious and, like all races who have been kept in subjection, suspicious and difficult to know. Then there were the German-Bohemians, few in number but influential by their commercial standing and, like all Germans, slow to appreciate the change in their position. Their contempt for the Czechs, however, was tempered by their financial stake in the new Republic. Belonging to the German group were the Prague Jews, German in culture, supporting the German opera and German drama and music, and divided in their loyalties to the old régime and the new. Lastly, there were those members of the Austrian nobility who, owning vast estates in Bohemia, had accepted Czechoslovak nationality. They ranged from millionaire landowners like Prince Schwarzenberg, with his fifty-three castles and 750,000 acres of land, to minor Counts with small country estates. Some, like the Kinskys and the Lobkowitzes, who were of Czech stock, might have been willing to assist the new state if a place, comporting with their lineage and self-esteem, had been offered to them. But the new Republic was essentially democratic. Its Prime Minister was a Socialist. Its President was the son of a coachman. In the eyes of the nobility it was, if not a Bolshevik régime, the next thing to it.

True, the estates of the nobility were now being subjected to expropriation, an expropriation, too, for which the Czechoslovak Government fixed its own price. In the circumstances it would have been too much to expect loyalty from a class which previously had enjoyed semi-regal state and which was now reduced to impotence. But for their own misfortunes the big landowners had only themselves to blame. As a class they had suffered from inbreeding. In their scheme of things quarterings were infinitely more important than brains. Proud of a lineage which went back to Charlemagne, if not to the Garden of Eden, they hated the Germans, disliked the Hungarians, and looked down on the Czechs as excellent servants unfit for any other occupation. They might have been willing to marry their daughters to a Hohenzollern Prince, but from a heraldic point of view they would have regarded the marriage as a mésalliance. Themselves the finest shots in the world, they liked the sporting qualities of the English. At the same time they secretly regarded our peers and peeresses as a bogus nobility, because of the chorus girl and merchant stock which has kept it virile. And when the Duke of Portland came to Prague on a visit, he was labelled behind his back the Duke of Cement, presumably on the assumption that his title had something to do with Portland cement.

In their own case virility was at a premium. Where it was present, it was generally due to some left-handed influence over its origin. They were a pleasant, charming, and hospitable class, and because of the social amenities which they provided their influence among the foreign diplomatists was greater than it should have been. For, with all their advantages of education and wealth, they had reached a stage of decadence which even without the war must, sooner or later, have undermined their privileged position. In their sheltered existence they had never rubbed shoulders with the world. Unlike the German Junkers, they had not even fought for their country. True, they had been in uniform. But the bulk of them had been on the staff and not in the front-line trenches. It was their accepted privilege. For centuries they had filled the chief administrative posts both in the army and navy and in the civil administration. From their ranks came the Berchtholds, the Czernins, the Dumbas. Since Metternich the quality had declined. Aristocrats by divine right, they had all the mental laziness of the Russian nobility without one-tenth of the talent. Now, when their Rome was falling in ruins before their eyes, their effort to help themselves was confined to sighs for the departed glory of the Habsburgs and to cheap sneers at their new masters. Nor, except in the case of the younger generation, had the revolution wrought any violent change in their mode of existence. Their arable land was in process of being taken away from them. But they had kept their forests and their sugar factories. They could still give shooting parties and entertain their friends. Above all, they benefited from the sound administration of the Czech finances. They were infinitely better off than their brothers and cousins (for they were all inter-related) in Austria. Compared with the fate of the Russian nobility, their lot seemed pleasant enough. It was perhaps on this account that they had learnt nothing from the war. In Vienna the revolution had ruined the aristocracy, compelling the younger sons to break with its most cherished traditions and to enter the American marriage market. In Prague the only effect of the war had been to quicken the process of decadence and to destroy what remained of their moral fibre.

Admittedly, they were amusing, and, when they came to Prague, there was keen competition among the foreign diplomatists for invitations to their parties. In those early days the chief critic of the new régime among the nobility was Count Adalbert Sternberg, a florid, rather coarse-looking genius, who but for an excessive self-indulgence, might have played the part of a Winston Churchill in Austro-Hungarian politics. A famous duellist, a brilliant linguist who could conduct a political discussion in six languages, and an historian and a poet, he was known to friends and enemies as "Monshi." When I knew him, his brain had begun to suffer from his excesses, and he was no longer to be taken seriously. But his wit, fearless and spicy, amused his friends, and he had a European reputation as a practical joker. It was one of the sights of Vienna to see him toddle from Sacher's down the Kaertnerstrasse dragging a mechanical toy behind him. At parties, therefore, he was in great demand. He would come in rather late and at once start scratching his behind. He would then make a profound bow. "Princess," he would say very gravely, "I must apologise. I have been in agony all day. Last night I slept at the Hotel de Saxe. Slept did I say? I did not close an eye. This morning I asked the reception clerk who had occupied my room the previous night. The answer was: 'a Czech minister.'" The scratching pantomime would be renewed, and even the little Countesses giggled. His star turn, however, was his visiting card which he produced on all festive occasions. Both the Austrian and the Czech Republics had abolished titles and, although not even the officials paid any attention to the decree, "Monshi" had had special visiting cards printed in order to meet the new situation. The wording was as follows:

"Adalbert Sternberg
Ennobled by Charlemagne 798
Disennobled by Karl Renner 1918"

Karl Renner was the Socialist Chancellor of the new Austrian Republic.

Although "Monshi" was scarcely a representative member of the old nobility, his attitude was typical enough of the post-war attitude of his class. In this atmosphere it was easy enough to understand why the monarchy had collapsed. If a Habsburg restoration meant putting this class back into power, there would be no restoration in our life-time. Thrones are not lost or won so much by kings as by the courtiers who support them. Convinced that there would be no violent swingback of the pendulum, I concentrated my attention on the Czechs.

My first impressions were not altogether favourable. I had come to Prague from Russia and expected to find something very similar to Russia. With my knowledge of Russian the language, although more different than I had anticipated, presented no great difficulty. Indeed, I picked it up too easily ever to become really proficient. In every other respect, however, the contrast between Czech and Russian was startling. East of the Rhine the Czechs are frequently referred to as the Germans of the Slavs. Admittedly, they have acquired certain Teutonic qualities from their long association with Germanic races. Actually, a better comparison is with the Lowland Scot. Like the Scot, the Czech is thrifty, hard-working, and ambitious. He has none of that reckless expansiveness which in Russian is called "shirokaya natura." He is hospitable enough when occasion demands, but wastes no money on entertainment for the joy of entertaining. Trained by years of suppression to conceal his feelings, to laugh when he wants to cry and to cry when he is really laughing, he is difficult to fathom. Once one has plumbed his depth, one finds sterling qualities of grit and courage. He has a fine physique, is one of the best gymnasts in the world, and has a passionate love of the hills and streams of his country. Beneath his practical material exterior he has a soul for poetry. His love and understanding of music are inborn, and it is a sore point with the Austrians that both Mozart and Wagner found Prague infinitely more receptive to their genius than Vienna.

His worst fault is scarcely of his own making. Circumstances have made him a provincial. In 1920 the hall-mark of provincialism was stamped on everything that belonged to him. Like the Lowland Scot, too, he had a fine conceit of himself. Perhaps this conceit was more apparent than real, for both the French and ourselves had come to Prague firmly convinced that we were the creators of this new Republic and that the Czechs owed everything to the victorious Allies. There is nothing more irritating to the benefited than the expectancy of gratitude on the part of the benefactor, and the Czechs, who, not without some justice, considered that they had made their own revolution, were inclined to resent an attitude of patronizing superiority which I now realise must have been irksome.

To mix the old nobility with the new Czech democracy is a task which has defeated every diplomatist in Prague with one exception. Some have begun with good intentions. Others, like the French, have been frankly pro-Czech. Others again, who had no particular interest in placating the Czechs and who were frankly out for a good time, have ranged themselves on the side of the nobility. But Sir George Clerk, my new chief, is the only man who has succeeded in maintaining a proper balance between the two contending factions.

He came to Prague just a fortnight after my arrival, and Prague at once sat up and took notice. For weeks his name had been on the front page of every Central European newspaper. He was the man whom the Allies had sent to Budapest to send the Bolshevik dictator Bela Kun about his business and to install a national government in his place. He had carried out his task with complete success. He was then in his forty-sixth year. Tall, silver-haired, and bemonocled, he had a figure which was the pride of his tailor and the envy of his friends. The perfect stage diplomatist, you will say. And why not? Representation is one of the accepted functions of diplomacy, and a slim figure and a neat trouser leg is a better support to diplomatic argument than gold-laced obesity.

As I watched him driving up to the Hradčany to present his credentials, a troop of Sokols riding in advance of his carriage, the bayonets of the guard of honour glinting in the February sun, I felt a thrill of pride. In the course of centuries many famous historical personages had made that steep ascent to present their homage to the Luxembourgs and the Habsburgs, but none, I dare swear, with such elegance and with so well-cut a uniform as the first British Minister to the free Republic of Czechoslovakia. Alongside the squat khaki- and blue-trousered figures of the Czech and French generals, he looked like a thoroughbred in a field of hacks. With that incurable passion for imitation which accompanies my devotion to those whom I like to serve, I began for the first time in my life to take an interest in clothes. The interest communicated itself from the secretaries to the chauffeurs, from the chauffeurs to the Chancery servants, and from the Chancery servants to the messengers. During Sir George's term of office we were the best-dressed Legation in Prague.

This blatant eulogy of the sartorial is not meant to be so flippant as it reads. In Russia I had witnessed a proletarian revolution. It had been everything that individual likes and dislikes may choose to call it. But it had been on the grand scale. It had not been petty. Here I was assisting in a petit-bourgeois revolution with all the pretentiousness and some of the ridiculousness inseparable from every petit-bourgeois revolution. In the transformation of the bourgeois into the minister and high state official it was as well that the Czechs should have a model and a mentor.

In those early days in Prague Sir George was the accepted arbiter of etiquette and deportment. A keen shot and angler, he fixed the rules for the management of the diplomatic shoots which the Czech Government arranged for our benefit. At football matches he taught the Czechs how to be resigned in defeat and magnanimous in victory. Sometimes when our own First League sides, more especially, a Scottish League side, were being massacred on the playing fields of Sparta and of Slavia, the two famous Czech clubs, the silver-grey moustache would tremble and the delicately tinted face would turn an ashen grey. Afterwards, he would tell me that the refereeing was disgraceful (more often than not, it was), that the winning Czech goal had been flagrantly offside. After all, he was a Scot, and football Floddens are as distasteful to us as the real thing. But before the Czechs no word escaped his lips, and when the rout of our professionals was complete he would turn to Dr. Beneš and congratulate him with a charming old-world courtesy which I found hard to imitate. At Davis Cup matches he was in his element, and whether as umpire or as linesman he fulfilled his duties with a combination of firmness and expansiveness that quelled the temperamental exuberances of the local Tildens and Perrys.

But in those heated duels, which we fought out, far from the eye of any spectator, on the private tennis court of Dr. Beneš in the early hours of the morning, he would relax from his self-imposed discipline, and the human, which is in all of us, would assert itself. Fierce, tense encounters they were: Beneš and one of his secretaries against Sir George and myself. Sir George, accurate in service, proficient in the chop, but rather too stately in movement and too uncontrolled in his drive, had to give seven years to Beneš, who without a tennis shot in his racket had all the fitness of a life-long teetotaller and non-smoker. The contests were always wonderfully even. When I had been betimes to bed, the robustness of my inelegant assault generally turned the scales in our favour. There were other days, when, coming straight from a Nachtlokal to the tennis court, I faltered. On these occasions gloom would descend on my partner. A faint damn would escape from his lips. Then, as I double-faulted for the third time in succession, he would hand me the balls and whisper hoarsely: "Pull yourself together, man. You aren't going to let us be beaten by those fellows." I pulled in vain. Beneš, bounding like Borotra and agile as a monkey, had a horrible knack of returning everything except the hardest drive, and, when I drove, the ball would rattle fullpitch against the wire-netting twenty-yards behind the base-line. My final effort would be received in stony silence.

Poor Sir George! I must have tried him highly. Yet he had a heart of gold, and his irritation never survived the first flash of thoroughly justifiable temper. He had something more than a kind heart. He had a first-class brain and a judgment of men and affairs that was rarely at fault. He was, too, the best "mixer" that I have ever met in the higher ranks of diplomacy. I have known him now for seventeen years. Never has he failed to give me the soundest advice—advice which, if taken in time, might have saved me from more than one catastrophe. I am therefore one of his admirers. But not even his worst enemy could have failed to praise the skill with which he handled a very delicate situation in Prague. He was a loyal friend to the Czechs, who soon learnt to appreciate his merits and to rely upon his advice. A man of liberal views, he was able to guide Czech Chauvinism into quieter channels. His personal relations with President Masaryk and Dr. Beneš were more intimate than those of any other diplomatist in Prague, and, although France was and still is the guardian Power of Czechoslovakia, it was to Sir George and not to the French Minister that the Czech statesmen came when they were in doubt what course to pursue. His counsel was always on the side of moderation. He smoothed out difficulties between the Austrians and the Czechs. He made the Hungarian lion drink Tokay at his table with the Slovak lamb. If the Succession States of Central Europe have not yet established that form of economic co-operation which is essential to their future welfare and which, in the case of Austria, is the only alternative to the Anschluss, it is not for want of friendly and tactful advice on the part of the then British Minister in Prague.

With the nobility he succeeded in establishing a thoroughly satisfactory modus vivendi. He gave no encouragement to their intrigues and monarchist ambitions. On the contrary, he showed them quite plainly that he had no sympathy with restoration schemes and that the existence of the Czechoslovak State was a fact which had to be accepted. But he invited them to his house, dined and wined, and played and shot with them. He advised those members of the aristocracy who had Czech blood in their veins to send their sons into the Czech diplomatic service. His advice was not always taken. Reconciliation, in fact, was slow and uphill work. But when the nobility realised exactly where he stood, they respected him and accepted him on his own merits. He was the first and for a long time the only foreign diplomatist whom they elected as honorary member of their ultra-exclusive club. In the end he was able to do far more to alleviate their political hardships than any avowed supporter of their cause could have done, and if to-day the Czech nobility still enjoy some of the fat of their former possessions it is indirectly due to Sir George, whose sage counsel did much to restrain the original predatory instincts of the Czech Land Reform Office.

If none of his successors has succeeded in building the same bridge between the old and the new in Prague, I must admit that his first efforts in this direction ended in a fiasco. Soon after his arrival he decided to give a gala dinner to which all the leading Czechs and nobles were to be invited. It was to be a kind of Gargantuan peace-offering, and we worked hard to make it a success. Nearly a hundred invitations were sent out. They included the whole Czech Cabinet and their wives, the speakers of the Chamber of Deputies and of the Senate, the Party leaders, and the chief Princes and Princesses, not to mention Counts and Countesses, of Bohemia. An army of cooks, waiters, and extra footmen was engaged. The wines included the priceless Tokay which Sir George had been given by the grateful Hungarians for his services in driving out Bela Kun. With immense care we arranged the seating of the guests. At that time the Czechs had not established any rules of precedence. Doubtless, they had been too busy with more important affairs. We had therefore to make our own. But, as it was an official dinner, obviously the places of honour had to be reserved for the members of the Czech Government. This point had been tactfully explained to the members of the nobility beforehand.

For days on end the whole Legation staff had toiled laboriously, checking the acceptances and refusals and writing out place-cards. It was no easy task. The nobility had replied with exemplary promptitude and in the prescribed manner. The Czech replies had come by every known form of modern communication: by telephone, by telegram, by typewritten letter. Some ministers had accepted for themselves without any mention of the intentions of their wives. Some had not replied at all.

My own contribution had been an elaborate table-plan, with the name of every guest and his official title written out in the neatest of block letters. Strange names they were—four or five consonants to every vowel. And as I wrestled with the Hrdličkas, the Strimpls, the Syrovys, the indispensable Bubela, our talented and good-natured Czech secretary, read out each name to me, letter by letter, with infinite patience. At last our preparations seemed fool-proof. At six o'clock we made a final tour of inspection of the table. The chefs expressed their satisfaction and confidence. The champagne was cooled to exact temperature. The string quartette had been positioned so that its cadences would please the ear without disturbing the flow of conversation. The floral decorations were a glory of pink and white. The dining-room, long and narrow with panelled walls, was lit by a hundred candles. Our labours had not been in vain. Not for three centuries had Prague seen anything like this.

I went home to dress and at eight-fifteen I took my place behind Sir George and Lady Clerk with the rest of the Legation staff. We were an imposing assembly. Lady Clerk was supported by Cynthia Seymour and Irene Boyle. Sir George was flanked by Coulson, magnificent in the tartan trews of the King's Own Scottish Borderers, Latter, Bubela and myself. Dinner was at eight-thirty. At twenty-five minutes past eight, the first guest arrived. He was a noble. Between twenty-five and half-past eight, all the nobility had arrived. At half-past there was not a Czech in the room. Between half-past eight and nine o'clock odd assortments made their appearance. Already my optimism had begun to flag. I had noticed a malicious smile on the lips of the Princess Lobkowitz. Worse still, I had realised that my table-plan would have to undergo an eleventh-hour operation. Czechs, who had refused or not answered, had arrived. Some, who had accepted for their wives, had left them at home. Others, who had refused, had brought them with them. Between nine and a quarter past a few more stragglers put in their appearance. At a quarter past, two ministers were still missing. With fear in my heart I looked at Sir George. He was pale but outwardly calm. Ultra-dignified but inwardly vastly amused, the nobility had settled down in the best points of vantage to watch the fun. For myself, I was in a sweat. I had been dashing backwards and forwards between the reception-rooms and the dining-room in a feverish effort to bring some order into my wretched table-plan. I now rushed off to telephone to the missing ministers.

While I was ringing up the exchange, one minister arrived with his wife who had not accepted. I could not get on to the other minister. At twenty-five past nine he came in very sheepishly, his face red with nervousness and his new shoes creaking loudly on the parquetted floor. My heart went out to him. I would sooner have faced a dozen firing squads than have to run the gauntlet of those staring well-born eyes.

We sat down to dinner just after nine-thirty. It went off better than I expected. The food, it is true, was spoilt. The soup was cold. Sir George's remedy was champagne and more champagne. Fortunately, neither the Czechs nor the "Blacks" were teetotallers, and after a silent beginning tongues flowed as freely as the Roederer itself. But the two groups did not mix, and the experiment was not repeated. Later on, indeed, Sir George was eminently successful in blending aristocrat with democrat at intimate luncheons, but for the rest of his stay in Prague Legation parties were divided carefully into Czech parties and "Black" parties.

CHAPTER THREE

I CAME to Prague with pro-Czech sympathies. They survived my stay there. I am pro-Czech to this day, partly, because I am a champion of the rights of small nations; partly, because so many of my countrymen were snobs who condemned the Czechs offhand without knowing them; but, chiefly, because of my admiration for the Czech leaders.

Six of them were men of exceptional merit. They were President Masaryk, Dr. Beneš, Dr. Švehla, Dr. Rašin, Dr. Kramař, and M. Tusar. I was privileged to be on terms of intimacy with all six.

Thomas Masaryk is to-day the most picturesque figure in Europe. I could write a tome about his career, his virtues, his influence for good. Here I shall try to describe him in a series of cinematic pictures.

My first picture is of a young Slovak boy. His father is a Slovak coachman, his mother a German peasant woman. He has been brought up in the humblest circumstances. His only learning has been acquired at the village school. He has one asset. He is bilingual, speaking Slovak and German with equal facility. Now at the age of sixteen he has been sent off to Vienna to earn his living. He is apprenticed to a Viennese locksmith. His evenings are spent in laborious study. Every penny he can spare is spent on books. But he is a good workman. He earns the praise of his employer, and perhaps but for a fortunate accident Masaryk, the President, might now be Masaryk, the skilful Viennese locksmith. A fellow apprentice steals his books and sells them, and without his books the young Masaryk cannot live in Vienna. His soul is starved, and he returns home. His father is displeased. He cannot afford to feed an extra mouth. He apprentices his son to a local blacksmith named Beneš. There is a portent in the name. For six months the young Masaryk learns to forge in order that forty years later he may teach the young Edward Beneš to forge the independence of his country.

My second picture is twenty years later. Masaryk is now a professor in Prague—a post which he accepted with diffidence because of his insufficient knowledge of the Czech language! He is a member of the Austrian Parliament. He is a great scholar with an international reputation as a philosopher. An Austrian Police President, let it be recorded, has helped him to free himself from manual labour and to devote his life to learning. A Jew, who commits suicide, leaves him a substantial legacy. He professes himself a Socialist in the higher sense of the word; he has little sympathy with the narrow intolerance of the Social-Democrats. He has written a book against Marx. Above all, however, he is a seeker after truth and an implacable enemy of every form of injustice. The year is 1899. Austria-Hungary is in a ferment. An unfortunate Jew called Hilsner has been accused of the ritual murder of a Bohemian peasant-girl. The alleged murder is the signal for a wild outburst of anti-Semitism. The populace, stirred up by anti-Semitic agitators, organises a series of pogroms against the Jews, who appeal to Masaryk to defend them. Masaryk does not hesitate. He examines the case, convinces himself that the charge is baseless, and then in his newspaper, the *Čas,* tears to shreds the evidence, supported by forged documents, of the witnesses and exposes the corruption of the judges. He suffers severely. So high does feeling run that his own students organise demonstrations against him, while by the majority of his countrymen he is denounced as the paid servant of the Jews. His efforts, too, are of no avail. Hilsner is sentenced to imprisonment for life.

Again the scene moves forward ten years. Again Masaryk is championing the cause of justice against the weight of public opinion. This time his challenge is flung down to the Imperial Government and to the Catholic Church. Again he is defending a man who is not of his own race. Dr. Wahrmund, a German Professor at the University of Innsbruck, has been deprived by the Austrian Government of his chair because of a lecture in which he has criticised the Roman Catholic Church for its interference with the teaching of science. Masaryk takes up the case. Although inspired by a profound faith in God and although himself the purest and most disinterested of men, he is regarded by the clericals as little better than anti-Christ. At the next Parliamentary elections the Catholics urge their followers to reject him in the form of this litany: "Those who love their country, do not vote for Masaryk! Those who love their wives, do not vote for Masaryk! Those who believe in Christ, do not vote for Masaryk!" It is the spirit of the old Habsburg Austria. But we are now in 1911. Masaryk is returned with a majority of nearly a thousand votes.

My final picture is of the Masaryk as I know him, the Masaryk of the last thirteen years, Masaryk the Anglophil, Masaryk the Good, Masaryk the Sage of Prague. I see him now in his library in the Hradčany, where I first met him, a dignified, gentle scholar with white beard and a lean, erect, athletic figure. The massive forehead has shrunk a little, but the kind, grey eyes look one straight in the face. Here, one feels, is a man who has never had to lie.

In Plato's Republic kings were philosophers. Here in Prague is a philosopher who is almost a king. Rows of books, reaching to the high ceiling, look down on him. They are in half-a-dozen languages, but English books predominate. The President speaks English almost perfectly. He himself is the living embodiment of the English ideal of high thinking and simple living. To-day, the summit of his material ambition is to ride again on the top of a London bus and to look down once more on the bustle of the London streets. We talk of his adventures during the war—in England and in Russia where alas! although we were there at the same time, we never met. He tells me of the disguises that he adopted in order to avoid capture. For, during the war, this straightforward, highly cultured philosopher was a conspirator and a revolutionary, who, if he had fallen into Austrian or German hands, would have suffered a traitor's death.

He tells me how he travelled to Russia on an American passport made out in the name of Bertram. Fortunately, his steamer escaped the vigilance of the German submarines. Even in wartime deception does not come easily to the inherently honest. When he arrives in St. Petersburg and opens his kit-bag, he finds that all his collars are marked "T. G. Masaryk."

He talks without a trace of affectation or vanity. He is a man of peace and goodwill, desirous of living at peace with his neighbours and willing to remedy the injustices of the Peace Treaty. He is no Pan-Slavist, no Imperialist, and, although his work of conciliation has been hampered by the chauvinist elements among his own people, the value of his moderating influence on the fiery course of Central European politics during the last fifteen years has been inestimable.

Mr. H. G. Wells once told me that he considered Masaryk and Lenin the two greatest men he had ever met. Certainly, the Czechoslovak President is the most inspiring moral force with which I have ever come into contact. Yet in his make-up the moral is to some extent dependent on the physical. The man's bodily fitness is astounding. I have one very vivid memory of that same library in the Hradčany. Its floor is covered with a valuable Eastern carpet. An Indian Maharajah is present. With his foot he points to some hidden beauty of the texture. With the agility of a boy the octogenarian President bends down and examines the wefts so closely and so intently that the Maharajah begins to wonder if the old gentleman has had a stroke and cannot raise himself again. The President sets the Indian's fears at rest by springing lightly to his feet. For years a system of gymnastics invented by Dr. Tyrš and practiced by the whole nation has fostered the national spirit of the Czechs. President Masaryk still does the Tyrš exercises every morning, can still at eighty-five touch his toes without bending his knees. His physical fitness is due, partly, to the ascetic nature of his life—he eats sparingly and never touches alcohol—and, partly, to his passion for riding. My own riding days are done, and, during my stay in Czechoslovakia, a proper sense of the ridiculousness of my seat on a horse made me decline all invitations to ride with the President.

It is now seventeen years since one day in Moscow I received a telegram from our Foreign Office. It contained a request that I should at once approach Trotsky with a view to securing a free passage out of Russia for the Czech troops in that country. The telegram referred to a man called Beneš—a name which in my ignorance I assumed was pronounced "Beans." He was then secretary of the Czech Council in Paris. When in 1920 I came to Prague, I found him installed as the Foreign Minister of the new Czechoslovak Republic. There he has remained ever since. I christened him "Beans," and "Beans" I expect he remains to the members of the British Legation in Prague to this day.

I have known Dr. Beneš for fifteen years. I have been engaged with him in delicate negotiations on several occasions. Once his word has been given, he has invariably fulfilled his promise even when the fulfilment has provoked the severe displeasure of his own Parliament.

He is so well known that here I need touch only on the high spots of his career. The son of a poor country peasant-farmer, he was sent, at great sacrifice on the father's part, to the University of Prague. Here he came under the influence of Professor Masaryk, an influence which was to alter his whole outlook on life and to which he owes the first-fruits of his political success. It was Masaryk who picked him out as the spear-head of the liberation movement. It was Masaryk who persuaded the young student, at the end of his first year at the university, to spend the next three years abroad.

He set out in 1905 for Paris with no other means in his pocket than the journey-money granted to him by the Prague branch of the "Alliance Française." His life was full of hardships. He lived by his pen, but, although his output was large, the Czech Liberal and Socialist periodicals for which he wrote were not in a position to remunerate the young student very highly. It was in Paris that he acquired that iron self-discipline which has made him to-day one of the most strenuous workers in the world. In 1908 he was awarded the degree of doctor of law by the University of Dijon. The thesis, which won him the honour, showed in what channels his mind was working. It was entitled: "The Austrian Problem and the Czech Question: A study of the political struggles of the Slav nationalities in Austria." In 1908, too, he spent several months in London, living in a room close to the British Museum. In London he made a study of the drink question and there acquired that horror of alcoholism which makes him to-day a warm sympathiser with the Prohibition movement. He came back to Prague in the same year and from then until the outbreak of the war his time was divided between political journalism and his professional duties at the university. During all these years, however, he was preparing himself for the life-struggle for which he felt he had been chosen and which from the beginning he had foreseen would be inevitable. Then came July, 1914, and the young Beneš, just turned thirty, was face to face with his destiny. With a complete disregard of all personal risk he threw himself into the struggle with all the ardour of his restless energy. "Per aspera ad astra" was his motto, and he became immediately one of the most active members of the Maffia, the famous Czech secret society, which rendered signal services to the Allies during the war. Twice, during 1914 and 1915, he undertook perilous journeys on false passports to Switzerland in order to confer with Masaryk. Finally, one dark night in September, 1915, with the Austrian police hot on his tracks, he slipped across the Bohemian frontier—and made his way to Paris.

It was his second visit. The young student of ten years before had come back to plead the cause of his people before the Allies. The story of those anxious two years during which the Czech leaders were fighting for recognition has been told often. And of these Czech leaders Beneš, the youngest, was the most active. Twice he was arrested on his way between France and England as an Austrian spy. He met with many rebuffs, but his patience never failed him. He had one slogan: break Germany on her weakest flank. He never tired of repeating it. At last the Allies listened, and in November, 1918, the young Czech professor had created a living state out of an abstract idea. For the realisation of this triumph the chief credit must be given to President Masaryk. His unselfish idealism was the inspiring force of all his followers. His, too, was the brain which guided and shaped the whole movement. The sword, however, was the sword of Beneš. Without his untiring energy and his fearless thrust the plan could never have been put into execution. For a reward he was put in charge of the

Czechoslovak Foreign Office, and on October 28, 1918, he entered upon his new duties as the youngest foreign minister of modern times.

The work which had to be accomplished was stupendous. A whole service had to be created out of material that was raw beyond words. In the ranks of the Austro-Hungarian bureaucracy few Czechs had ever risen beyond the grade of a second-division clerk. Unlike the aristocracy in Poland, the Bohemian aristocracy was frankly hostile to the new state, and a diplomatic personnel had to be formed from men, few of whom had ever worn a dress-coat in their lives. Central Europe, too, was in a chaotic state when the young Czechoslovak Minister returned to his native city after the Peace Conference. A Bolshevik Government had seized the supreme power in Hungary. Vienna, an immobile body bereft of all its limbs, lay bleeding and unable and even unwilling to help itself. In the Succession States, which had reaped the full reward of the victory of the Allies, the flames of patriotism, fanned by the military agents of France, threatened to spread into a blaze of senseless hate. Within a few months the voice of the pessimist was already strident. In London, and even in Paris, financiers, bound by business connections of long standing with Vienna, looked aghast on the impending ruin. The old order in Central Europe was not slow to exploit this situation, and Allied observers asked themselves with increasing premonition: "Had there been a terrible mistake? How could these new nations, with their governments built up from the ranks of ex-waiters and peasants, ever make good?"

It is the great service of Dr. Beneš to his countrymen that by his powers of organization and by his own personal talents he has gained for Czechoslovakia a prestige among the councils of nations out of all proportion to its size and strength. No statesman in Europe to-day knows his job so well. I remember his first meeting with Mr. Baldwin in 1923. Lord Curzon introduced the two men. "Here," he said, "is the little man for whom we send when we are in trouble. And, by Jove, he always puts us right."

The truth is that Dr. Beneš is far better equipped for diplomacy than many of the amateur ministers of Downing Street or the

Quai d'Orsay. In the game of foreign affairs a small nation is always at a disadvantage. Only a Great Power can afford the luxury of ignorance. The diplomatist of a small nation must know everything, must speak all languages, and must study as a fine art the psychology of both his friends and his enemies.

Among the diplomatists of Central Europe Dr. Beneš is the most expert and most talented. He knows the atmosphere of every capital in Europe. He is more at home in the Council of the League of Nations than within the walls of his own Parliament. This, in fact, is his strength and his weakness. His success is due to natural ability harnessed to incessant application. No German has ever worked so hard. No Slav has ever led so spartan a life. He rises at seven and works without rest until far into the night. He eats very sparingly. He has never touched alcohol or tobacco. His capacity for taking pains has triumphed over all the disadvantages of his poverty. He has had to learn foreign languages in his scanty hours of leisure, and, although his linguistic abilities are not to be compared with those of a pre-war Tsarist diplomatist, he has acquired a knowledge of French, German, Russian, Italian, and English, which, had he been an English minister, would have won him a reputation for omniscience. A great footballer in his youth, he has a wiry athletic figure. To-day, at fifty, he still seems able to work sixteen hours a day and to retain his physical fitness. And with all his success he remains a modest, little man, calm, logical, almost apologetic, and always smiling. The smile is misleading. He is a good friend. He can be a formidable enemy.

There is a tendency in England to regard Dr. Beneš as a puppet of the French. This view is exaggerated. True, he owes much to France, and, in the present state of Europe, he relies for security on the military strength of France. But his policy is dictated, first and foremost, by the needs of his own country. That policy has two objects: (1) to secure the consolidation of the new Republic by cutting the chains which bound it to the old Austro-Hungarian monarchy, and (2) to establish a new economic order in Central Europe, which, while leaving unimpaired the political liberties of the new Succession States, will restore something of the economic entity of the old régime. In his own words, it was the policy of "first destroy and then create." The work of destruction has been successfully—all too successfully—completed. The tariff restrictions, which to-day encircle the Succession States like a Chinese wall, impeding the natural flow of trade, are the direct result of that destruction. It is perhaps the chief defect of Dr. Beneš's statesmanship that the work of creation has been gravely retarded. He is not the first revolutionary who has found the work of destruction easier than the work of restoration.

It would be absurd to hold Dr. Beneš responsible for the existing chaos in Central Europe. Contrary to the general English opinion, his name is not synonymous with Czechoslovakia. He has enemies in his own country. At all times he has had considerable difficulty with his own Parliament and from the beginning his attitude towards Austria and Hungary has been more liberal than that of many of his compatriots. Although he might be forgiven for having personal grievances against the old régime (during the war his wife was imprisoned and locked up with ordinary streetwalkers by the Austro-Hungarian Government for no other reason than that she was the wife of Beneš), he is essentially a man of peace who will always prefer the cipher codes of diplomacy to the rattle of the sabre.

The other Czechoslovak leaders are little known in England. Their influence, however, has been as great as that of Masaryk and Beneš—in domestic politics perhaps even greater. For the first ten years the real master of Czech politics was the late Antonin Švehla, the leader of the powerful Agrarian or peasants' party. He is worth a place in any portrait-gallery of post-war European statesmen. Prime Minister for five years, Švehla was the complete antithesis of Beneš. He had a horror of publicity, hated public speaking, and kept himself in the background as much as possible. But both in office and out of it his influence in the council chamber and in the Parliamentary lobbies was supreme.

I was, I think, the first foreigner to establish personal relations with him. In appearance a Pickwickian figure with a round bespectacled, benevolent face, he impressed me by his Anglo-Saxon phlegm. Once he had expropriated the estates of the big landowners in order to satisfy his peasants, he took a firm stand against the exaggerated nationalism of the Chauvinists and advocated conciliatory measures towards the German minority. The presence of German ministers to-day in the Government coalition is mainly the result of Švehla's tact and genius for compromise.

A thoroughly practical politician, Švehla was a very attractive figure who might have played an immense part in the refashioning of Central Europe. Unfortunately, as a result of taking no exercise, never resting from work, and smoking cigars all day, he broke down in health completely six years ago. He died in 1934. After the President he enjoyed more respect among his countrymen than any other Czech. He would have made an admirable successor to Masaryk.

Perhaps the most interesting personality, however, and, certainly, the greatest revolutionary whom Czechoslovakia has produced was Dr. Rašin, the first Minister of Finance. In my capacity as Commercial Secretary I had frequent access to, and many duels with, Alois Rašin. He was a fighter. As short as Beneš but stouter and more solid, he had a fine mouth and nose, a Louis Napoleon beard, an immense forehead, and eyes that would have quelled a tiger.

In his own sphere Alois Rašin was a remarkable man, perhaps even a great man. He had his defects. In politics he was narrow-minded and ultra-national. In 1893, when still a young man who had just finished his university career, he was arrested by the Austrian police for belonging to a secret society and was condemned to two years' hard labour and deprived of his degree as a doctor of law. During the war he had been condemned to death for treason, but even with the sentence hanging over his head he had never retracted.

As Minister of Finance of the new Republic he stood out among the Finance Ministers of Central Europe like a giant in Lilliput. A Francophil in politics, he was a whole-hearted admirer of England and of English methods in finance. His whole effort was devoted to the task of making expenditure conform with revenue, of inculcating thrift in the minds of his countrymen, and of covering all deficits by taxation and not by borrowing. "Only Puritan simplicity," he used to tell me, "can extricate the nations of Europe from the misfortunes arising out of the war." And with grim resolution he set himself to oppose the orgy of expenditure which resulted from the boom years following on the Armistice. He taxed his people as no people in Europe except the English have been taxed. He was attacked by the Socialists. He was attacked by his own capitalists, who resented his incursions into their profits. He heeded nobody, feared nobody. He had a plan, where his critics had only vague objectives, and by sheer will power and personal magnetism he overcame all opposition. When the printing presses of Vienna began to work overtime, he saved the finances of his own country by boldly separating the Czech currency from the Austrian. He had foreseen the probability of a currency collapse in Austria and Germany and at the time of the Armistice he advocated the appointment of an Allied Financial Commission whose functions would be to sit in the State banks in Berlin and in Vienna in order to control inflation. His advice, however, was not taken, and he never forgave Mr. Lloyd George, whom, rightly or wrongly, he blamed for the rejection of his proposal.

His character was pure gold. He was open as a book and spoke his mind with a frankness which won the respect of his enemies. As a worker he was indefatigable, and he never tired of preaching the gospel of work to his fellow citizens. "Because we are a small people," he once told me, "we must be filled with the idea that each one of us must do the work of two men. Only in this way can we become a great people." Ten years of strenuous personal effort brought its own reward. In 1922, first of all the nations of Europe, Czechoslovakia was able to float a public loan on the London market. A few months later the man to whom more than to any other individual the Czechs owe their financial stability was struck down by the bullet of a mentally deficient Communist. He died as bravely as he had lived, leaving behind him a tradition which has been faithfully followed by his successors.

No picture of Czechoslovak life in those early post-war days would be complete without some reference to Dr. Karel Kramař, the one Czech statesman, with the possible exception of Masaryk, whose name was known before the war to the outside world.

A tall, handsome, cultured man with a striking head of stubbly white hair, fine features, and a pointed beard, Kramař had been one of the great pre-war figures in the Austrian Reichsrat where his fiery oratory rarely failed to fill the benches. In the Austrian Parliament the Czechs played the same rôle as the Irish in the House of Commons, and Kramař was the Austrian Parnell. Rich and widely travelled, he was the accepted champion of his people. Like Rašin, he had been arrested and condemned to death by the Austrian Government during the war. But for the death of the Emperor Franz Josef he would probably have gone down to history with Hus as the greatest of Czech martyrs. On the accession of Charles I he received the benefit of the general amnesty granted to political prisoners by the young Emperor.

For the sake of his own place in history it might have been better for him if he had faced the firing squad. When I arrived in Prague, he had just resigned his post of honour as the first Prime Minister of the new Czechoslovakia. His rather short forehead and his firm jaw betokened obstinacy, and his character, redeemed by great personal charm, was a mixture of erudition and pig-headedness. He had been an obstinate figure at the Peace Conference. He was as obstinate in his own Cabinet, where his reactionary capitalist views clashed hopelessly with the radical and socialist tendencies of his colleagues. He was one of the Czechs to whom I had a letter of introduction. It had been given to me by Prince Lvoff, my old Moscow friend and the first Prime Minister of Russia after the abdication of the Tsar. I could not have had a better introduction, for Kramař was more Russian than the Russians—a Pan-Slavist who believed that the best safeguard for his country's independence was a strong Russia. Married to the daughter of a rich Moscow manufacturer, he loathed the Bolsheviks with an implacable hatred. He was, of course, an interventionist and in 1919 was a warm supporter of Mr. Winston Churchill. It was his Russian policy and his complete absorption in Russian affairs, which, more even than his die-hard attitude towards home affairs, ruined his career in his own country.

His luxurious villa on the left wing of the Hradčany Hill overlooking the river was and still is a home for every anti-Bolshevik

Russian. He was a charming host and a brilliant conversationalist. We always spoke Russian together and, although I disagreed fundamentally with his views, it was hard to avoid talking about Russia. It was almost worse when we discussed Czechoslovakia. His jealousy of Masaryk and his hatred of Beneš were scarcely concealed, and gradually I dropped out of his life.

To-day, he lives in the reflected glory of his pre-war career. He is still the fierce anti-German, whose life has been spent in the glorious task of freeing his country from its foreign yoke. Since his resignation he has never taken office again. He is now seventy-four, and his career is ended. In spite of his rather childish vanity I felt strangely drawn towards him. His fate has been like a Greek tragedy. After wandering for many years in a foreign land, he entered into his kingdom, had his brief reign of glory, and then his own countrymen rejected him. His pride has softened the bitterness of his closing years. He has never winced in public. He still believes in the fundamental soundness of his views and in the ultimate triumph of his cause. When this lone, proud and lovable figure has passed from the stage, his country will forget the post-war Kramař and remember only the Reichsrat orator who for thirty years fought his country's battle with brilliant forensic skill and indomitable courage.

My last Czech portrait is of Vlastimil Tusar, the former leader of the Czech Social-Democrat Party and the Prime Minister of Czechoslovakia at the time of my arrival. I have kept Tusar to the end, because in many respects he was the most far-seeing of all the Czechs and because, if he had been blessed with better health and stronger physique, he might have done more than any one now living for the pacification of Central Europe.

Tusar was an extraordinarily attractive personality, shy and modest but very human when one penetrated the barriers of his reserve. He had a lame leg, and his whole expression reflected the pain of his physical discomfort. Small and of poor physique, he had a drooping silky moustache, a complexion as white as wax, and the gentlest of watery blue eyes. He was the son of a tailor and was more or less self-educated. But his vision and his understanding were the result of a long and varied experience in the school of life. He knew Vienna as well as he knew Prague. He had rubbed shoulders with nearly all the international Socialists of Europe and in the process his own Socialism had mellowed until it was scarcely recognisable.

I remember one glorious evening with him just after his resignation. I had been to one of the numerous official receptions. There had been the usual champagne, the usual victory celebration speeches, and the usual toasts to the glorious Allies. Bored with the monotony of these futilities, I had gone on to a cabaret, had taken a box by myself and was engaged in watching the gyrations of a Viennese dancer, when suddenly I spotted Tusar in the box next to me. He was alone. There was a full bottle of white wine in front of him. He, too, had been bored by the official party and had slipped away. He waved to me to join him, and for two hours I listened to one of the best and most entertaining human histories I have ever heard. Simply and without a trace of vanity he told me his life story: his early struggles to earn his daily bread, his experiences as a young Socialist in Vienna, his marriage, his escapes during the war, his rise to power, and his ambitions. He had no illusions about the permanence of the victory sentiment or of the value of Allied support. He had already retreated from glory, if, indeed, he had ever been there. He was an anti-militarist without the fanaticism of the sentimental pacifist. But he was a man without hates, holding that national hate was the foster-mother of all wars, and he had no wish to see his country made the cat's-paw of any Great Power. "In the present state of Central Europe," he said, "we require an army to preserve order. But it is a costly experiment. The French wish to see us strong. Yet they sell us their dud war material and make us pay a high price for it." Not even excepting Masaryk he was the one Czech who could view the Central European problem as a whole, dispassionately and not from the narrow angle of Czech nationalism. Although not possessed of one-tenth the erudition of a Kramář or a Beneš, he saw more clearly than any Czech that the future prosperity of Czechoslovakia would depend to a very large extent on his countrymen's ability to placate the minority races of the Republic. He was therefore a warm advocate of a policy of conciliation not only towards the German Bohemians but also towards the Germans of the Reich. He was one of the few Czechs who mistrusted the French alliance.

He was most entertaining on the subject of the great European Socialists. In his search for knowledge he had dabbled at one time with Bolshevism and had met both Lenin and Trotsky in pre-war days in Vienna. "What did you think of Lenin?" I asked. "We respected him," he answered simply. "Most of all we respected his independence. He was beholden to no man." "And Trotsky?" I asked. "Ah!" he replied, "when Trotsky came along the street, we crossed to the other side. He was always trying to borrow money."

Tusar's tolerance and breadth of vision was to some extent the result of his marriage. His wife was a baker's daughter—a blonde Viennese who played her rôle of Madame Sans-Gêne in the new Republic with infectious gaiety and disarming enthusiasm. She enjoyed the privileges of her new position; the fine dresses, which it gave to her, the title of Frau Minister-President. Above all, she liked entertaining and, of course, dancing.

At official parties the Czechs had an official minister of ceremonies, a good-natured lawyer, who took his duties with the seriousness of a ballet-master. Not so Madame Tusar, who replaced ceremonial by an all-conquering good nature. General Pellé, the French chief of the Czech General Staff and a hero of the Marne, would not be dancing. She would push him into the arms of an admiring Czech, and off they would go trotting gravely round the ball-room. She would defeat even the dignity of my own Minister. With arms akimbo she would stand before his six-foot of immaculate elegance, while her eyes would flash a message which conveyed the German equivalent of "what about it?" She never met with a rebuff. Indeed, only a curmudgeon could have resisted such genuine light-heartedness. I flatter myself that in the waltz I was her favourite partner. She was rather plump. But where is the Viennese who cannot waltz? In any case her figure was admirably suited to my own burly squatness. And there, in that same palace, where the ill-fated Charles, the last Emperor of Austria, had lived with his tutor as a boy, the orchestra would strike up

"The Blue Danube," her arm would wave a Napoleonic command, and I would brace myself for what was, in fact, a test of endurance.

We would begin decorously, almost slowly. Then, as the other couples began to withdraw, she would order the band to increase the tempo. My right arm would sink lower, until it grasped her waist in a "rugger" tackle. Then, reversing in ever narrowing circles until we could almost have spun round a plate, we pursued our feverish course until we had the floor to ourselves. When at last Viennese blood could stand no more, giddy and reeling I would lead her to the wall. The bystanders would clap their hands. Then, with her heart beating audibly and her blue eyes shining, she would give my hand a last grateful squeeze and whisper rapturously: "Gott im Himmel. Das war schoen!"

She was years younger than her husband, who treated her like a doll. But in her own way I think she influenced him in favour of her own suffering country. Hate of the Habsburg system. Hate of the big landowners and the big capitalists who had exploited Bohemia's wealth for the benefit of Vienna. That one could understand in a Czech. But hatred of the warm-hearted Viennese people was a culpable prejudice, which may yet react unfavourably on the Czechs themselves. Tusar was free of this prejudice. Two years after my arrival in Prague, he went as Czechoslovak Minister to Berlin, where both Herr Stresemann and Lord D'Abernon, then at the peak of his power in Berlin, had the highest opinion of his statesmanship. He died at his post in 1924.

Obviously, Czechoslovakia cannot always expect to produce men of the exceptional qualities of the six men whom I have described. Of these six only Dr. Beneš is comparatively young—only Dr. Beneš enjoys robust health. Three are dead, and already pessimists both inside and outside the Republic are anticipating the calamity which may follow when the remaining three disappear from the political stage.

Those who know the Czechs will not share this pessimism. Englishmen, far more than Americans, are inclined to overlook the fact that in Austria-Hungary, as in Russia, the dynasty and the ruling class connected with it were going towards their inevitable doom. The war hastened a natural process; the Peace

Treaties merely unloosed the forces which were already straining at the leash. The Czechs, at any rate, have made good their claims to independence. At a time when Central Europe was a kind of witches' cauldron bubbling over with corruption, debauchery, dishonesty and decadence, they furnished the one justification of a nation's vitality. They produced the men—and I write without exaggeration—the exceptional men whom the moment demanded. At a time when a whole world was crumbling round them, they were not afraid to build. They may not have built perfectly. But I feel sure that they have built solidly.

CHAPTER FOUR

I ENJOYED my first year in Prague or Praha, as the Czechs call it. After my first three months I went home for a fortnight to England for the birth of my son. In August my wife came out to join me and to choose a flat which would accommodate the addition to our household and provide the necessary air and light for an English nursery. After a long and troublesome search we found a roomy furnished flat close to the Kinsky Gardens on the Hradčany side of the river. We engaged a staff of servants including a model Czech chauffeur and Marie, a Czech cook, who remained with me for six years and who in fifteen months taught my son to gurgle in Czech. Then, having settled the question of our future residence, my wife went home in November, returning in the following April with my boy and an English nurse.

It was our first experience of diplomatic life in a small capital, and for a time at any rate the novelty blinded my eyes to the meanness of what is, in effect, a belittling and narrow existence. Life was cheap. Both Czechs and Allies were still living on the champagne of victory, and finding my feet in strange surroundings provided sufficient work to keep me out of mischief. My diplomatic colleagues were exotic and varied. The creation of a whole series of new states had added greatly to their number, and many like the Poles, the Letts, and the Esthonians were new to the job. The bulk of them were more ornamental than useful. With a natural instinct for maintaining the balance of power we English sided with the Americans in order to counteract the influence of the French, who with a little marquis and a couple of counts in their mission had the advantage not only of numbers but also of titles.

The Americans, however, had the money and in Alan Winslow,

a fair-haired, blue-eyed airman, who had lost an arm in the war, the good looks. For their Legation they had the famous Schoenborn Palace. Their minister was Richard Crane, the original son of an original father. I had met Charles Crane, the father, in Russia. He was a rich Chicago sanitary ware manufacturer with an interest in diplomacy, education, and Russian church music. He had been for years a profound admirer of President Masaryk and at one time had employed Jan Masaryk, the President's son and now Czechoslovak Minister in London, in his Chicago factory. During my stay in Prague he visited Czechoslovakia several times and was, I think, the first American to come to Europe via the Siberian railway after the Bolshevik revolution. Both he and his son were gentle and hospitable Anglophils. Alan Winslow was almost one of ourselves. McCabe, the military attaché, was an Irish-American with a sense of humour and a good-humoured contempt for diplomatists, whom he christened "the white-spat brigade." He had been a fine boxer and even in middle age preferred a straight blow to an argument. He created a minor sensation by slapping the face of an Austrian prince of unimpeachable lineage but of questionable morals. Warm-hearted and generous, he was a grand fellow. Indeed, all the Americans—and with their Food missions and other relief organisations they made a brave showing—were a very cheery lot. As they themselves said, they were the boys who put the "ha-ha" into Praha.

In our own Legation most of the work was done by Sir George Clerk, an industrious and punctilious chief, and by the precise and efficient Latter. I had an infinite capacity for looking busy. John Henry Stopford Birch, our First Secretary, provided that leisured dignity which supplies the necessary brake to the impetuousness of the over-zealous. More stories are told of John Henry, now Minister in Central America, than of any other member of the British diplomatic service. An excellent linguist with a somewhat Spanish appearance, he had served in half the capitals of the world and had succeeded in satisfying all his chiefs with a minimum expenditure of energy and trouble to himself. In his youth he had been one of the lesser lights that rule the night, and both as a master of the tango and the Viennese waltz and as a connoisseur of cocktails he added to the gaiety of our social existence. He was a man whom no one could help liking.

Even that stern disciplinarian, Lord Kitchener, had yielded to the subtlety of his charm. John Henry had been under the great man in Cairo and for the first time in his life was in some danger of being over-worked. Then one morning, as Lord Kitchener was giving a breakfast-party on the Residency verandah, a buggy pulled up outside the high garden wall. Out clambered a squat figure in full evening dress. Just as it was sprawling over the wall, Lord Kitchener looked up. For a moment his eyebrows bristled in an apprehensive query. Then he recognised John Henry and burst into a roar of laughter. From that moment John Henry was immune from all attempts by Lord Kitchener to cramp the soul of diplomacy with military discipline.

John Henry's arrival in Prague also bore the stamp of originality. Within twenty-four hours he had requested and had been granted a week-end's leave in order to go to Vienna. Monday came but without John Henry. By Wednesday Sir George Clerk began to grow restive. His fingers played a rapid succession of staccato semiquavers on his desk. "Where was Birch?" I did not know. As the days passed, Sir George's face, which on occasions can be sterner than that of any man I know, began to assume a set expression. On the following Sunday morning he sent for me. "I hear that Birch has come back," he said. "I'll see him after luncheon." He looked and was very angry. I think he had postponed the interview in order that his wrath might not influence his judgment. With the fellow-feeling of one undisciplined nature for another, I rushed off to warn John Henry. He was magnificently unperturbed. We lunched well and slowly. After coffee and brandy I drove him back to the Legation and waited in the Chancery, while he went upstairs to see the Minister. In twenty minutes he came down again. He looked hot, but there was a twinkle in his eyes. He was whistling softly the refrain of the latest Viennese song "In der kleinen American Bar." "Well?" I said. "All right," he replied laconically. "But," I stammered, "what on earth did you say?" "I told the truth," said John Henry. "And the truth?" I asked. "Well, I told him that I had gone to Vienna to buy a car. It *was* the truth." "Yes," I said, "but that's no excuse for over-staying your leave." "I agree," said John Henry. "But you see the car had to be painted, and, as I had to drive it back, I had to wait until the paint dried." "But why didn't you telegraph?" I asked. "I did," said John Henry solemnly. In those early post-war days in Central Europe telegrams did not always arrive. John Henry, I felt, was the man for a crisis.

For all his careless nonchalance it was indeed true. He had done sterling work during the war in Madrid. Three years later in Tokio he was to win the golden opinion of Sir Charles Eliot for his work during the Tokio earthquake. His stay in Prague lasted just under a year. It was distinguished by one minor athletic triumph. In a rash moment I had made a large bet with Alan Winslow that the British Legation would beat the American Legation at tennis. After much wrangling it was arranged that the contest should be a doubles match of seven sets to be decided in two parts: the first to be played on any court of our choosing and the second on the court of the American Legation. The American pair was a lop-sided combination. Alan Winslow, with his one arm, was severely handicapped. But his partner, a tall, fair-haired Swedish-American, was two classes better than any one we could produce. We had some difficulty in selecting our pair. Indifferent tennis-player as I was, I picked myself both on the grounds of physical fitness and because I had the most at stake. Our other choice was John Henry, who had a good eye, had been a useful cricketer at Eton, and was still our best performer at the scientific but not very exacting game of Chancery cricket. Strenuous physical exercise, however, was now no longer his strong suit, and his staying powers were more than doubtful. We persuaded him, however, to do a little training. It consisted in his going to bed before midnight for one night, and the next day on a side-court of the Czech Lawn-Tennis Club we finished the first part of the match, played without spectators, with an advantage of three sets to one. We had only to win one set in the concluding part to collect the honour and the money. When we went up to the American Legation on the following afternoon, we found a large gathering of diplomatists including our own Minister. The story of the bet had gone the rounds, and the American Minister had given a tea-party in order to see the fun.

It was then that I first noticed or, to be more accurate, that my attention was first drawn to John Henry's tennis kit. It was the immaculate Sir George, always zealous for the dignity and honour of Britain, who directed my line of vision. "Those trousers!" he hissed. "Where on earth did they come from?" I looked. Certainly they were trousers. They were, too, in perfect repair—neither too tight nor too loose and provided with the requisite number of buttons. It was their colour which had offended Sir George's propriety. They were, in fact, a mottled study in black and white. John Henry had not played tennis since he left Madrid. He had packed his tennis trousers among his boots and boot polish. They had lain for months in some old bag and had been resuscitated for this great occasion. I now realised that against the background of the women's white frocks John Henry's trousers were an eyesore. The thought that my partner looked more like a bicycle tramp on the music-halls than a Tilden made me self-conscious, and largely owing to my erratic play we lost the first two sets. This made us three sets all with a final set to come to decide the issue. I was resigned to defeat. Already I saw myself signing that cheque for fifty pounds which I could so ill afford.

It was then that John Henry went Berserk. I have said that he was the man in a crisis, and, summoning all his reserves of nervous energy, he took complete command of the situation. Dashing from side to side, he drove the enemy and his partner off the court. In an ordinary match I should have been convulsed with laughter. As it was, my feelings were a mixture of admiration and fear—admiration for that round sweaty figure in the ridiculous trousers, who, with the fire of a Crusader in his eyes, was in the process of adding fifty pounds to my bank account, and fear, a justified and genuine fear, of physical danger to myself from John Henry's ubiquitous racket. As I staggered back on retreat towards the spectators, I smiled at Sir George. There was no answering smile. "Play up, man," he whispered sternly. The lust of victory had communicated itself from our First Secretary to our Minister Plenipotentiary. Gradually we climbed to match ball. The enemy drove a high lob into the far corner of my side of our court, and my knees trembled. With a roar of "Mine!" John Henry made three bounds and almost off my nose crashed a glorious volley right between the advancing Americans. The victory clinched, John Henry beamed. The spectators clapped, Sir George's face was transfigured. Forgotten was the iniquity of John Henry's trousers. With slow dignity he walked towards our champion. "Well played, Birch," he said gratefully.

Dear John Henry, if ever you become an Ambassador, never will you enjoy so sweet a triumph as on that summer afternoon in 1920 in the hanging gardens of the Schoenborn Palace.

One of the great dangers which zealous diplomatists incur in a small capital is loss of perspective. They become absorbed in local politics. They are inclined to attribute to purely local events an importance which they are far from possessing in world affairs. In Prague this danger was averted in our own case by the visits which we received periodically from distinguished and representative British citizens. With praiseworthy enterprise they came to study that amazing mosaic of peoples—11,000,000 Germans, 10,000,000 Hungarians, 21,000,000 Slavs and various odd millions of Roumanians, Jews and Italians—of which the former Austro-Hungarian monarchy was composed and which was then and still is so little understood by our countrymen. In those days a visit of twenty-four hours enabled one to speak with authority in the Cabinet or in the Council of the League of Nations. In 1920, therefore, the ambitious and far-sighted found their way to Prague.

First, there was Sir Samuel Hoare, who, zealous for new fields to conquer in the estate of foreign affairs, had established himself as a kind of patron saint of the Czechs. He was followed hotly by Lord D'Abernon, an impressive figure in a doublebreasted blue suit and a stiff white shirt, on the cuffs of which he jotted down his memoranda of important conversations. It was the duty of his private secretary to prevent the shirt and the cuffs from being sent to the wash until the notes had been faithfully entered in his Lordship's famous diary. Lord D'Abernon, then just beginning his reign of glory in Berlin, impressed me as the greatest

Ambassador I have ever met. His carelessness in dress and his loose collar, nearly always detached from its stud, and floating tie detracted nothing from the nobility of his commanding presence. There was always a far-away expression in his eyes, doubtless cultivated in order to increase the impression of disinterested detachment which he sought to give to all his utterances. But he spoke as one having authority, and his conversation was first-class —witty and to the point. He had, too, strong views of his own and, but for the intransigence of the French, might have given to the German Republic the permanence and stability which it has never acquired. Certainly no Ambassador of modern times has ever wielded such influence over the statesmen of the country to which he was accredited. During his seven years in Berlin the German Government rarely if ever issued a Note without first discussing its terms with this most unorthodox of British Ambassadors and accepting his advice.

If Lord D'Abernon won my admiration, his private secretary, "Tich" Whelan, impressed me no less favourably. "Tich," who went everywhere with his chief, was and is a great character—the Napoleon of all private secretaries. He had nothing to do with the Foreign Office. Lord D'Abernon, who, contrary to prevailing rumour, relied very little on his diplomatic staff and dictated all his despatches himself, had picked him out specially for his Berlin mission. He relied a good deal on Whelan, whom he always addressed as "Corporal," and in his hours of boredom unbent before him. It was "Tich" who daily wrote up to Lord D'Abernon's dictation the diary record of the great man's ambassadorship. When the task was completed, Lord D'Abernon would rise, shake his shoulders like a great bear, and say: "Corporal, we will now play billiards." Then the six-foot three of the Ambassador would engage in a solemn contest with the five-foot two of the private secretary, who with flushed face and puffed-out chest would spread-eagle himself across the table with a cue more than twice as long as himself. It was an unequal contest, but it brought joy and relaxation to the Ambassador and increased the hero-worship of the private secretary. "Tich" is now, more than any one else, the right hand of Lord Beaverbrook. I hope that some day he will write a memoir of his experiences with both his chiefs. It should be a very human document.

The most amusing of these visits was a corporate one—a delegation of members of the British intelligentsia, who at the invitation of the Czechoslovak Government descended on us in order to witness with their own eyes the progress of the new Republic. It was a distinguished delegation. It included Mr. H. G. Wells, Lord Dunsany, Sir Henry Wood, Mr. Clifford Sharp, the former editor of the *New Statesman,* the ubiquitous Sir Harry Brittain, Mr. Philip Page, the musical critic, and many other celebrities, both male and female, whose fame was at the time unknown to me and whose names have therefore eluded my memory and my diary. This visit, the first of its kind, was organised on the grand scale. There was the usual round of luncheons and dinners with appropriate speeches. Sir George gave a magnificent Venetian fête—with free champagne and cigars—in the glorious garden of the Legation. The Czechs provided the requisite number of motor-cars and their best English-speaking guides. The visit, I feel sure, must have produced beneficial results, if for no other reason than that it sowed the seeds of Mr. Wells's lasting admiration for President Masaryk. Lord Dunsany, too, must have been favourably impressed. During the four days of his stay, his guide, perplexed perhaps by his first encounter with an Irish peer, insisted on addressing him on all occasions as "Our Lord."

The proceedings began and ended on a Ruritanian note. When the delegates' train pulled up at the Wilson station, the conductor had forgotten to wake Mr. Page. The platform was crowded with Czech dignitaries—representatives of the Foreign Office, the Army and the City Fathers who had assembled to welcome the distinguished English visitors. They could not be kept waiting. Mr. Page was equal to the occasion. Unshaven and unwashed, he hastily put on his boots and his hat. Then, putting on a huge overcoat over his pyjamas, he stepped down on to the platform and took his place among his brother delegates to a roar of "Na zdar," which is the Czech for Heil, from the cheering Czechs. It was midsummer and the heat was tropical, and Mr. Page, the heavy-weight of the delegation, was at once singled out as the typical John Bull. I take off my hat to Mr. Page. His dignity never relaxed. He strode down the platform with the slow majesty of the late Sir Herbert Beerbohm Tree. He shook hands with the Lord Mayor. He saluted the Generals. He bowed gravely to the beauty chorus in peasant costumes which presented him with a bouquet of carnations. Then, with his striped pyjama trousers fluttering bravely in the sunshine, he took his place in the open carriage and, still saluting, drove through the streets, lined with the tumultuously cheering populace, to his hotel on the famous Square of St. Wenceslaus. It was an epic performance—a supreme example of English presence of mind. The Czechs noticed nothing. Perhaps I do them an injustice. I should have said that they noticed nothing incongruous. Two weeks after the visit a new fashion made its presence felt on the streets of Prague. It took the form of black and white striped flannel trousers.

If Mr. Page's pyjamas were the overture to this visit, Mr. Wells's cherries provided a thrilling finale. Tired by three days of incessant feasting and conducted tours to museums and government buildings, Mr. Wells, who is the embodiment of physical fitness, had decided to do a little sight-seeing on his own. With Mr. Page he had walked briskly out to the neighbouring countryside. The day was hot—oppressively hot, and, as "H. G." sat on the fourth milestone mopping his brow, his observant eye noticed a cherry tree heavy wth luscious fruit. In all innocence he raised his hand and helped himself to the gifts which a bountiful nature had so generously provided.

Now Czechoslovakia is not only a great industrial country. It is also admirably farmed, every inch of soil being put to profitable use. A striking feature of the Czech agricultural system is the row of fruit trees which line each side of the road. They were planted by the order of Napoleon at the time of Austerlitz and Wagram. The trees are the property of the close-fisted Czech peasantry and during the fruit season they are zealously guarded by sentinels, who are concealed in little shelters built of leafy branches. As "H. G." gathered his cherries while he might, he was duly spotted by one of these guards. There was a village close by, and the guard, impressed by Mr. Wells's robust figure, went for help.

Presently he returned with a small army of irate villagers of both sexes. The men rolled back their sleeves. The women opened the proceedings with a volley of abuse. Fortunately, H. G. is no linguist. Otherwise, his ears might have tingled. The attitude of the peasantry, however, was clear enough. It was menacing, and, yielding to superior force, Mr. Wells allowed himself to be piloted towards the village. Happily for the good name of Czechoslovakia and the physical comfort of Mr. Wells, there was no lynching, no undignified incarceration. A deus ex machina arrived in a motor-car. It was Mr. Wells's guide, who, alarmed by the disappearance of his charge, had been scouring the country and had at last tracked him down.

We had numerous other distinguished visitors. They ranged from soldiers like General du Cane and economists like Sir George Paish, already prophesying gloom and disaster from the huge tariff walls which were being erected between the Succession States, to great noblemen like the Duke of Portland.

Members and ex-members of Parliament were also fairly frequent. Of these the most interesting was the former member for Lincoln, the notorious Trebitsch-Lincoln. Trebitsch, the only foreign spy who has ever become a member of the House of Commons, was then mixed up in the German secret organisation "Konsul," which, run by Captain Ehrhardt and Colonel Bauer, was carrying on a subversive campaign against the German Republic. Its aims embraced the restoration of the monarchy both in Germany and in Hungary. Trebitsch had stopped in Prague on his way from Munich to Budapest. Reports in our possession stated that his planned visit to Budapest was in connection with an attempt to restore the Emperor Karl as King of Hungary.

Our ex-member of the House of Commons did not call at the Legation. One of our Intelligence officers, however, called at Trebitsch's hotel. It was a cat-burglar call, carried out at considerable personal risk and during Trebitsch's absence. It consisted in a crawl along a third-floor ledge from a room specially hired to Trebitsch's quarters. The fruits of this unofficial visit was a series of documents revealing the ex-M.P. as a sworn enemy of the British Empire and as an arch-plotter against the peace of Europe.

Not all our visitors were British subjects. There was also a considerable coming and going of well-known Russians. Chief of them was Boris Savinkoff, the famous Social-Revolutionary, who had been Minister of War under Kerensky. Savinkoff came to Prague twice during these early post-war years. He was accompanied by Sidney Reilly, the British secret service agent, who, after a miraculous escape from the clutches of the Bolsheviks in 1918, was to be shot down a few years later by Bolshevik frontier guards, while attempting to cross from Finland into Russia. Both men were full of a scheme for organising a peasant revolt in Russia. But the rôles were now reversed. Reilly, who had always worshipped Savinkoff, was now the real leader. Savinkoff himself was now a bundle of nerves. Sometimes, under the influence of brandy, the old fire would come into his eyes, and he could summon up some of the old energy. But his spirit was broken. There were great hollows under his eyes, and the sallow complexion had become almost yellow. He was accompanied, too, by two or three Russians in whom I felt little confidence, and, although I entertained him and enjoyed his conversation, I felt that he was a very uncertain shadow of his former self.

Kerensky, too, was another Russian who came frequently to Prague, where a small group of his colleagues, including Chernoff and Zenzinoff, was publishing a Russian newspaper. Kerensky, whom I have always liked, and Savinkoff were now poles apart, and, although both men came to Prague to enlist the sympathy and the financial support of the Czechs, their aims and objects were different, and their roads never crossed. The Czechs, who as Slavs were very generous to the Russian refugees in their midst, sympathised more with Kerensky than with Savinkoff. They were not to be drawn into any interventionist adventures, and I shared their view. Kerensky, too, I saw several times. Our conversations, however, were more of the past than of the future. As far as Russia was concerned, I felt that we both belonged irrevocably to the past. Had not the hard-working Latter summed up my character unerringly when he said that I was living in the past and on my past!

Another visit which revived more pleasant memories of Russia was the arrival of the Moscow Art Theatre on a short Central European tour. They came in full force with the great Stanislavsky, Lilina, his wife, Knipper, the widow of Chekoff, Kachaloff, Alexandroff and all the heroes of my early Moscow days. It was through my old friend, Lykiardopoulos, the former secretary of the Art Theatre, that I had first come into touch with the Russian intelligentsia. For the two years before the war I had been stage-struck. My evenings had been spent within the walls of that staid and sober building in the Kammergersky Street where no applause was allowed—only tears and unaccompanied by sobs. I had conducted many famous Englishmen, including Mr. H. G. Wells and Mr. Granville Barker, to their first view of "The Cherry Orchard," "Hamlet" with Gordon Craig's scenery, and Gorki's "The Lowest Depths." I had known personally nearly all the members of this famous company in which there were no stars and in which every actor played alternately and with unfailing perfection the rôle of hero or of super. Now in the welter of sentiment provoked by this sudden resurrection of the past I nearly lost my head—and my heart. I went to every performance in Prague. The repertory included nothing new—only my old favourites which in my mood of the moment was all that I demanded. I spent my spare time with the company. When they moved on to Zagreb, I took a week's local leave and went with them.

It was my first visit to the Croat capital and to Yugoslavia. It was spring, and the lilac was already in bloom. Was my enthusiasm entirely inspired by my artistic predilections or even by the evocation of my own short reign of glory in Russia? Certainly I enjoyed my conversations with the white-haired Stanislavsky. Politics had no interest for him. He never discussed them. He still lived in and for the theatre. He was, I think, unhappy out of Russia. He had been disappointed in his audiences abroad. European art had shocked him. It was so mercenary. Only in Croatia had he found anything approaching the same reverence for the theatre as an interpretation of life as he had inculcated in his Moscow admirers. I enjoyed, too, drinking vodka, eating Russian food, and talking over old times and hearing news of old friends from the other members of the company.

But there was also Mlle. X. I dare not give her name. I remembered her first appearance in Moscow during the war. She was then a young girl of nineteen. Now a finished actress, she had developed into the finest type of Russian woman—intense, yet strong, temperamental but self-reliant. I had known her slightly in Moscow. In Prague we had renewed our acquaintance. Now in Zagreb, where she was cut off from all her friends and where opportunity and my own insistence had thrown us together, I was to learn to know her better than one knows many people in a life-time. For a whole week I was her constant companion. At midday, when she was free, I drove her out to the glorious Croatian countryside. We lunched out of doors in the warm Southern sunshine on caviare sandwiches and sweet Croatian wine. From the hillside we looked down on the dark blue waters of the Pivlitzer lakes. We gathered posies of vetch and cornflowers in the lush Croatian meadows. At night I drove her to and from the theatre. I filled her dressing-room with flowers. But the romance was all on my side. In her profession she played such tragic parts as Irina in Chekoff's "Three Sisters." There was real tragedy in her large brown eyes, which, when they looked at you, seemed to read into your soul compelling truth and honesty. She had left her own romance in Moscow. Very simply she told me her story, her hopes of marriage, the difficulty of finding housing accommodation, the lack of privacy. Yet this was her life, and one had to make the best of it. Her heart was full of hope in the future, and her one preoccupation was counting the days until she might go back to Moscow. She, too, was unhappy out of Russia. She had full confidence in herself, and she gave me her own confidence with such faith that self-respect compelled me to restrain the sentimental impulses which were tugging at my heart-strings. She lived in an hotel called "The Three Crows," and from the beginning I felt that this sinister signboard presaged ill-omen to my suit. Yet, when we parted, I had my reward. There was a film of tears over her eyes, as we said goodbye. "Roman Romanovitch," she said in a tone of finality which brooked no contradiction, "we shall never meet again. But I shall remember your kindness and your restraint all my life. It will be my most pleasant recollection of a journey in a land of ghosts." It was an idyllic friendship, which with the years has perhaps assumed too romantic a proportion in my memory. Yet at the time it left me with a feeling of discontent at the uselessness of my own life and with an immense desire to return to Russia. More poignantly than ever before I realised how little happiness depended on material prosperity and, still less, on political systems.

CHAPTER FIVE

TO-DAY, I feel that I sadly neglected the opportunity of advancement which these visits afforded. The Russians, of course, I did not count. Russia was now outside the orb of my minor diplomatic constellation. But promotion in any government service abroad is often accelerated by the favourable reports brought back to London by influential and important visitors. In Moscow my rapid rise had been largely due to flattering praise of this nature. Politicians, bankers, soldiers, business men, who came to Russia, were always afflicted by a certain diffidence and difficulty of orientation. At no time has Russia ever been an easy country for the stranger within its gates. My local knowledge enabled me to help my distinguished compatriots in whatever sphere their business or their pleasures lay. They returned to England. They went to the Foreign Office—in certain cases it was not even difficult to suggest this procedure—and, in recounting their own triumphs to the Permanent Under-Secretary or perhaps even to the Foreign Secretary himself, they would add as a grateful afterthought that in Moscow there was a young man who knew his way about and who was devilishly well-informed. And gradually the accumulation of evidence of this sort would secure for the young man a series of good marks which in the end counted for merit and promotion.

In Prague I had the same opportunities and, doubtless, if I had been more assiduous in my efforts to avail myself of them, they would have borne good results. I blame myself for my indolent negligence. But there were extenuating circumstances. It was not merely that I had lost the little ambition I once possessed. It was not merely that in Moscow I had been cock of my own farmyard and that in Prague I was only one of the subordinates of an efficient and extremely intelligent minister. There was a difference in the attitude of the distinguished visitors themselves. In Russia they had not been ashamed to confess their ignorance. They had been eager and, indeed, grateful for information. They came to Prague as representatives of the victorious Allies. They demanded gratitude from the new Succession States and subservience from defeated and truncated Austria and Hungary. And, although Central Europe was more complex and demanded more intimate knowledge than Russia ever did, they did not hesitate to advance their own views and their own remedies with unblushing self-assurance.

Victory is the tonic of self-confidence. Unfortunately, the remedies varied in the case of the individual visitors. Some were pro-Czech and others anti-Czech. Their attitude was determined largely by the treatment which they received at the frontier station. Some saw the only hope of salvation in the restoration of the Habsburgs. Others demanded redress for Hungary. Others again were advocates of the Anschluss and were in favour of incorporating Austria in Germany. Later, when Mussolini came into power, there was a movement against the Balkanisation of Central Europe and in favour of giving a free hand to the Fascist Duce, even if it meant handling over the Dalmatian Coast to Italy. There were others—and they were the sanest—who advocated some form of economic federation, which would restore the economic entity of the former Austro-Hungarian monarchy.

The variance of these views was reflected to some extent in the attitude of our own Legations in Central Europe. In Prague Sir George Clerk realised and, as far as a guarantee of their political independence was concerned, sympathised with the aspirations of the virile Czechs. In Vienna Sir Francis Lindley had his hands full with the problem of assuring the economic existence of the Austrian Republic. He would have been less than human if he had not laid stress on the Austrian point of view. Sir Thomas Hohler was the recipient of Hungarian grievances in Budapest. In Belgrade Sir Alban Young and, later, Sir Howard Kennard were confronted with daily evidence of a triune nation, which, divided against itself in internal politics, was yet united by a common hate of Italy and a common fear of Italian aggression. But on the whole local British diplomacy favoured a general solution of the problem, and in any case its effort was exercised in favour of restraint and moderation. It was well-meaning but almost helpless in face of the French policy, which, standing boldly for the maintenance of the Peace Treaties, sought military alliances with the Czechoslovaks, the Jugoslavs and the Rumanians for the continued subjection of the defeated.

Naturally I had my own views. I have always held the opinion that even without the war the collapse of the Austro-Hungarian monarchy was inevitable. I could see no sense in a restoration which would be violently opposed by the twenty-one million Slavs and Roumanians who had been liberated by the Peace Treaties. The Habsburgs, too, were like the Romanoffs. They had no candidate capable of sustaining the rôle. In any case a Habsburg restoration meant a restoration of the feudal nobility, and I could see no virility in the charming but effete Austrian aristocracy. I was in favour of a proper frontier readjustment in favour of Hungary. But when I asked myself whether any Hungarian would be satisfied with a strictly just revision, I was forced to answer "no." I did not share the enthusiasm of many British residents in Hungary for the virtues of the Hungarians. In some respects they were an anomaly in Europe—a Mongol race among Aryans. They had a bad record in their treatment of other nationalities. Even Kossuth, the hero of their own liberation movement, had been uncompromising towards the Slavs. "Croat nationality," he declared in 1848, "I know no Croat nationality." Hungary has changed little since 1848. I could not forget that in the pre-war Hungarian Parliament 10,000,000 Hungarians had 407 deputies, while the 8,000,000 Slavs and Roumanians had only 6! Moreover, Hungary, an agricultural country, is dominated by a feudal aristocracy. How long, I asked myself, can this unnatural state of affairs be maintained when on every side of her frontier the peasants have come into possession of the land? Can the Hungarian system last in the new Europe? Will it survive the introduction of the secret ballot in Hungary?

As regards Austria, the Anschluss was superficially an attractive proposition—just the thing, in fact, to satisfy those English politicians, and there are more of them than most people imagine, who take their foreign politics from the headlines of the popular Press. It justified itself on ethnological lines. Was not the name of the new Austrian Republic Deutsch-Oesterreich—German Austria? Allowing for slight differences of accent, both Germans and Austrians spoke the same language.

Austria, said the Anschluss advocates with sound reason, cannot exist economically by herself. Let her incorporate herself with Germany, and one of the cankers of Central Europe will be healed. When one came to look into the question more closely, one found a hundred difficulties. In my own case it was not merely fear of the revival of German dreams of a vast Teutonic Mittel-Europa which raised doubts in my mind. What worried me was the uncomfortable suspicion that in her heart of hearts Austria did not really want the Anschluss. There were Austrians who genuinely believed in the Anschluss. There were others who paid lip-service to it, partly as a policy of despair and partly as a lever with which to wring concession from the Allies. There were many Austrians who would sooner face starvation than subservience to Prussia. Their number was not to be gauged by the votes cast in the elections. Austrian antipathy to Germany, above all, Viennese antipathy to Berlin, was deep-rooted. It had been intensified rather than lessened by the lessons of the war. That it had not disappeared even during the worst period of Austria's economic distress was clear to any one who was on sufficiently intimate terms with Austrians to be regarded as a friend and not as a target for propaganda.

What I believe to be even to-day the predominating Austrian point of view with regard to the Anschluss was put very succinctly by the late Dr. Seipel in a private conversation with a banker friend of mine. Dr. Seipel, indisputably the greatest statesman whom Austria has produced since the war, said: "We are of German stock. Therefore we must welcome union with our blood-brothers. We are, however, Austrians. We must therefore preserve our independence and our civilisation. The Anschluss is something which we must always advocate but never put into effect." Actually, during the period of my stay in Central Europe the attitude toward the Anschluss varied with the trade barometer. When economic conditions were intolerably bad, ninety per cent of the Austrians were for the Anschluss. When they were tolerably good, ninety per cent were against it. As for giving a free hand to Mussolini, well, I am no military expert. But when it comes to deciding what is a Great Power and what is not, I have in my diaries notes of conversations with German and Allied officers of high rank who have seen both the Italian and the Yugoslav armies. There was not one who would care to lay odds on Italy's chances in a war against Yugoslavia.

For my own part I favoured any scheme which, while safeguarding the political liberties of the new States, would help to restore the free flow of trade between the Succession States and which would put an end to the ridiculous system of Chinese walls behind which Hungary, an agricultural state, was erecting an uneconomic textile industry while Czechoslovakia, her neighbour and a huge industrial country, was trying to increase her agricultural production. The old Austro-Hungarian monarchy had many faults. It was well buried. But it had been a natural economic entity. Here was economic autarchy gone mad. There were many Allied representatives who saw the folly of this outrage on Nature. There was the story of the two villages on the Czechoslovak-Hungarian frontier. For a thousand years one village produced corn but had no fuel for the winter. The other had fuel but no grain. The inhabitants of Tarpa exchanged their grain for the wood blocks of Berehovo, and both villages were happy. Then, after the war, came the gentlemen of the Boundary Commission. They drew a line between Berehovo and Tarpa, placing the first in Czechoslovakia and the second in Hungary. The insensate folly of customs barriers and closed doors did the rest. Since 1919 the good foresters of Berehovo have starved and the honest peasants of Tarpa have frozen.

While I favoured a gradual breaking down of the barriers, I was opposed to the intervention of the Great Powers and to the idea of big conferences. From the beginning the influence of the

Great Powers, who have used the Succession States for their own ends and abetted them in many of their worst follies, has been nefarious. From the first moment of its existence Geneva has been little more than a waste-paper basket for protests and a debating ground for mutual recriminations. Why not, I said, let the Succession States settle their own differences? Let their delegates be locked up in some suitable retreat, call off the French and the Italians, and let them remain there until they produced some workable arrangement. Alas! even this was impossible.

Like many other people I wrote innumerable memoranda on this subject. I spoke with Czechs, Hungarians, Bulgarians, Austrians, Roumanians, and Yugoslavs. There were reasonable people in all four countries, but they were swamped in the morass of national chauvinism and international hate. The Czechs accepted the ideal of economic co-operation, but they played for postponement. In Hungary, too, there were men who realised that one day Hungarians would have to trade with Czechs and Czechs with Hungarians, but these were faint voices in the great national chorus of "Nem, nem, soya! (no, no, never!)" which, if it means anything more than patriotic hot-air, means that Hungary will never be satisfied until she has recovered her former frontiers and her mastery over the 10,000,000 Slavs and Roumanians whom she formerly kept in subjection. The Yugoslavs, dominated by Belgrade, which is the most parochial of all European capitals, were suspicious of any form of internationalism. There economics, finance and industry were controlled by the Serbian militarists, who said bluntly: "What we have, we hold." Nobody paid any attention to the unfortunate Austria, who welcomed economic co-operation in almost any form. From a military point of view Austria was too weak. Here was the rub. What chance had sanity and common sense against the natural greed and money-lust of man? Here was a new Central Europe—a better and fairer Central Europe than the pre-war map. Yet here was every one talking and acting in terms of military force; the Czechs, the Roumanians, and the Yugoslavs arming to the teeth to retain not only their just but also their unjust gains; the Austrians and, especially, the Hungarians seeking every opportunity to re-arm in order to reassert their domination and to re-establish their own former rule of injustice. Could any one reconcile this conglomeration of peoples who had hated one another for centuries? Could there be any settlement in Central Europe without war or, indeed, a succession of wars?

I recalled Napoleon's conversation at St. Helena with the British naval captain, who had made a voyage of exploration to the Loochoo Islands. Napoleon questioned him closely on the military qualities of the islanders. "They have no arms," replied the Englishman. "No arms!" said Napoleon. "You mean no cannon?" "Neither cannon, nor muskets, nor swords, nor arms of any kind," said the captain. "How then do they fight?" asked the astonished Napoleon. "They don't fight, sir," replied the naval captain. "You see, they have no money."

Overweening national ambition, expressed in terms of money and property, was the chief obstacle not only to peace but to co-operation in Central Europe. Every one admitted the necessity of economic co-operation. No nation, no individual, was prepared to sacrifice one inch of territory, one krone of property, for the common good.

As the months passed, I became more sceptical and more cynical. That was why when members of Parliament came to Prague I took them to the Sekt-Pavilion, to Gri-Gri, to the Chapeau Rouge, or to the Russian gipsies instead of to the battlefields of the White Mountain and the Bohemian Historical Museum. Disillusionment is the quickest descent to indolence and indifference.

The truth is that, although we were assisting at the birth of a new Europe and participating in what history will call a revolution, political excitements were few and far between. Even the war had had its dull moments. But in that grim struggle there was always a definite end in view, and in the united pressure to achieve results one's private life was a matter of minor consequence—even to one's self. The post-war atmosphere brought with it an inevitable relaxation and a definite relapse into egotism.

One flare-up, reminiscent of the war excitement, we did have. This was in October, 1921, when the Emperor Karl made his ill-fated attempt to regain his throne in Hungary. It was the second alarm. In March of the same year he had left his villa on the Lake of Geneva and had made a clandestine visit to Budapest. He had had a dramatic interview with Admiral Horthy, the Hungarian Regent, who had convinced him of the inopportuneness of any attempt at restoration. On the 5th of April he had left again for Switzerland. The Allies had been angry. Under pressure the Swiss Government had imposed new conditions for his residence in Switzerland. The ex-Emperor had promised to give three days' notice of any change of "place of exile." Now on October 21 he had broken his word. Telling his entourage that he would not be home that night, as he and the Empress wished to celebrate the anniversary of their marriage in the Bernese Oberland, he had set out by aeroplane for Hungary. The same evening he had arrived at Sopron. At 9 P.M. we received the news that he was on his way to Budapest.

The excitement in Prague was intense. The Czech Government issued a mobilisation order. That night, for the first time since the war, our Legation staff worked until early in the morning ciphering and deciphering telegrams. The affair, however, fizzled out without a shot being fired. On the 24th of October, the one "loyal" battalion, which had gone over to Karl, was surrounded and disarmed by Hungarian troops. The ex-Emperor himself was put under restraint. A week later he was taken away by H.M.S. *Glow-worm,* the British monitor on the Danube, to be conveyed later by cruiser to his last exile in Madeira.

Karl is the most tragic figure of all the royalties deposed by the war. His apologists are sentimental about his good intentions and his lost opportunities. Like the Jacobites in the eighteenth century, they lay great stress on his noble character and on his humaneness in desiring to avoid bloodshed in the interest of peace. Even Anatole France, no lover of kings, has paid a warm tribute to the young Emperor's pacifism. "The Emperor Charles," he wrote, "offered peace. He is the only honest man who has appeared during the course of this war. And we did not listen to him."

That Karl meant well few even of his enemies will doubt.

He hated the German militarists, and the German General Staff, fearful of the possible consequences of his pro-Ally sympathies, loathed him in return. It may be questioned, however, if he possessed the strength of character which alone would have enabled him to dominate so difficult a situation. The young Emperor was a dreamer rather than a man of action. He lived in a world that had already crumbled even before he ascended his throne. In this connection the ex-Kaiser of Germany told me a significant story. I imagine that he had it direct from ex-Tsar Ferdinand of Bulgaria. In 1918 Ferdinand and Karl met. In his deep bass voice Tsar Ferdinand brought a Job's comfort. "Things are going very badly for us," he said. "Our thrones are tottering. But you will be the first to go." "Nonsense," replied the young Emperor. "I am stronger than Charles V." The argument was ended by Tsar Ferdinand. "Revolution or no revolution," said that cheerful cynic, "let us go and eat."

In Karl's case history will wish to know why, without preparation and without any assurances of support, he was so foolish as to undertake that fatal journey to Hungary in October, 1921. The answer must be that like most weak and well-meaning monarchs, he was surrounded by incompetent advisers.

Apart from this one thrilling interlude, our political life became drab and colourless. Diplomacy was now concerned more with economics and finance than with the drama of war, and it was inevitable that the generation which had survived the five years from 1914 to 1919 should find the post-war period monotonous and unexciting. At first we showed a praiseworthy but ineffective energy. We wrote voluminous reports. Every month we sent to the Foreign Office a long analysis of the situation. After the first two years, however, we found ourselves repeating the same recommendations, the same obvious commonplaces. Then one day our monthly reports ceased from a natural inanition and there was no protest from London. Almost insensibly I began to realise that we were assisting in a curious process of disintegration, the end of which was not in sight and over which we had no control. For those who like generalities woven round personalities I should say that, if the ex-Kaiser, as the living symbol of German militarism, had been mainly responsible for the war, M. Clemenceau, typifying those Frenchmen who hold that the Prussian is a blond beast to be held in eternal subjection, had been the architect of a peace the consequences of which to Europe could not be foreseen but which sooner or later were bound to be disastrous. At the same time there was a puzzling contrast of destruction with construction which made it almost impossible to distinguish between progress and retrogression.

For the Central Europe of those post-war years was not the horror of starvation and misery which it has generally been pictured in Western Europe and in the United States. The Czechs, busily engaged in building their new Jerusalem, were collectively and individually prosperous. If there were starving children in Slovakia and in Sub-Carpathian Russia, new millionaires were being made in Prague. Even the dispossessed landowners found means of adapting themselves to the new situation. They formed their forests into private companies. In return for shares they handed over their best areas to sugar companies. Their freedom of action was restricted, but they were and are to-day better off than their prototypes in Austria and Germany and even in England. Men, too, who had been waiters and clerks, had become ministers and high officials, and the dignity of their new position created a vast expenditure on furniture, clothes, motor-cars, and the other essentials of official representation. The factories worked at full time. Four and a half years of blockade had left Central Europe shoeless and shirtless. To meet the demand, stimulated by peace, there was employment for all. Before the war the riches of Bohemia had gone to swell the coffers of Vienna. Now the Czechs, in full possession of their wealth, could afford the luxury of a well-clothed army and of a well-paid Civil Service of their own. Moreover, as seventy-five per cent of the industry of the former Austro-Hungarian monarchy was concentrated in Bohemia and Moravia, the Czechs were in a position to satisfy the needs of their starving neighbours. They took every advantage of a situation which brought to them a real prosperity. Except for the fact that the Yugoslavs lacked the financial acumen of the Czechs, Belgrade represented a somewhat similar picture. Concession hunters swarmed in both capitals. There was intense Stock Exchange activity. Flotation followed flotation with bewildering rapidity.

In Budapest and especially in Vienna there was a very different state of affairs. The contrast of wealth and poverty was startling and pitiful. Yet here, too, after an initial period of starvation and profound misery there was a wave of prosperity. True, it was an unhealthy prosperity, due to an almost unrestricted use of the printing presses for currency purposes. Yet it produced an orgy of expenditure. In Vienna the middle classes were in despair. Generals, left with one uniform and their orders, begged in the streets. The pawnshops overflowed with the treasures of the dispossessed aristocracy and were bought up for a song by French, English and Italian bargain-hunters. At the same time a Socialist administration was providing the Viennese workmen with dwellings which would have roused envy in the breast of even a Ford mechanic. Above all, the collapse of the exchange afforded universal opportunities of getting rich quickly. It produced, too, a new type of profiteer more rapacious and more successful than any of the war-profiteers.

An English accountant, who was in Vienna at the time of the stabilisation, proved by an analysis of the figures that during one part of the inflation period it was possible to make a fortune of one million sterling in six months' time with an initial capital of £100. The process was simple. One deposited one's hundred pounds with the Credit-Anstalt and borrowed Austrian kronen against them at the rate of 100 kronen to the pound. One then walked across the road to the Wienerbankverein and bought a hundred pounds with the 10,000 Austrian kronen. One then had £200 and one owed 10,000 crowns. As the exchange fell, one borrowed more crowns against the £200 and bought more pounds with the borrowed crowns. By the time the exchange had fallen from 100 crowns to 100,000 to the £1, one had amassed a sterling fortune and one's debt in crowns was almost wiped out.

England has heard of the Stinneses of Germany. It knows little or nothing of the currency kings of Austria. Yet for a period of three or four years the Castigliones and the Bosels of

Vienna lived on a scale far beyond the expenditure of the most extravagant American millionaire. They bought palaces with the same ease as they bought foreign currency. They filled their new homes with art treasures. Nothing was beyond the reach of their purse: princely gold plate, the linen of counts, the wines of Habsburgs. Both state and aristocracy were only too glad to find a buyer for their former trappings, and the mushroom millionaires spent their money royally. Proud Austrian princes who visited Castiglione's palace were waited on by their former footmen and looked down upon by their former Van Dycks and Titians. This speculation period was insensate. It was disastrous to Austria. But, while it lasted, it was not without a kind of Saturnalian magnificence.

The currency kings, too, had imitators in every town of Central Europe. In the main streets every second house was a bank which was a euphemism for a foreign exchange bureau. The most successful speculators were the Jews. It was not that the Christians were more patriotic or more virtuous, but merely that the Semites understood the intricate operations of foreign exchange almost by second nature and were the quicker and the surer calculators. Later, currency stabilisation and government restrictions on the sale of foreign exchange were to sweep away these mushroom growths almost in a night, sending the millionaires back to the office stools and grocers' counters where they had started. The fortunes vanished even more quickly than they had been made. To-day, there are Austrian clerks working in London banks who once owned their own finance house and the Rolls Royces and beautiful mistresses that went with it.

This orgy of speculation was attended by that laxity of morals which comes invariably with sudden wealth and with sudden misfortune. With the new rich it was a case of "easily made, easily spent," with the new poor a question of despair. As in Russia just before the revolution, the former ruling class, seeing their world crumbling under their feet, were determined to drown their sorrow in champagne before the fall of the exchange had turned their last crowns into useless paper. To meet this need for distraction there was an army of purveyors of amusement. Night life flourished as never before. Central Europe, which before and during the war had scarcely known the cocktail, was now to be introduced to that insidious concoction by returning emigrants, and American bars were as numerous as cockroaches in a Russian kitchen. For every new bank there was a new Nachtlokal with a name as exotic as the mood of the moment. Budapest had its tsiganes, its "Green Cockatoo," its "Parisien Grill," where corypheans, who, having satisfied honour and police regulations by a rapid appearance on the stage, took their places at the supper-tables and assisted the waiters in the "grilling" of the guests. As its Regent was a sailor and as Hungary herself had no seaboard, its smartest Nachtlokal in those days was called the Admiral-Bar. Vienna, too, had its Parisien, where at a price one ate caviare and drank French champagne, while rickets-stricken children in Meidling lacked milk and even potatoes, its Tabarin, its Chapeau Rouge, and a hundred other establishments with French names. Even Belgrade, where night life had never risen above the level of the bawdy house, had its "Luxor," its "Palace," its "Casino."

Prague, however, with its sounder currency, showed the greatest transformation. When I arrived at the end of 1919, there was hardly a Nachtlokal in the place. Within a year and a half they were to be numbered by the score. To Prague, too, came all the best talent: the best Russian gipsies from St. Petersburg and Moscow, who, having followed the fortunes of the Russian "Whites," were now exiles; Hungarians, with shining teeth and flashing Mongolian eyes; dark and light-fingered Roumanians, unsurpassed in extracting the last dollar note from their victims and generally with a pimp protector in the background who hounded them to their work and cursed when they came back with an empty purse; Germans, Poles, Italians, Scandinavians and, indeed more than half the nationalities of Europe. Supreme, however, both in artistry and attractiveness were the inimitable Viennese—gay, happy-go-lucky, dance-mad, and generally honest.

Finally, on the purely male side there were the spurious princes and bogus counts and the American and West Indian negro musicians. The snobbish instincts of the new democracy had to be titillated. Most programmes therefore had their aristocratic dancing pairs: Lola d'Annunzio and the Marchese di Ventimiglia or —and perhaps these were genuine—Graf and Gräfin Rosenkrantz. The negro had come with the cocktail and with jazz. He was received and accepted by every one including the young aristocrats without any manifestations of colour prejudice. There were establishments to suit every purse and every taste. In the better Nachtlokals of Vienna, Budapest and Prague the clientele was cosmopolitan and even distinguished. If the currency speculators predominated, there were also diplomatists, bankers, officers, and even ministers. There was nothing indecent about those places. Certainly, there was nothing even faintly resembling the spectacular display of exotic vices which are flaunted before the visitor in Paris and Berlin. On Sundays the Czechs took their wives to see the stage performances and suffered no shock to their moral system. In the Balkans things were rather different. Here we were a little nearer the East. In Serbian eyes women who frequented cabarets were no better than they ought to be, and in a Belgrade Nachtlokal there was always a risk of a brawl. One might be knifed or—what was worse—kissed by a Macedonian Komitadji leader.

To-day, the post-war carnival has ended. It is unlikely to return in our life-time. But while it lasted, it provided an orgy of expenditure and of unhealthy excitement which will intrigue the curiosity of the future historian. One might have thought that in this vitiated atmosphere Communism would have flourished. Genuine Communism, however, is a creed which demands as much self-sacrifice and self-denial as the most ascetic forms of Christianity, and, fortunately, among the Communists of Central Europe there was no one with the will-power and the self-discipline of a Lenin. They, too, had their Nachtlokals.

I do not mean to suggest that the whole population of Central Europe was infected by this wave of extravagance and self-indulgence. In all countries there were men whose self-discipline was admirable and who worked sixteen hours a day for their country's good and even for the general benefit of mankind. They included Czechs like Beneš, lean, efficient, ambitious, and hungry for their country's advancement and the great Viennese scientists who, in spite of all hardships, maintained the high reputation of their native city as one of the great centres of research. Spiritual life never dies. Otherwise civilisation would cease. But the impression which those post-war years have crystallised in my mind is one of gross materialism in which, as a whole, personal interests were ruthlessly pursued even to the detriment of national interests and similarly narrow national interests to the detriment of the common interests of the Succession States. The Austro-Hungarian monarchy had not crashed in the storm of war like a giant oak. Rather was it in course of decomposition, and the ants, tumbling and pushing each other out of the way, were now busy with the corpse. It was a demoralising atmosphere—noxious both to the foreigner visitor and to the local population. It affected adversely all the Allied representatives in Central Europe. It affected, most of all, the English and the Americans, both unimaginative races, who are never at their best when removed from the powerful if narrowing restraint of their home public opinion.

CHAPTER SIX

IF there is any merit in the game of Rugby football as taught in the Scottish public schools, it is the lesson—driven in with frequent applications of the boot—that one must never cry over past disasters but grit one's teeth and get on with the game. It is an excellent philosophy for mankind. I am not given to mourning the lost opportunities which lie like a wilderness of weeds along the roadside of my journey through the world. I confess, however, that the Prague chapters of my life give me little cause for self-satisfaction. I could have arranged my existence on an almost ideal basis. Work in a British Legation is more exacting than it was before the war. But it is not strenuous. Owing to the disparity in age and rank between the different members of the staff there is no jealousy—none of that trampling over one's friend's dead body in order to gain advancement which characterises the more commercial and more competitive professions. As a whole, ambassadors and ministers are the most considerate and human of men.

In Prague a six-hour working day would have won for me a reputation for industry and reliability both with my chief and with the Foreign Office and the Department of Overseas Trade. I had ample spare time in which to write my books. In this manner I could have avoided the boredom and the temptations of city life, which I have always detested. To satisfy my love of nature there was within easy distance of Prague the most glorious countryside that even a Celt brought up in the Highlands of Scotland could desire.

Fortunately for my physical welfare and for the salvation of my immortal soul, I spent almost every week-end of my life in

Prague in the open air. Sir George Clerk combined a genuine love of nature with a passion for shooting and fishing, and in Czechoslovakia we could shoot and fish in ideal surroundings during every month in the year. From August to October there was partridge shooting in the vast sugar beet fields of Bohemia and Moravia. From the middle of October to the end of the year there was the finest pheasant shooting in the world. In January we shot duck or took part in a bloody and rather nauseating slaughter of hares. In February we could tempt the fierce huchen —the land-locked salmon of the Danube and its tributaries—in the icy waters of the Waag, and success was full compensation for the physical discomfort. In March we stalked the lordly capercailzie with a rifle as he courted his mate in the pine trees of the forest. It was a more sporting performance than it sounds. One entered the forest at dawn. One spotted the "Caper" by his hoarse love song. During those moments of rapture he was both deaf and blind, and one ran forward towards the sound. Suddenly the song would cease, and one stood still scarcely daring to breathe. The crash of a broken twig would send him soaring to safety. Then the song would start again, and one made a further advance until at last one could distinguish the mottled plumage of his breast against the dark background of the trees. Admittedly, the end was unworthy. One shot him sitting. But the stalk itself provided an experience which I found far more thrilling than the organised and just as murderous carnages of partridge and pheasants. In April there were woodcock in profusion. "Bags," if not so immense as in pre-war days, were on a scale unknown in England and Scotland. For the more venturesome there were bear and noble stags to be tracked in the Carpathians and chamois in the Tatra mountains. In the spring and in the summer there was trout-fishing in river, lake and mountain burn.

Sir George took full advantage of these opportunities, and on many occasions I accompanied him. We left the Legation on Friday afternoons in his high-powered car and within two and a half hours we were in the mountains far away from civilisation. He was a delightful companion with a profound knowledge of bird-life and a modest and charming manner of imparting it to others.

My shooting adventures would fill a book by themselves. Some, like the shoots provided by the aristocracy—splendid hosts and the finest "Shots" in the world—were a real lesson. Others, like the diplomatic shoots organised by the Czech Government on the properties of the Habsburgs, afforded a wonderful opportunity of seeing the country. The slaughter of vast quantities of partridges at Židlochovice in Moravia was a very minor thrill compared with the fact that I was shooting over the battleground of Austerlitz. We stayed, too, in the former palace of the Archduke Josef, and, as I opened the chest of drawers in my bedroom, I came across a drawerful of Habsburg miniatures—pathetic reminders of the past which had been packed away and, apparently, forgotten.

Moreover, there was nothing democratic about the arrangement of the shoot. There was no drawing for places. The best stands were reserved invariably for the Ministers, and humble secretaries like myself walked up with the beaters or were posted on the extreme flanks. Sir George Clerk had a glorious time, but the secretaries, at any rate, enjoyed the feeling of greater personal security. For, if Sir George was a more than useful shot, some of the other heads of missions had a highly dangerous technique. Some held their gun at an angle which made one glad to be well out of range. Others had an unfortunate habit of shooting into the coverts, and, as a beater clapped his hands to his outraged posterior, a human yell would be added to the "click-clack" of the beaters' sticks. Fortunately, there were no serious casualties, but Richard Crane, the American Minister, who had never shot before, had had his first victim—a hare—stuffed and mounted. Alan Winslow, his secretary, used to keep us in fits of laughter by solemnly pretending to trace in the stuffed hare's features a sinister resemblance to a young beater who had received the spent contents of a ministerial cartridge in the chest and who had been carried, more frightened than hurt, from the scene of action.

If these government shoots provided both amusement and historical instruction, our greatest enjoyment was the small rough shoots we arranged for ourselves. John Cecil and Frank Aveling, who had succeeded Birch and Latter on our staff, were both keen shots and, alone or accompanied by one of the American secretaries, we enjoyed ourselves hugely.

Historically, however, my most interesting experiences were the shoots at Konopišt, the home of the former Archduke Franz Ferdinand and the scene of his famous interview with the ex-Kaiser a few weeks before his assassination and the outbreak of the Great War. Both the house and the arrangement of the coverts threw an illuminating light on the character of the murdered Archduke. In Central Europe to-day there are many Habsburg supporters who hold that the real cause of the war was the fact that the Emperor Franz Josef lived too long. The Archduke Franz Ferdinand, who was loathed by the Hungarians, favoured the establishment of a Triune Kingdom in which the Southern Slavs would have had equal rights. Had he come to the throne in 1910, he might have created a federal Austria, and there would have been no war. According to this theory, it was Serbian fears that this scheme would wreck all hopes of a Great Serbia which were responsible for the Archduke's murder. After seeing Konopišt, I have always wondered whether the Archduke's mental deficiencies were not at least as great as those of other Habsburgs. His lust for killing was certainly abnormal. His passion for records exceeded anything achieved in this direction by the late Marquis of Ripon. He shot with seven guns and four loaders. His temper was violent if by some error of judgment on the part of the keepers the shoot failed to realise expectations. Admittedly, his marksmanship was superb. On one occasion he shot over 4,000 head of game to his own gun—or guns—in one day. But he shot so much that in the end his hearing was permanently affected. In his later years, when out shooting, he wore a bandage round his ears and a rubber pad on his shoulder. At Konopišt everything was arranged for slaughter, and the final covert, close to the house, provided a carnage on the machine-gun scale of the last war.

The castle itself was a vast mausoleum for the perpetuation of the Archduke's prowess. His trophies of the chase exceeded

300,000 head of game. Not all are included in the museum of Konopišt, but over 6,000 head of deer are assembled under one roof in a little lodge which the local inhabitants call "The Palace of Horns." Every head is carefully numbered, and a little birchwood plaque bears the date and place-name of the killing. In the living rooms of the castle were more heads, more trophies, set off by a rich collection of arms and countless statues and bronzes all representing St. George in the act of slaying the dragon. The contrast between the peaceful rose gardens outside and this zoological museum and arsenal left an indelible impression on my mind. No future historian of the war should begin his task without a visit to Konopišt. The love of killing birds and animals is shared by many Englishmen. In the Archduke Franz Ferdinand it amounted to a mania. The Konopišt of to-day contains one other curious memento of the past. It is the Christmas-card sent by the ex-Kaiser to the Archduke's children on the occasion of the first Christmas of the war. Carefully preserved under glass it is written in the ex-Kaiser's own hand. The writing, bold and clear, runs as follows: "We have avenged your dear parents. The Justice of God has triumphed."

There was some question of the propriety of our shooting at Konopišt. The Habsburgs having been dethroned, the Imperial estates had become Czech national property. But Konopišt had been the private property of the late Archduke, and in the eyes of the aristocracy and supporters of the old régime it was still private property. Many diplomatic representatives were indisposed or had another engagement whenever they were invited to take part in a Konopišt shoot.

Some of our experiences were truly Ruritarian. On one occasion we received an invitation to go down to stay with Henry Cartwright, who had been on our Military Mission in Vienna and Prague and was now our Consul at Bratislava. He had promised us that we should catch a huchen and shoot a chamois, and, Henry being a man of his word, we naturally accepted. He was a splendid fellow, tall, good-looking, and with a commanding presence. A former captain in the Middlesex Regiment, he had had a wonderful war record, had been captured and terribly treated by the Germans, and, after an incredible number of attempts, had finally succeeded in escaping. Now, at this time, he was the uncrowned king of Bratislava, respected and looked up to by the five antagonistic Hungarian, German, Jewish, Czech and Slovak elements which composed the hybrid population of the town. When we arrived at our destination—a little village on the Waag River, we noticed that the local population treated Henry with a respect which the Czechs had never paid to our Minister, let alone to ourselves, in Prague. It was the kind of reverence which Roman sycophants might have accorded to Caligula in the days when he was aping Jupiter. The man who was providing us with the fishing and the chamois was a small Hungarian squire. He welcomed us cordially enough as Cartwright's friends, but to Henry himself his attitude was the quintessence of deferential awe. In the absence of the requisite red carpet, he was almost prepared to lay himself at Henry's feet rather than allow the rough stones of the Slovak roads to soil the great man's shoes.

Our first efforts in this sporting paradise were to be devoted to huchen fishing, and our procession or rather Cartwright's to the river was regal. One keeper carried his bag, another his rod, while the local squire, with many bows and flourishes of his hat, explained just where the best huchen lay and how they were certain to fall to the right bait—a Zopf, or pig-tail, of worms surmounted by a swivelled cap. A Hungarian, however, may bring three inexperienced Englishmen to the river, he may give to them rods, bait, and the best advice, but he cannot persuade the huchen to attach themselves to the hook. We laboured manfully but in vain, and at the end of a strenuous day were glad to get back to our host's house, where an enormous dinner, preceded by slivowitz (plum vodka) and washed down by local wines, awaited us. Our host was very upset. Continuing to ignore us, he was profoundly apologetic to Cartwright. Then his face brightened. To-morrow would be all right. The chamois were there. His keepers had worked them toward a neighbouring height. To-morrow, His Highness would bag three or four. We exchanged glances. Hungarians were Orientals. Therefore they were flatterers. But "Highness"—this was going a little too far.

It was during dinner that the bubble of Henry's transient glory was pricked. My wife sat on the squire's left (Cartwright of course sat on his right), and, during one of the rare intervals when he was not plying Henry with food or wine, he said to her in an awe-stricken whisper: "What relation is His Highness to the King?" My wife looked puzzled. She knows no Hungarian. The Magyar knew no English. Her German is not exactly a gift from God. The Hungarian's was little better. "Which highness to what King?" she asked. The Hungarian explained. "Why, your Duke to your King, of course," he said. He waved an expansive and almost possessive arm towards Cartwright. My wife shook her head. "But he's no Duke," she said. This time it was the turn of the Hungarian to express surprise. For a moment a startled look came into his eyes. Then he smiled. Women, of course, were ignorant creatures. From the depths of a pocket-book he produced his ace of trumps and put his finger to his lips. "Look," he whispered. The evidence of my wife's insanity and of his own omniscience was one of Cartwright's official cards. It was inscribed as follows:

CAPTAIN HENRY CARTWRIGHT,
DUKE OF CAMBRIDGE'S OWN.

"Now," said the squire triumphantly, "please tell me what relation your Duke is to your King." At last my wife saw the light. The squire had interpreted the card as Henry Cartwright, Duke of Cambridge. It was not a very grotesque error. These were hard times for royalties. The Hungarian had seen some of his own Archdukes reduced to taking jobs on the music-halls. Why should not an English royalty undertake the highly honourable and important duties of British Consul in Bratislava?

Laboriously but very quietly she explained to the squire that Cartwright had been an officer in the British army and that his regiment, the Middlesex, was known as "The Duke of Cambridge's Own." Even to-day we all find it hard to forgive her. She might at least have waited until we had had our chamois shoot. As it was, the shoot was a farce. We walked for miles. We crawled on our bellies. We waded through mountain torrents. We scanned the crags with our binoculars. But we saw no chamois. I realised why even before we had set out. The Hungarian was still polite, but the glory had gone from his deference. Chamois were for Dukes and not for Consuls. He had adapted himself to the new circumstances. In the early morning the same keepers, who had so laboriously assembled the chamois for our ducal benefit, had shooed them back into safer and more remote fastnesses.

Another shoot, which provided me with an adventure, was at St. Joachimsthal, the famous radium spa in the heart of the Erzgebirge. It was from the pitch-blende of St. Joachimsthal that Monsieur and Madame Curie made their great discovery, and to-day the little township has the largest radium-mine in the world. The place, however, has a far longer history. During the sixteenth century the town enjoyed a prosperity which can be compared with that of Klondyke or Ballarat in more modern times. In 1516 the discovery of silver caused a typical miners' rush to the valley, and the chronicles of the time describe the cry which was heard all over Germany and Bohemia and even as far as Venice:

*"Ins Thal, Ins Thal,
Mit Mutter, mit All!"*

It was from the silver mine of St. Joachimsthal that was coined the first "Thaler," a word which is the origin of the modern dollar. In fifteen years the population rose from one thousand to over twenty thousand. Alas! the silver soon gave out, and the glory of the township departed. The district, too, became embroiled in the religious wars which terminated in the Battle of the White Mountain in 1620. During this struggle St. Joachimsthal, inspired by its priest Mathesius, the disciple of Luther, embraced the anti-Catholic and anti-Habsburg faith. With the suppression of Bohemian independence many of its inhabitants were driven into exile, while the last of the Schlicks, the overlords of the district who had created its prosperity, were executed together with twenty-six of the leading Protestant nobles of Bohemia in order to satisfy the Habsburg thirst for vengeance.

Just before the war an English company built a huge hotel at St. Joachimsthal in order to exploit the radium cure, which gives immense relief to sufferers from gout and rheumatism. When we went there in the early post-war years, the hotel, which has since been bought by the Czechoslovak Government, was closed, and we lived in a little annex. The scenery and the air were magnificent. There were stretches of moor where one could imagine one was in Scotland, and the streams and lochans, which abound in the neighbourhood, were full of lusty trout, which fought with the gameness one should expect from fish bred in these radio-active waters. We had also some very fair rough-shooting, the rarebit of which was a wild duck lake which we always took at the end of the day.

In those days we had the place more or less to ourselves, and, as we were the annex's best customers, we were pampered by every one. On one occasion, however, we came down to dinner after a long day's partridge shooting to find our favourite corner of the dining-room occupied by a party of three men. We took another table and had hardly swallowed our soup, when the waiter brought us a message from the newcomers. Would we be so good as to refrain from staring? The party in the opposite corner did not like it. The message came from Prince George, the former Crown Prince of Serbia and the eccentric elder brother of King Alexander of Yugoslavia. As we had taken no notice of the Prince or of his party, the message rankled. The situation was beautifully handled by Jack Cecil, who, in the absence of Sir George Clerk on leave, was in charge of the Legation. Sending for the manager, he requested him to inform the Prince's equerry that we were members of the British Legation, that we were not in the habit of staring, and that, unless an explanation was forthcoming, a complaint would be made to the Czechoslovak Foreign Office. I am bound to say that we received a handsome apology. After dinner the Prince's doctor, a pleasant-mannered and cultured Serb, came over to us and explained that the Prince was in St. Joachimsthal for a cure, that his nerves were in a bad state, that the waiter had misunderstood the message, which, in fact, was nothing more than a request to the manager for a private dining-room: in a word, that the last thing His Royal Highness had intended or desired was to insult his allies, the British. The doctor smiled and bowed. We bowed and smiled back. From that moment all was peace.

This was my first and only meeting with Prince George. Later, when I went to Yugoslavia, I was to hear many tales of his wild escapades, of his strange life among the Serbian fishermen on the Danube, and of the restraint which his kingly brother had imposed upon his liberty. In the sinister atmosphere of Yugoslav politics it was difficult to ascertain the truth. Was he the irresponsible eccentric whom the government supporters pictured him to be or was he a victim of one of those personal feuds which have stained the history of the royal families of Serbia? Even to-day he has a certain number of adherents and sympathisers in Yugoslavia. At the time I felt sorry for him. He seemed a restless, unhappy man.

CHAPTER SEVEN

FAR more than the organised "shoots," however, or these pleasant outings with my colleagues I liked the fishing. I have rubbed shoulders with all kinds and conditions of men in every part of the world. I am what is known as a "good mixer." I have more acquaintances than most men. Yet I object strongly to being called a gregarious person. Even to-day I dread meeting new people. At all times in my life I have had a craving for solitude which, the more it is unsatisfied, becomes almost a mania. Trout-fishing is the spur which forces me to seek that solitude. I fish not so much to catch fish as to be alone. I dislike anglers collectively. I would sooner catch perch on a worm by myself than a dozen salmon on fly with a rod on either side of me and half a village watching me from the bridge. I like trout-fishing because it brings me all those things which I miss so much in the cities: the clean, pure air, the smell of peat, of fresh-cut hay, the rustle of the birch trees, the cry of the curlews, and the cool sound of running water in the quiet places. Above all, I like fishing because it affords an escape from unhealthy luxury and from temptation and because it satisfies most completely the needs of my spiritual life.

Czechoslovakia—and, indeed, all Central Europe—was an ideal refuge for the angler, and, when my soul was sick with the fever which attacks all those who live in cities, I went into retreat by the riverside. For three months in every year I was completely happy. Nor did I have to go far to find my happiness. Within an hour by car from Prague there was a dry-fly stream—a tiny tributary of the Elbe, which flowed through pleasant meadowland with a fairy-like background formed by the castle and vineyards of Melnik. Within the same easy reach there was a small lake fed by a brook in the heart of a deer forest, where the "plop" of a rising trout was the only sound to break the stillness of the pines. Farther afield, to the north-west, were the streams of the Riesengebirge. Here we had a charming English hostess, the late Baroness Koenigswaerter, who at Schloss Kwasney provided us with all the comforts of an English country-house. Here, amid glorious Highland scenery, we had three streams at our disposal, and here I cast my first fly on the waters of Bohemia. Yet Fate nearly robbed me of this pleasure and diplomacy of one of its greatest exponents. We had set out in Sir George's new car—a high-powered Austro-Daimler driven by the Legation chauffeur called Nobilis. Suddenly, as he was letting the car all out on a flat stretch of the Koeniggraetz road, a front wheel came off. My heart was in my mouth, as I saw the wheel shoot forward like a low shell from a field-gun. How Nobilis—a great character with the moustachios and the arrogant bearing of a D'Artagnan—kept the car on the road was a miracle. Yet he performed it, and, shattered and thankful, I walked two hundred yards down the road to rescue the erring wheel. To the west there was Joachimsthal with its three lakes.

Better than the lakes were the two streams which were within easy reach of the little mountain town. One was in the valley below and flowed through the park of Schlackenwerth, once the home of the Herzog of Toscana. The other—and it was my favourite—was on the mountain plateau and ran through some four miles of treeless moorland. Here one felt like Jack after he had climbed his Beanstalk. Only here there were no ogres and no castle. One never saw a living soul the whole day, and, if the trout were small, their appetite was insatiable. My first visit to Joachimsthal furnished another motoring adventure. I had set out in my own rather indifferent car. I had gallantly offered a lift to Cynthia Seymour and Irene Boyle, who wished to spend a few days in the mountains. They did it more realistically than they expected. I lost my way and, after scaling most of the heights of the Erzgebirge, had to pull up, with the approach of night, at the side of a mountain road. Here, numbed with cold and half-famished, we waited until dawn. But the fishing was ample compensation for our hardships. Within half-an-hour of our arrival I was on the first lake. With my second or third cast I hooked and landed three trout at once. Their aggregate weight was four-and-a-half pounds, and each fish exceeded a pound!

My dream-river of Bohemia was the Otava, a stream which is photographed in my memory as the ideal of all a trout-fisher can desire. It has its setting in the silence of the Sumava, which is the Czech name for the Bohemian forest, and almost every yard of the water makes perfect fishing. It is indeed a noble river—nobler, because of its unspoilt solitude, than the Spey. On a high wooded hill opposite the hut, in which we used to sleep, stands Rabi, a ruined castle, where five hundred years ago Žižka, the Cromwell of the Czechs and the greatest European soldier of his day, lost his eye while fighting against the Catholic forces of the Emperor. The river, now tumbling riotously over the boulders, now swirling darkly into long, deep pools shelved by rocky precipices, still shelters a few salmon, the gallant survivors of the army which sets out every year from the North Sea up the Elbe through the bilge water of Hamburg, past the barge traffic of Dresden, through the sluices and locks of Prague, on the 800 miles journey to the ancient spawning beds in the Bohemian forest. Only some twenty fish get through every year, but this journey must surely be the greatest Odyssey of any modern salmon. Fish with such admirable housing instincts deserve a better fate than capture by mere man, and, although one or two were hooked, no Otava salmon was ever taken on rod and line in my time. I fear, however, that their end was ignominious. The local peasants used to take them out in the winter with a prong, and, since the building of the new locks at Prague, I doubt if the annual journey is now possible.

I have taken many good baskets from the Otava. Yet, for some unknown reason the trout were "dour" to rise, and all too frequently my flies earned the contempt of the Czech professional fisher who, with a wire trace and a coarse minnow tackle, would hurl on to the bank the two and three pounders which persistently defied my Greenwell and my 3x cast. On the other hand, the grayling—in these waters a very sporting fish and incomparably superior to his lethargic English cousin—are super-excellent. There are several stretches on the river where the dry-fly can be used with effect, but, as the best grayling lie in the shallow running water, the wet fly is more killing. The fish run from ½ lb. to 2 lbs. and on a good day one can count on a brace of 1½ pounders in every dozen. The Otava grayling are at their best from October 15th to November 15th, but much depends on the weather, and an early winter can curtail the season. They make, too, first-class eating. Indeed, there is no more pleasant recollection in my fishing diary than of a certain November day on the Otava with a frosty, blood-red sun glowing on the white walls of Rabi Castle, the air just keen enough to tingle one's cheeks, a complete absence of wind, and nothing to mar the smooth course of the water save the tiny rings made by the feeding fish. A heavy basket and a light heart, and then supper in the warm shelter of our hut with fresh-killed grayling fried in butter and a generous mug of real Pilsener. If it was not trout fishing, it was the finest substitute that can be found in Europe.

Our host on the Otava was Mr. Liška, a philosopher and a sportsman who deserves a page to himself in the annals of fishing. Heavy of build and slow of speech, Pan Liška loved his stream, stocked it, and guarded it with an obstinacy which baffled the predatory instincts of the Czech Land Office and of the vote-catching advocates of "everything for the peasants." He belonged to the old school of anglers. He tied his own flies, invented his own hooks, and made his own rods. He did more. In the long winter nights he learnt English in order to be able to read in the original Izaak Walton and such moderns as Halford and Dunne. One of the earliest treatises on angling was written by a Czech bishop called Dubravius. In 1926 Pan Liška gave to the world the first serious study of trout-fishing ever compiled in the Czech language. It is dedicated to Sir George Clerk and is well worth translating. For this modern Dubravius had many original ideas about the angler's craft, and it will come as a shock to Englishmen to know that he considered we still have much to learn from the Germans about the habits of trout. Pan Liška is now over seventy. He is a splendid type of Czech and one of those real anglers who are as happy without their rod as with it. In this life he has found the secret of happiness in the contemplation of running water, and, as his character is pure gold, he will one day fish in the limpid waters of Elysium.

My own zest for the contemplative life led me beyond the confines of Czechoslovakia. In May 1920 I took a week's local leave and with a grim disregard of rules and regulations crossed into Germany, which I had not visited since before the war. My objective was Munich and my intention was to fish the mountain streams of the Bavarian Alps. My visit, however, nearly ended in failure. I had left Prague in a blaze of almost summer heat to arrive the same evening in Munich in a snowstorm. As the mountains were deep in snow, all hope of fishing was gone. Professor Heintz, the only Bavarian I knew, was in Berlin. My holiday seemed wasted.

Necessity, however, is the main-spring of ingenuity, and, full of determination, I set out for the Fisheries Department of the Bavarian Ministry of Agriculture. There I was received by a benign, long-bearded professor, in a threadbare frock-coat, who knew everything about the life-habits of the trout and nothing about fishing. He was polite, but pessimistic. Still, he gave me a card to a certain Herr S——, and with sinking hopes I ordered my taxi-driver to take me to Herr S——'s office. At first Herr S—— was not encouraging. The only fishing that was of any value in Bavaria was in private hands, and permission was difficult to obtain. In any case nearly all the streams came from the Alps, and owing to the weather it would be days before they could clear. Here was the end of all hope.

Herr S——, however, was friendly. He was the honorary Consul-General of a foreign Power. I had been in the British Consular service. He had been in Japan. So had I. A community of interests kept us talking, and then I showed him my fly-box. The dry-flies did it. He had never seen a dry-fly before. For one long minute he fidgeted nervously with the papers on his desk. Something was troubling his mind. Out it came at last, slowly and cautiously, after much reflection. "I have a stretch of water myself not very far from Munich—a stream which rises from a spring and does not come from the mountains. If you like I can take you there to-morrow. You will be one of the first Englishmen—but not the first British Consul—to fish my water. During the war I took Sir Roger Casement, when your Government had set a price on his head, to try his luck with our Bavarian trout. He was a very fine fisher."

And this is the story of my introduction to the Bavarian Semt—my favourite among all the streams I have fished in many parts of the world. Since that cold May morning when I landed 27 trout weighing 23 lbs., I have visited the Semt every year. I have fished it wet. I have fished it dry. And always the stream has yielded its toll of 15 to 20 trout averaging approximately a pound. It has, too, a May-fly rise, and one never-to-be-forgotten June evening there yielded me six trout weighing fourteen pounds. But it is not the trout that attract me solely to the Semt. It is the lure of the stream itself. It is set in the most picturesque scenery of all Bavaria. In summer the broad meadow-land through which it runs is a carpet of wild flowers. Its waters are as clear as the finest glass, and it flows at an even depth with a soothing and majestic laziness. Above all, it is a sanctuary, almost free from the intrusion of man, for every form of wild life. Water-voles, with eyes like two black pins in a cushion of brown velvet, watch unscared from the river-beds. Kingfishers flash like a streak of blue through flights of startled teal and mallard. Half-way between the two foot-bridges there is a small beaver farm kept by a retired German officer. In the background, closing in the whole picture, loom the snow-crested summits of the Bavarian Alps, and in the evening red-deer and even golden eagles come down from the mountains to seek the friendly shelter of this warm-scented valley. Here a man may fish and smoke and think out the things that are worth while. I would not change it for any other stream in the world.

Petri Heil is the usual form of greeting among German anglers. May St. Peter reward Herr S——, whose friendship has stood the test of the fifteen most difficult years in Anglo-German history. I owe him much. He taught me to know and to love Munich in all the vicissitudes of its post-war existence. I have lived there at a time when it was almost impossible to spend more than a pound a day, when the best suite in my hotel worked out at rather less than thirty-five shillings a week, and when for the sum of ten shillings I could roam the countryside from morning to evening in a high-powered car. I have dined more expensively in Walterspiel's than in any other restaurant in the world. I have seen the streets and squares of Munich a model of order and cleanliness and peopled by honest citizens going about their business as though there had never been a war. I have seen them thronged by pale-faced students and underfed workmen marching in ragged order and singing patriotic songs in an effort to recapture the lost spirit of Germany.

Twelve years ago, at the corner of the Kellerstrasse, I saw a little black-haired man in riding-boots and a cheap brown waterproof haranguing a mixed crowd of some two hundred men and women from a soap-box. He was bare-headed. He spoke in short, jerky sentences. The crowd changed every few minutes. Some jeered. Some laughed and moved on. Some stayed to listen. Then a policeman came up and ordered the rabble to move on. There were scowls and curses. But the crowd dispersed. The little man was Herr Hitler. Two years later I drank my Steinkrug of Munich beer in the Buerger Beer Cellar and was shown the hole in the ceiling into which Herr Hitler discharged his pistol as the signal for the outbreak of his ill-fated Putsch of 1923. It was on this occasion that the wit of ex-King Ferdinand of Bulgaria saved him from a beating. He was sitting in his car outside the Hotel Regina, when some young Nazis came up and took him by the collar. "Let's throw out this ugly Jew and take his car," they said. The king looked at them mournfully. "Gentlemen," he said, "I have, it is true, a prominent nasal organ, but I am no Jew. I am Tsar Ferdinand, temporarily, alas! without a throne." Munich laughed then at this schoolboy Putsch and Europe laughed with it.

I have seen the decline of the Bavarian aristocrats, many of whom have been forced by the collapse of the mark to eke out their reduced income by taking in young English girls of good family. In a small way I may claim to have been instrumental in renewing the old pre-war glory of Munich as a finishing school for young English girls. It was I who persuaded Lord and Lady Rosslyn to send their daughter Mary to Count and Countess Harrach's. Since then many others have followed in her steps. I have talked with the business men of Munich, the artists, the writers. I have noted the slow erosion of the democratic spirit under the strain of deferred hope. I have seen the gradual decline of a charming capital which owed its artistic glory to its Court. I have watched with sympathy the efforts of its citizens to maintain the best traditions of its opera, of its theatre, and its painting. I have wasted my money on its night-life. With the German prototypes of my own lost generation I have done the round of those subterranean cabarets, where exotic vice flourished as it always flourishes in times of human distress and where men and women sin by night and sleep by day. I have watched the rise of the new generation, browned by the sun, hardened by football and athletics, and magnificent in physique. I have learnt to know and like the Bavarian peasant—with his sturdy legs, his green stockings, and his green-corded short trews—a real Highlander and closely allied by a common heritage of mountains, loch and stream, with the clansmen of my own country. There is almost no phase of Munich and Bavarian life that I have not known, and to-day both town and country have a permanent place in my affections.

All this I owe to my chance meeting with Herr S——. But my greatest debt to Herr S——is the recapture of that respect for the German people which I had acquired in my student days in Berlin and which, like most English admirers of Germany, I had lost in 1914. And, at a time when it was dangerous to raise one's voice on behalf of Germany in the clubs of London, I began to question not only in my own mind but to my friends who had influence in high places the wisdom of the Treaty of Versailles. With men like Herr S——, who in those days represented the solidest part of the German people, a removal of the most flagrant injustices of the Treaty would have laid the foundations of a lasting peace and would have stabilised Republican sentiment in Germany for years. Unfortunately, there was no man of sufficient vision and power in England to take the bold course, and by a long series of drifting postponements the British Government, almost against its will, found itself trailing behind France in support of the Treaty and of a senseless prolongation of the impossible. When the change in sentiment came, it was already too late.

I take no credit for my own altered views. Long before I made my first visit to Munich, there were Englishmen whose feelings had already undergone the same revulsion. The first seeds of Anglo-German post-war friendship were planted by the officers and men of the British Army of Occupation in the Rhineland.

CHAPTER EIGHT

AS disillusionment began to shatter my ideals, there came a gradual weakening of my own moral fibre. So long as my leisure hours were confined to dining with my diplomatic colleagues, to listening to excellent music which was always provided at Madame Beneš's receptions, and to pleasant excursions to the Bohemian countryside, I was safe. But by the end of my first two years, I had exhausted the social amenities of Prague. I grew tired of handing tea-cake to ministers' wives and of dancing with débutantes who had nothing to say. Everywhere I went I saw the same people, heard the same conversation, listened to the same scandal. In the summer I went to Marienbad and Karlsbad, and the cosmopolitan society of over-fed Rajahs, bilious Jews and dyspeptic Germans made even less appeal to me. True, I could always escape my own shadow. Apart from my shooting and fishing haunts, there was Woleschowitz with its tennis courts and its private golf course. Woleschowitz was the country home of Baron Ringhoffer, the railway King of Czechoslovakia and a German-Bohemian who combined a mania for sport with the hospitality of a Russian Grand Duke.

To the members of our Legation the Baron and his wife were amazingly kind, and many were the pleasant week-ends that I spent there in an orgy of golf and tennis. It was at Woleschowitz that I first met Karel Koželuh, to-day the partner of Tilden and at one time the greatest tennis player in the world. He belonged to a family of natural ball-game players, to whom every game from ice-hockey to ping-pong came easily. He had begun his tennis career as a ball-boy to the Ringhoffers. In 1920 he was the Baron's private trainer. But it was the private golf course—complete with

English professional and girl-caddies—which was my chief delight. Michiels, the Dutch Minister, who has played in the British Amateur Championship, was our chief star. Both in singles and in foursomes, in which I partnered Sir George against the Baron and the Dutchman, we had many strenuous encounters. The Baron himself was a majestic personality both off and especially on the golf course. He played with the seriousness of an American training for the open championship. He carried, too, as many clubs. His sportsmanship was impeccable. I have met few men who were so complacent in defeat and so modest in victory. Weighing seventeen stone in his pyjamas, he combined the power of a Tolley with the figure of Lord Castlerosse and could hit the ball as far as any man living. On his day he was a useful ten. But his day came only once a month. When he was off it, the whole game was held up on every teeing ground. After minute instructions the caddie would tee the ball to the exact height. Then the Baron would plant his feet firmly on the ground, hand his cigar to his cigar caddie, and shake himself like a big Newfoundland. He would take his driver—a club too heavy for ordinary giants but in his hands a flail of the avenger. There would be a roaring swish. Then with a crack like a pistol shot the ball would soar away to the right until it found its burial place in the pheasant coverts. The Baron's face betrayed neither annoyance nor sorrow. Without moving, he nodded to the caddie. Another ball was teed up. Again the flail whistled through the air. This time the ball would land with a mammoth pull in the rhododendron bushes of the garden. The process would be repeated four or five times with the same stolid precision until at last hands, feet, hips, swing, and force would combine in perfect rhythm, and the ball would sail majestically through the air, carry the second shot traps, and roll on and on until it finished in the middle of the green some three hundred and fifty yards away. The stern seriousness of the Baron's face would then relax into a seraphic smile. What matter if he had played nine from the tee. If he holed his putt, he would duly enter a ten on his card. But in his mind he had done an eagle two, and for the rest of the day he was happy.

Woleschowitz was a godsend in more ways than hospitality.

It was for many years the only golf course within a hundred miles of Prague. Soon after the war British sporting enterprise made an endeavour to remedy this state of affairs, and, forming an Anglo-Czech committee, we actually reached the length of laying out a nine-holed course with real greens on the Stromovka, the Hyde Park of Prague.

The French Military Mission must have been alarmed by this manifestation of Anglo-Czech fraternisation, for before the course was even opened the greens and fairway were turned into a morass of hoof marks by the French cavalry officers. Apparently, the land which the Czechs had given us for the golf-course had also been allotted to the French officers for riding practice, and they were not prepared to abandon one inch of their rights to the sacrés anglais. The course died in childbirth.

Would that I myself had been content with such simple pleasures. The Prague of those early post-war years never slept. The temptations of its night-life were both varied and facile, and I yielded to them with a zeal which came dangerously near to developing into a habit. Perhaps it was the reaction of the war. Perhaps the excess of nervous energy from which I have always suffered was partly responsible. At any rate, there was a restlessness in my soul which could be satisfied only by sweet champagne and garish lights. In the cabarets of Prague there was a new world to explore, and I surveyed every corner of it with unremitting diligence.

On mature reflection I think the music was most to blame. Except to dance to, I have always loathed American music. On the other hand, I have never been able to resist the peculiar intoxication of those minor melodies which work such havoc with the heart and pocket of the Slavs, the Viennese, and, I suppose, the Celts. There is a tale that, when a Czech child is born, the parents put a coin and a violin string in the cradle. If the child grasps the coin first, the parents train it as a thief. If it takes hold of the string, it will become a good violinist. I make no reflections on the honesty of the Czechs. But I can testify that in the Gri-Gris, the Sekt-Pavilions, the Alhambras, and the Chapeaux Rouges of Prague there were pianists and violinists, who lacked only the opportunity to become famous virtuosos. At Zavrel's, the one smart restaurant of Prague, there was Pan Blaške, rivalled only by Hecht of Vienna as a violin exponent of Viennese music. At the Sekt-Pavilion there was Herr Loeffelholz, a young Jew, who played dance music while he composed symphonies and who, when the other guests were gone, would pour out to us on the keys of his champagne-stained piano the storms and longings of his soul.

Above all, there were Wolff and Bureš. Bureš, a pale, fair-haired Czech, who had been a prisoner in Russia, was a violinist who could reduce a room crowded with giggling girls and drunken speculators to an exalted silence. Wolff was the broken genius of Central Europe—a pianist with the soul of Chopin and a taste for old brandy. He had passed out of the Prague Conservatory with the highest honours. Then the war had interrupted his career, and he had drifted into night-life. When I met him first, he could not have been more than thirty. But already his heavy mottled face was scarred with lines, and his tiny black eyes bore a tell-tale redness which spoke of sleepless nights and deep carouses. His life was all tragedy. He knew his own genius, but could not escape from the prison of his physical defects. He loved with a passionate, constant, and hopeless longing one of the Animier-Damen* of the cabaret in which he played. When the "animating lady" of his affections was sitting with some particularly obnoxious customer, Wolff would be consumed with a violent jealousy. He could make no scene. He gave her all his money, but it was not enough to take her or him out of nightlife. And when he was jealous, he went to his brandy bottle and drank stolidly, intentionally, to drown his rage.

Yet he could play as I have heard no one play. Not even the best gipsies of Russia could induce in the same degree that intoxication of melancholy which makes a man pledge his soul and his last penny of credit in his uncontrolled desire to prolong the exaltation of the moment. I used to engage Wolff for Sir George

---

* Animier-Dame is the euphemism which the proprietors of Central European Nachtlokals give to the young girls who act as dancing-partners and table companions to the guests in these establishments.

Clerk's parties at the Legation. I had to buy him off for the night from his employer and during the evening I had to take care that no domestic quarrel should endanger his sobriety. He had many triumphs during which Princesses sat at his feet and begged for more. There were other occasions when the brandy had done its work, and, long before the party was over, the short, squat figure would sway dangerously on its stool and, as brain and hand failed to connect, the stubbly fingers would blur the notes. He was never boisterous or objectionable. But a stupid, self-satisfied grin on that strangely mobile face told its own tale.

At times like these Sir George would be angry. He would take me aside and say firmly: "This is the last time we can have Wolff here." The little man, however, was as popular in society as he was in his Nachtlokal. And when Princess Schwarzenberg or some other dame de la noblesse would say to Sir George: "Next week you'll give a party, won't you, and you'll have Wolff," Sir George would relent. At the next party Wolff would be back in his place, superb, smiling, repentant but unchanged.

These, however, were not the proper occasions on which to hear Wolff. His kingdom was the Chapeau Rouge, his hour of audience three in the morning. For Jack Cecil and me, listening to Wolff became a kind of ritual. After official parties we would seek him out as an escape from boredom. Sometimes the room would be empty, and he would come forward to greet us, rubbing his podgy hands and bowing like a Spanish grandee. We could tell if other guests were present as soon as we entered the building. From the cloak-room we could see him seated at his piano. He would see us, look up, and shrug his shoulders contemptuously. Translated into robust Czech, the gesture meant that there were a few soulless morons present but that he would soon get rid of them. But guests or no guests, from the moment we came in he played for us. Certainly, we paid—handsomely and foolishly. But Wolff always gave full value for his money. We gave no orders. Automatically the waiter set a bottle of champagne on our table. Automatically he gave a bottle of brandy to Wolff's band. Automatically he brought a fresh bottle as soon as the previous one was empty. We would lean forward with elbows firmly planted on the table, and Wolff would begin. If he had a new Viennese Leid, he would try it first in order to see if it met with our approval. It rarely did. It was the old favourites that we and Wolff himself liked best; slow, sentimental waltz-songs with idiotic words but played by Wolff with a delicious languor which lifted them out of the commonplace. Most of them were by Jewish composers and as popular in Prague and Budapest as in Vienna. Certainly, I never heard any Viennese play them with the same ecstatic melancholy as Wolff played them. Strangely enough, the tunes, like "Wien, Wien, Du Stadt meiner Träume," which have since become popular in London, were those which we liked least. Wolff's repertory was inexhaustible, and to-day I have forgotten the names of many of his songs. Some like "Servus Du" and "Im Prater blühen die Bäume" I shall remember as long as memory lasts. As the brandy mellowed him, he would forget us, send Bureš and the 'cellist out of the room, and seek an outlet for his emotion in the nobler music of his own country: plaintive songs by Fibich and Smetana in which one could hear the rill of mountain streams and feel the hopeless longing of a people whose destiny has been frustrated for three centuries. He would end his concert with Suk's "Love Song." His broad back would sway from side to side, as his fingers lingered over the notes in an effort to extract their full sweetness. He would remain bent over the piano, long after the last note had died away. Then, rising from his seat, he would shuffle clumsily over to our table and sit down beside us. There were tears in his eyes. There was a moist film over my own.

As we fed him on sausages and black coffee, he would talk on every subject under the sun. If he was foolish in his own conduct, he was wise about life. He was a patriot, but there was much in the attitude of his countrymen of which he disapproved. "Why all this hate?" he would say. "Why should I dislike a man because he's a Hungarian or an Austrian? There are good people and bad people in every country, and a good Austrian is a better man to me than a bad Czech. We're up to-day, and they are down. To-morrow, it may be their turn, and our sons and daughters will be sorry too late. The trouble with us Czechs is that we are too provincial. Still, we have good qualities. We learn quickly. Pray God that we learn in time." The words were very much the same as I have heard President Masaryk use in private conversation on more than one occasion. They find an echo in the heart of many Austrians, Czechs, Hungarians and Yugoslavs, but, seemingly, they are never heard in the Parliaments and Council Chambers of Central Europe.

Sometimes, too, he would talk of his ambitions. They were modest enough: a little farm in the country with a few acres of land, the pale, faded girl of his heart, and peace in which to write his own compositions. Poor Wolff! His hopes would never be realised. He was a prisoner of his own attractive yet impossible temperament. He would never write even a popular Schlager. During our stay in Prague, he was, I think, the only cabaret leader who did not present us with a Lockhart Lied or a Cecil March especially composed in our honour and, of course, for his own monetary compensation.

When at last we made signs of moving, Wolff would spring to his feet. "One moment, please," he would say. He would stumble back to his piano. Bureš and the 'cellist would take their places. All three would raise their glasses and drink our health. Then Wolff would nod. It was the signal for the last tune. It was always the same: Oscar Straus's "There are things that we all must forget." Slowly, languorously, they would play through the long verse. But it was the chorus, repeated pianissimo with Bureš's harmonics dominating, which was the consummation of our desire of the moment.

> "Noch einmal zum Abschied dein Händchen mir gib,
> Nur einmal noch sag' mir: 'Ich hab' dich so lieb!'
> Nur einmal noch schling' meinen Arm ich um dich,
> Und dann, mein Schatz, vergesse mich, vergesse mich!"

>> ("Just once again give me your hand to press,
>> Just whisper once again: 'I love you so.'
>> Let me enfold you in one last caress,
>> And then forget me, love, forget and go.")

Out we went into the night, striving to retain by silence a mood which had already passed. If it was winter, we went home. But in the spring we would take a car and drive down to the river. It was—and must be for any one—an unforgettable experience. Standing on the Bridge of the Legions, we would look up at the high hill of the Hradčany on the other side of the Vltava. In the dark grey light it looked black and more like a forest than a fortress. Even the outline was undistinguishable. Behind us was the drab grey mass of modern Prague; below the river so still and silent that it scarcely seemed to move. Then as the first streaks of dawn broke the uniformity of the grey pall, the shapeless mass of the Hradčany unfolded itself until it looked like a ghost ship sailing on a sea of black. The islands, green with trees, revealed themselves. A tiny breath of air ruffled the leaves bringing with it the cloying fragrance of the lime-trees. Then, long before we could see the sun, the Hradčany was flooded with light, beginning with the dome of St. Vitus and ending with the palaces and churches of the Mala Strana until every window shone like gold, while the rest of the city remained in darkness.

From my early youth I have had an instinctive capacity for extracting the full flavour from an experience, and I have no false regrets about these long nights with Wolff. There were other nights that were less profitably spent: wild parties in which we joined up with the Americans, descended on a Nachtlokal, and took command of the proceedings. The Central European cabarets of these days were very much alike. There was the main room with boxes, supper tables, and a stage. The performers were of every nationality. Most of them were women, and most of the turns were song-and-dance acts, varied by juggling, acrobatics and performing animals. The stage show lasted until one o'clock. Then the main floor was cleared of its tables, and there was dancing. There was no lack of partners. Every woman performer had a clause in her contract engaging her to remain in the establishment until it closed. As there were no licensing hours and as dawn was the usual closing-time, the proprietors prospered.

There was one cabaret king of those days who, when I first came to Prague, was a waiter in a restaurant. To-day, he is a rich householder, owning a couple of streets and half-a-dozen hotels of his own. The Mimis, the Liesels, the Madelines, the Käthes, and the Hansis, who laid the foundation of this wealth, did not fare so well. Some, doubtless, married into respectability. One or two have since achieved fame on the legitimate stage. One young Russian girl, who earned her first money on the parqueted floor of the Prague Sekt-Pavilion, is now the leading light-comedy actress of Berlin. The talented dancer who is now the chief ornament of Budapest musical comedy began her career as a girl of sixteen in the same establishment. These, however, were the exceptions. The reign of the others were short. Unable to lift themselves out of the ruck, they drifted from the semi-respectability of Prague, Vienna and Budapest to the more exacting sordidness of the Balkans until finally they passed into oblivion and worse in the dance-halls of Alexandria, Cairo and Constantinople.

To us this life offered an outlet for high spirits rather than for romantic adventures. We danced hectically. We mastered the intriguing rhythm of the Viennese waltz. We conducted the orchestra. We played the drums and the piano and even the violin, according to our individual talents. We balanced ourselves on two champagne bottles—a favourite stunt of my own which, when performed on the top of a high bar, never failed to win me many bets. The departure of a colleague was always an excuse for a party, and we celebrated the farewell of Ruggieri, the charming Italian diplomatist, by lowering him on a rope-ladder of tablecloths from an upstairs-box of a Nachtlokal on to the stage below. He now occupies a post of high responsibility in Fascist diplomacy, and I shudder to think how easily a great career might have been cut short if Czech linen had proved less durable or if one of our hurriedly tied knots had come undone.

Occasionally, there were rows. Their origin was nearly always a national anthem. In a place like Prague, where the hates of the war and of the peace still survived, the playing of national anthems in Nachtlokals was rightly forbidden. Perhaps just because it was forbidden, it was an irresistible temptation. We ourselves had no trouble. There was, however, one fracas which, if it had been made public, must have ended disastrously for many of us.

One evening a young French officer, an amusing companion and an excellent soldier, was giving a party in one of the smaller Nachtlokals. Most of the other tables were occupied by members of the diplomatic corps, including Jack Cecil and myself. The only strangers in the room were two powerfully built but placid-looking men who I thought were Austrians and who were sitting at a table by themselves. The French officer, who was in his most cheerful mood, signalled to the band to play the Marseillaise. We all stood up. The strangers remained seated. In an instant the Frenchman's good humour vanished. "Gentlemen," he shouted. "The Marseillaise! Stand up!" Then, as the strangers made no move, he hurled a plate at their table to enforce his request. The bigger stranger rose and took two steps across the room. The Frenchman advanced to meet him. There was a swift exchange of blows, and in a second the Frenchman was lying on the floor with as clean a knock-out as I have ever seen delivered in the prize-ring. With the blow the situation had become serious. As soon as he came to his senses, the Frenchman, who was a noted swordsman, was dangerously correct. He had been struck. There was only one way in which he could avenge the insult to his country and to himself. He would send his seconds. To make matters worse, the strangers were Czechs. They kept their tempers and they spoke with an icy self-control which filled me with forebodings. They knew the laws of their own country. They had been provoked. Every one present would testify to their behaviour. Let the police be summoned and a protocole be made. The arrogant Frenchman should be taught a lesson.

The situation looked serious. The Czechs were within their rights. If the matter came to the ears of the authorities, there would be serious trouble for all of us. Cecil and I took a hand in the affair. While Cecil argued with the Frenchman, I poured sweet reasonableness on the Czechs. Fortunately, they were good fellows at heart, and in the end there was a general reconciliation with drinks all round.

I do not wish to convey the impression that our life in Prague was a succession of orgies or that we turned day into night to the detriment of our work. Diplomatists work much harder to-day than they did before the war. They travel more. They rub shoulders with all kinds and conditions of people and they have a far wider knowledge of men and affairs than their pre-war predecessors. But no picture of the early post-war life in Central Europe would be complete without some mention of the extraordinary atmosphere in which we lived and of which hard work and hard living, feverish gaiety and intellectual endeavour, selfish ambition and reckless extravagance, were the component elements. It was an atmosphere which affected great and small, young and old, junior secretaries and ministers, soulless speculators and staid City bankers. It was perhaps the inevitable reaction to war discipline, but it characterised life in all the Central European capitals. It was not only the champagne of victory. It was also the anodyne of defeat.

Nevertheless, there were long periods during which I took myself and my work very seriously. I read voraciously everything that had been written on Central Europe. I worked at my Czech until I could read with pleasure and follow the Czech drama with understanding. When, too, under the influence of the repentance of repletion, the Calvinist spirit reasserted itself in me, I would pack my bag with Bohemian histories and ethnographical treatises and betake myself to the country for a long week-end's reading. At the end of my first two years I had a first-hand knowledge of the politico-economic and cultural life of Czechoslovakia. I was on terms of intimacy with most of the leading politicians in every Party, and I had learnt more Czech than perhaps any other diplomatist in Prague. I had, too, a fairly comprehensive understanding of the whole Central European problem and had formed a concrete view of the dangers that lay ahead. I had visited Berlin, Munich, Dresden, Vienna, Budapest and Zagreb. I had found new friends among my former enemies. At thirty-five I had not curbed my spirit of irresponsibility. My energy, however, was unimpaired. If my ideals had suffered, my judgments were tempered by richer experience. Greater diligence, it is true, might have brought greater knowledge, but, on the whole, I knew my Central European "muttons" as well as most people. And, when my colleagues faked a ciphered telegram from the Foreign Office requesting me to carry out an inspection of the Czechoslovak navy, I turned the laugh against them by setting out solemnly on what was a natural and very proper task. The Czechs had a navy —a flotilla of gunboats on the Danube!

Yet, I found little satisfaction in my work. During the war local knowledge had at moments commanded a premium of attention and reward. Peace was a slow process of reconstruction, in which there was little outlet for ambition. Czechoslovakia was a small country—an island of prosperity in a sea of chaos, and in the turmoil over German reparations the Foreign Office at home were only too glad if from Prague there was nothing to report. Telegrams in those days meant trouble, and in those early postwar years Czechoslovakia, thanks to the sound administration of her finances, was pleasantly free from political vexations.

When I grew tired of politics—and in those days every one including the women talked politics, I found a pleasant relief in exploring the literary and artistic world of Prague. Not in vain did Berlioz call the Czechs the most musical people in the world, and with the acquisition of national independence Czech music came into its own. In Prague, in addition to several excellent concert halls, there were three theatres which gave opera—the Czech National Theatre, the German Theatre, and the charming old Stavovské Theatre sacred to music-lovers by its Mozart traditions.

I made a pious study of Mozart. The house in which he stayed was just behind my flat at the foot of the wooded Petřin Hill and was a favourite haunt of mine on summer evenings. In Mozart's time the house had nestled among vineyards. Now it was surrounded by factory chimneys, but the one-storeyed villa and its charming garden remain almost as they were. It was here that he composed Don Juan, and, as I strolled beneath the chestnut trees and acacias, I used to picture to myself the scene when on the eve of the first performance Mozart was locked in his room and told to remain there until he had delivered the promised overture of which he had not written a single line. Sustained by bowls of punch, the wonder-boy worked all through the autumn night, while from hour to hour his friends tiptoed into the garden to see if the light was still burning in his window. In the morning he delivered the manuscript. It was performed unrehearsed the same night with Mozart himself conducting and was received with tumultuous applause.

This first performance of Don Juan in the Prague Stavovské was the greatest operatic triumph of Mozart's life. Mozart himself was grateful to the Czechs. "This opera," he used to say, "is not for the Viennese but for the people of Prague and more still for me and my friends." The Czechs, too, are proud of their recognition of his genius and contrast their admiration with the indifference of the Viennese, who allowed him to starve and then buried him in a nameless pauper's grave. Even to-day there is no place in the world where Mozart's operas are given with such sympathy and understanding as in this old Prague theatre to whose comfortless red satin seats one finds one's way through the stalls of the Prague provision market.

There were other ghosts in Czechoslovakia which inspired me to indulge my incurable zest for literary pilgrimages. When I visited the Star Palace and the site of the Battle of the White Mountain, it was not of our own Stuart Elizabeth, the ill-fated Winter Queen of Prague, that I thought, but of Descartes, who in an adventurous ambition to see the world enlisted in the ranks of the Catholic army and came unscathed through that bloody day. It was, too, in trying to trace the literary route of Chateaubriand through Bohemia that I made my first real acquaintance with the Memoires d'Outre-Tombe, the most entrancing of all autobiographies and the literary bible of M. Paul Morand and many another French diplomatist.

My pilgrimages took me farther afield. When I went to Teplitz, it was not the château of the Clarys which attracted me but the town park where over a hundred years ago Beethoven walked with Goethe. And as they walked arm in arm, suddenly the Austrian Imperial family came in sight. Goethe withdrew to the side of the path and, with bowed head and hat in hand, waited reverently until they passed. But the rugged Beethoven strode forward, clearing his way through the Imperial procession, an emperor by the genius of his music accepted as such by the emperor of the proud Habsburg lineage.

At Dux, too, I spent more than one profitable afternoon, which should have been devoted to the inspection of factories, in visiting the Wallenstein Castle. There is nothing particularly attractive about the castle except its magnificent wooded park. The great Wallenstein of the Thirty-Years War never lived here, and his descendants have left the estate, which now belongs to the Czechoslovak Government. But it was here that Casanova spent the last thirteen years of his life as librarian to the Wallenstein of the day. It was here, too, that he developed that incredible intellectual activity on which rests his fame and which, indeed, entitles him to far more respect than all his amorous and perhaps rather fanciful adventures. He was sixty when he came to Dux. Wallenstein, an admirer of his literary work, had taken pity on his poverty. And to repay his benefactor the old adventurer not only catalogued the magnificent library but also maintained a literary activity so prodigious in its output and so extensive in its range of subjects that even the most prolific years of Goethe's life seem inactive in comparison. It was at Dux that Casanova wrote his Memoirs. They were written, as he himself said, to amuse his friends. They were only a pleasant relaxation from the countless works on science, mathematics, astrology, history, art, philosophy and poetry which flowed from his pen. Casanova, the libertine, is known to the prurient-minded the whole world over. Casanova, the virile scholar and man of letters, whose intellect no self-indulgence could impair, has never received the recognition to which his merits entitle him. He died and was buried at Dux, but, as in the case of Mozart, the whereabouts of his grave is unknown.

These literary pilgrimages impelled me to a literary activity of my own. I drew up the synopsis for a novel on diplomatic life. I actually began a history of Bohemia. Alas! for the short-lived ambitions of the complacent. Their execution was always postponed until the morrow. My theatrical ventures yielded more practical results. In Prague for the first and only time in my life, I appeared as an actor on the stage of a national theatre. True, the company was an amateur one, composed of members of the French Mission with the Dutch Minister and myself thrown in as ballast, and the performance was for the benefit of the Czech Red Cross. But we had a gala audience including Miss Masaryk, Dr. Beneš and the entire Czech Cabinet, and the play, Tristan Bernard's "L'Anglais tel qu'on le parle," went with a bang. I played the unflattering part of the English father who throws his weight about in a mixture of English oaths and bad French. But my grey check English suit was the pride of Prague and earned me a bouquet of orchids and carrots from an unknown admirer.

I fear that these unaccustomed rays of limelight must have affected my vanity. At any rate, they led me into an unjustified extravagance and into my first and only effort as an impresario. When a troupe of old friends from the Moscow ballet, headed by the talented Mlle. Frohmann, came to Prague, I persuaded Sir George Clerk to give a ballet entertainment at the Legation. With the Croat conductor I arranged the details of the programme. With Jack Cecil I prepared the stage. To see the show, Sir George had asked an audience composed of the élite of Bohemian society, and before the assembled princes and princesses my ballerinas betrayed a nervousness which they had never shown in Moscow. Their agitation was not groundless. Cecil and I had done our part badly. We had been too niggardly with the resin, and, as Mlle. Frohmann attempted her first ambitious series of fouettées, she slipped on the shining parquetry and hurt her ankle. The audience, however, knowing nothing of ballet technique, was not critical. Mlle. Frohmann carried on with great courage. The Spanish dance of Mlle. Bekefi, the daughter of the famous ballet-master, stirred the blood of even the most blasé princeling. And when with the mechanical doll dance, in which Jack Cecil and I carried Mlle. Frohmann and her brother on and off the stage like lay figures, the entertainment ended in an avalanche of flowers and applause, the élite of Bohemian society took my ballerinas figuratively and literally into their arms.

Indirectly, the Russians were the cause of my financial undoing and of my abandonment of my official career. Throughout my life I have always found Russian gipsy music the most irrestible of all human temptations. When the best Russian tsiganes, attracted by good Czech money, began to drift from Constantinople to Prague, I was an easy and willing prey. The troupe that assembled itself in those days under the management of Colonel Bogretsoff, a former aide-de-camp of the Grand Duke Nicholas, was a galaxy of all the talents. It included the famous Nastia Poliakova and her brother Dmitri, Gania, an old friend from the Moscow "Streilna," Fesenko, Morfessi and two or three minor stars. Its headquarters, appropriately enough, was the "Golden Goose" on the Wenceslaus Place. And here, all too often for the good of my pocket, I renewed the sentimental memories of my Russian past. These plaintive minor melodies were at once a mirror of my own wrecked ambitions and a link with Moura, from whom I was now completely shut off. I saw again the dark shadows of the Kremlin projected by the moon on the Moscow river. I heard again the pleasant, strangely quiet, sound of the sleigh traffic. I saw again the countryside with its endless plains and vast horizons with the red ball of the sun setting over the golden corn. I felt again the warm attraction of the Russian people with their strange contrasts of cruelty and human kindness, of laughter and of sadness, of past failings and of unfulfilled destiny. And with it all there came an irresistible longing to return to that Russia which an Englishman either hates or can never forget. In these moments I hated Prague and all Central and Western Europe and still more myself and my own weakness.

Jack Cecil was my favorite companion. Although he had never been in Russia, he approached what was, in fact, a rite in the proper spirit and treated the tsiganes with that old-world courtesy which all great artists expect. There were others who did not. As the fame of the gipsies grew, I was constantly being pestered with requests from distinguished English visitors to take them to a tsigane party. Rarely was the experiment successful. Some of my guests were bored. Others were profanely familiar, their attitude reminding me of those ill-bred tourists who enter a Muslim mosque without taking their shoes off. Once a beefy Member of Parliament, who had reached that stage which euphemistic American hostesses call "amply refreshed," burst into "Yoicks" and John Peel, as Gania was singing "Two Guitars."

The tsiganes were shocked. Jack Cecil closed the incident by gently removing the soulless politician from his seat and pushing him under the table where he remained peacefully for the rest of the evening.

There were a select few—and among these I include my own minister—whose sense of appreciation brought its own reward. On those occasions the gipsies were inspired. Once, too, a world-famous ballerina came to Prague. She dined with us and, being tired, left early. As I saw her home to her hotel, I said to her: "Nastia Poliakova is in Prague. Would you like to hear her?" The tired look disappeared from her eyes. She had not been in Russia for four years. That night Nastia sang as I have never heard her sing before or since. It was the tribute of one great artist to another. Nor would she or any of the gipsies accept any remuneration for their services. There were tears of nostalgia in the ballerina's eyes, and, as she said goodbye, she took the brooch, which she was wearing, from her breast and gave it to Nastia as a thanks-offering and as a memento of an hour which would never be recaptured. It was very Russian, very emotional, and completely natural.

The next day we had a visit from an English parson, and there was a service, complete with hymns and harmonium, in the Legation drawing-room. I played the hymns. One of them was "Peace, perfect Peace."

CHAPTER NINE

AS a very small boy I acquired a reputation for kind-hearted generosity through handing over to a beggar a shilling which had just been given to me by my grandmother. My brother, who was with me and who also received a shilling, but did not part with it, carried the tale home, and my relations patted me on the head as a shining example of the Christian virtue of charity. The reputation was unjustified. Freudians have since told me that my alleged generosity was merely the effect of a weak-willed inability to say "no", the weak will and the inability being due to a misdirected sex urge caused by adenoids.

Be this as it may, it was obvious even to myself that my irresponsibility in money matters was heading me straight towards a financial crash. Even with local champagne at a few shillings a bottle, night-life is an expensive amusement, and, although at the beginning life in Prague had been cheap enough on a falling krone, I had always lived above my means. Scorning to speculate on the exchange, I had existed on a lordly overdraft with a Czech bank which I reduced from time to time by gifts from my relations.

The crisis came in 1922 when I was least ready to meet it. Thanks to the energetic financial policy of Dr. Rašin, the Czech krone made a rapid recovery and, after having been 420 to the pound, rose in a few months to 120. I was in a desperate situation. My grandmother had died. My relations had lost nearly all their money in rubber. I dared not appeal to them again. Helpless as a leaf before the wind, I watched my overdraft rise automatically with the exchange and with no benefit to myself from £700 to over £2000 and trusted to my luck to work a miracle in my favour.

And, as it has happened so often in my life, my luck held.

One morning, as I sat in my office meditating resignation as the prelude to automatic ruin, the Chancery servant brought me in a card. It bore the name of Michael Spencer-Smith. My visitor brought with him a strange story. It began with an Austrian overdraft and a dream of Mr. Montagu Norman, the Governor of the Bank of England.

Before the war there had been a large bank called the Anglo-Oesterreichische Bank in Vienna—a Jewish concern with some English capital and with branches all over the old Austro-Hungarian monarchy. On pre-moratorium bills met by the Bank of England after the outbreak of the war the Austrian concern was now heavily indebted to the Bank of England and owing to the hopeless economic situation in Austria was not in a position to meet its obligations.

Partly with a view to liquidating this debt and still more to helping Austria, Mr. Norman had conceived a great scheme of converting the bank into an English bank and of using it as an instrument for the reconstruction of Central Europe. Michael Spencer-Smith had been sent out as the Governor's man of confidence to put the scheme into effect.

At that time Spencer-Smith was the youngest director of the Bank of England. He had had a meteoric career. Educated at Eton, he had gone on to Oxford where he had made friends with the present Lord Bearsted. He had entered the Shell Company, had been its general manager in Japan, and had subsequently become a partner in the firm of Lefevre & Co. Appointed a director of the Bank of England before he was forty, he was regarded as the most promising of all the younger financial lights in the City of London. Fair-haired, good-looking and remarkably tall, he was a man of great charm and the highest ideals. A typical Englishman, he knew no foreign languages and had had no experience of dealing with Continental Europeans.

As he unfolded his story slowly and deliberately, I realized instinctively that here was an opportunity for myself. It revealed itself almost immediately. Before he could put his scheme into effect, there was one almost insurmountable obstacle which had to be cleared away. All the assets of the Viennese bank were in Austrian Treasury notes which had been deposited in Prague. While the Austrians claimed that the notes were entitled to be valued in Czech currency, the Czechs were equally insistent that they were not.

This comic situation had a typically Central European origin. After the war the old Austrian currency had continued to run in the new Czechoslovakia. But in 1921, Dr. Rašin, the Czechoslovak Finance Minister, had created a new Czech currency by the simple process of stamping all Austrian bank-notes that were in Czechoslovak territory on a certain fixed date. The Austrians had known of Dr. Rašin's intentions, and the more far-seeing had rushed their bank-notes into Czechoslovakia before stamping day.

Unfortunately, the Jews in the Anglo-Oesterreichische Bank had been too far-seeing. Instead of sending bank-notes, they had transferred interest-bearing Treasury Notes. The Czechs had stamped the bank-notes. They had refused to accept the Treasury notes. Greed for interest had defeated its own ends. At that time the exchange value of the Czech krone was 120 to the £1. The Austrian krone exchange was over 300,000. If the 148,000,000 Treasury notes of the Anglo-Oesterreichische Bank had a Czech value, they were worth over £1,000,000. If they had an Austrian value, they were practically worthless. Without assets the Governor could not go ahead with his scheme.

This was the situation when Spencer-Smith enlisted my help. The negotiations that followed were long and difficult. I soon found that, as far as I was concerned, the doctor had been called in too late. The whole question of the validity of the Treasury notes had already been thrashed out. The matter had been referred to the Ambassadors' Conference, and the Conference had decided in Czechoslovakia's favour. Moreover, Spencer-Smith had come to Prague accompanied by Dr. Rosenberg and Dr. Simon, two Viennese directors of the bank, and at that time, foolishly but perhaps naturally, the Czechs regarded Viennese bankers with grave suspicion. Worse still, he had already seen Beneš and had tried to brow-beat him, and, although Dr. Beneš is a modest, little man, he is a jealous guardian of the sovereign rights of his people.

It was a tangle after my own heart. Here at last was an exciting battle of wits such as I had not fought since I left Russia. Nor in entering this fight were the English without a vantage ground. Spencer-Smith's admiration for Mr. Montagu Norman amounted to hero-worship—a tribute to the Governor's magnetism and a characteristic which I have since remarked in everyone who has served under that remarkable man. And the dream of the Governor and of Spencer-Smith was not without its attractive allure. As a sop to the nationalist susceptibilities of the new Succession States they were prepared to split up the former branches of the Anglo-Oesterreichische Bank into local banks: an Anglo-Czech bank in Czechoslovakia, and Anglo-Austrian bank in Vienna, and Anglo-Yugoslav bank in Yugoslavia, an Anglo-Hungarian bank in Hungary, and an Anglo-Rumanian bank in Rumania. All these banks would work together for the common good of Central Europe under the control of a central institution, of which the Bank of England would be the chief shareholder. It was to be a kind of miniature financial League of Nations with Mr. Norman in the rôle of President Wilson. True, the lofty idealism of this dream was not untinged with materialist interests. If the scheme were successful, it would give to England a financial footing in Central Europe which it had never previously possessed. It was the Governor's counter-stroke to the German Mittel-Europa thrust. Suspicious as he was of anything which came out of Vienna, Dr. Beneš was the last man in the world to fail to realize the benefits which a connection with the Bank of England might bring to his own country. In his scheme of things a military alliance with France and a financial alliance with England were the surest guarantees for his country's independence. Moreover, the goodwill of the Bank of England was the open sesame to the coffers of the City of London and to the establishment of Czechoslovakia's credit. Here was a tactical position which might be used with great advantage in my negotiations with the Czechs.

With Spencer-Smith I made one stipulation. Rosenberg and Simon, the two Viennese, must be kept in the background. It would be better if the preliminary negotiations with the Czechs were conducted by myself alone. Spencer-Smith agreed, and at once I carried the battle into the citadel of the Hradčany, avoiding the barbed wire entanglements of the Ministry of Finance and advancing direct on Dr. Beneš, whom I have always found not only a shrewd negotiator, but also a master of compromise and a man of his word even when keeping it has brought down the wrath of his countrymen on his head. Sir George Clerk prepared my way by recommending the scheme in one of those shrewd and disarmingly frank conversations which never failed to impress the Czechs.

From the start Dr. Beneš gave me a most sympathetic hearing, and I found an unexpected supporter in Dr. Hotowetz, the Minister of Commerce and one of the first Czechs to realise the importance and, indeed, the necessity of closer and freer trade relations between the Succession States. Reassured by Spencer-Smith that the proposed new Anglo-Czech bank would be a real Czech bank and not merely a subterfuge for maintaining Viennese financial domination in Prague, both men were warmly in favour of clinching the deal.

But when we came to the all-important question of the Treasury bonds the negotiations always broke down. Unless the bonds were given a Czech currency value, Mr. Montagu Norman would not and, in fact, could not proceed with his project. The Czechs were in an even more difficult position. They would willingly have paid the sum of £1,000,000 as the price of the Bank of England connection, but the constitutional means were not there. Moreover, they dared not admit that the Treasury bonds were entitled to Czech valuation. There were other banks and other individuals in Czechoslovakia who held Austrian Treasury bonds. If the Czechs made an exception in the case of our Treasury bonds, they would be forced to admit the claims of other holders.

Day after day I went to Dr. Beneš's room in the Hradčany or to see Dr. Hotowetz in the Ministry of Commerce. I went to the full length of my brief and a little beyond it. I drew a touching picture in which I portrayed the Old Lady of Threadneedle Street mothering the youngest and healthiest of Europe's children. Just as in Scottish history St. Andrews is famed for its slaughter of Archbishops and Cardinals, so, too, in Czech history the favourite method of getting rid of political undesirables used to be defenestration or throwing out of the window. As I looked out from Dr. Beneš's room, my eye caught that corner window of the Hradčany from which in 1618 the sturdy Czech patriots had thrown the bodies of the Catholic myrmidons of the Emperor Ferdinand into the yawning abyss below. I reminded Dr. Beneš of this stirring episode in his country's history, and I made a contrast. This was not a case for casting out old baggage. The old tyrants were gone. Here was a good fairy coming in by the window. It was an opportunity that no Czech dared neglect. It might never come again.

My eloquence was perhaps unnecessary. Dr. Beneš's imagination needed no prompting. He saw to the uttermost farthing the advantages of the situation. But when I returned in the morning to Spencer-Smith's rooms in the Passage Hotel there was little progress to report. Both parties were agreed on all points except the vital one of the Treasury bonds.

The situation seemed impossible. Even the astute Jewish minds of Rosenberg and Simon could suggest no satisfactory way out of the impasse. Simon, a former official of the Austrian Treasury, I liked. He was a little stocky clean-shaven man with close-cropped hair and a nimble mind, which jumped from subject to subject with bewildering rapidity. He was full of enthusiasms, which contrasted strangely with that cold impassiveness of the London banker which is both a sound tradition and a cloak for lack of imagination and, sometimes, for lack of ideas. Rosenberg was an enigma which I never solved. Short, fat, pasty-faced, with a thick black moustache, heavily-lidded eyes, and Nietzscheesque bushy eyebrows, he passed as one of the ablest minds in Central Europe. He had been a famous lawyer in Vienna. He had been one of the numerous Ministers of Finance of the new Austrian Republic. Now at the age of forty-six he had taken up banking in real earnest. He was the magician who was to restore the fortunes of the Anglo-Oesterreichische Bank. He had been to London in connection with the new scheme, had seen the Governor, and had made a great impression on all the City magnates whom he had met. To Spencer-Smith and to Ralph Hamlyn, the well-known London accountant, who had carried out the investigation into the affairs of the Anglo-Oesterreichische Bank, his scholarship, his Greek and Latin "tags," and his omniscient erudition were a source of wonder and admiration.

But there was something abnormal both in his appearance and his manner. I felt instinctively that behind those heavy rather sleeply looking eyes there lay a restless ambition and an inordinate vanity. I never liked him, and I imagine that the dislike was mutual. Of his talents, however, there could be no question. He could talk with authority on almost any subject, and, if he was brilliant rather than practical, the brilliancy was impressive. But even the scintillating Rosenberg could find no solution for our difficulties.

Then one day I had an idea. I knew nothing about finance. In my youth, when I had been manager of a rubber estate in Malaya, I had had to pay a Chinese clerk out of my own pocket to keep the estate accounts for me. In Russia my grandmother's cheques had saved me from financial ruin. In Prague I had put a load of debt on my shoulders which I could not shake off. Only a few weeks before Spencer-Smith's arrival, I had been in London on leave and had paid my first visit to a money-lender. The visit had proved fruitless, mainly because I had not learnt to put the proper value on my own past and future accomplishments which is the real technique of the approach to the money-lending fraternity. Nevertheless, we had discussed terms and gone into various questions of interest until my common sense revolted. All that remained in my mind of that interview was the impression that while ordinary capital doubled itself in fifteen years, a money-lender's capital doubled itself in fifteen months.

Suddenly, in the middle of my Prague negotiations, this vague recollection came to my rescue. Surely, if a loan at an abnormally high rate of interest could double itself in fifteen months, a loan at an abnormally low rate of interest would cancel itself in a short space of time. Bank rate in Prague at that time was about 10 per cent. If the Czech Government were to give us a loan of

148,000,000 Kronen (the equivalent of the Treasury bonds which the bank held) at 1 per cent, the loan would be equivalent to a gift.

I was incapable of working out the calculation but it seemed a great idea. The Czechs were more than eager to obtain the goodwill of the Bank of England. They were even prepared to do a back-door deal with the Anglo-Oesterreichische Bank and to recompense it for the loss of the Treasury bonds out of a government loan to be raised eventually in England. Spencer-Smith, however, would make no "junctim" between the loan and the Treasury bonds. The Czechs could not make us a present of the bonds. My loan idea seemed therefore not only the best but the only solution.

I put my idea tentatively to the Czechs. It seemed good to them. It offered an exit out of a constitutional labyrinth. It would form an excellent basis for discussion. Elated but still uncertain of success, I returned to Spencer-Smith's rooms in the Passage Hotel. I found him closeted with Rosenberg and Simon. So incoherently did I explain myself that for a moment Spencer-Smith must have thought that I had been drinking. Rosenberg, however, saw the light at once. As he was a Viennese, his first impulse was to suspect a Czech trap. He rose from his seat and began to walk up and down the room. While he bit his moustache in profound thought, my eyes photographed the whole scene in my mind: the rather dingy room with its small round table, its gaudy carpet, its cheap prints on the walls, its divan, its uncomfortable chairs, and its curtained alcove through which I could see the bed and bathroom of Spencer-Smith. East of the Rhine more business is done in the bar than in the boardroom. Here if I was not in a bar I was at least in the centre of Prague night life. Through the open window I could hear six orchestras playing simultaneously: one from the hotel restaurant, one from the Passage Bar, two from the "Golden Goose" next door, one from the Alhambra, the most elegant of Prague Nachtlokals below, and one from a bar across the road. Higher up the Square, looking down benignly on our deliberations, stood the huge statue of King Wenceslaus. My sense of the dramatic surged over me, blotting out all other thoughts. Suddenly one of the orchestras crashed into the popular song of the day until it dominated all the others:

"*Fein, fein, schmeckt uns der Wein,*
Wenn man zwansig ist und die Liebe.
Fein, fein, schmeckt uns der Wein,
Wenn man dreissig it, und auch die Liebe.
Wenn man vierzig ist, man noch gerne kuesst,
B'sonders wenn man auch sparsam gewesen ist,
Wenn man älter wird, ein wenig kalter wird,
Bleibt allein nur der Wein."

("Fine, fine, tastes the gold wine
When one's twenty and ready for love.
Fine, fine, tastes the gold wine,
When one's thirty and still full of love.
When one's forty, one still kisses gladly—
All the more if we've not lived too madly.
When, however, we're older and alas! rather colder,
There remains only wine, only wine.")

As I reflected on the incongruousness of the stage on which I was making my first entry into big business, I realised that Rosenberg was speaking. His words came slowly as if each one had been weighed and assayed before it was delivered. He spoke on many matters which I did not understand. But he was definitely in favour of the loan idea, and in the end his opinion prevailed.

I had nothing to do with the final settlement. The financial details of the deal were worked out by the experts, but it went through without a hitch. The English and the Viennese received a long-term loan, equivalent to the amount of the Treasury Bonds, at a nominal rate of interest. The Anglo-Oesterreichische Bank became an English concern with the title of the Anglo-Austrian Bank. The Czech branches were converted into an independent Anglo-Czechoslovak Bank with headquarters in Prague. Six months later, thanks to the good offices of Spencer-Smith, the Czechoslovak Government was able to float a State loan of £10,000,000 in London and New York and to establish its credit on the two great financial markets of the world.

Everyone had had his reward. Everyone was happy. Did I say everyone? Unrewarded remained the debt-ridden Commercial Secretary of His Britannic Majesty's Legation in Prague, who had been called in to mend a situation which had broken down and who had unwittingly stumbled on a satisfactory solution.

Let me say at once that neither the English nor the Viennese were ungrateful. Had I been in private employ, I could have stipulated, in the event of success, for a commission of 2½ per cent, and it would have been paid gladly. This would have given me a sum of £20,000, paid all my debts, and left me with a competence for life. Naturally my official position precluded any such bargain. Dr. Simon, however, proposed that I should be given a motor-car, but on this gift, too, officialdom imposed its ban. Almost it seemed as if the opportunity, which had presented itself so miraculously, was to be taken out of my grasp. Then, on the night he left Prague, Spencer-Smith asked me to dine with him. He had a proposal to make to me.

We dined at Zavrel's off caviare, baked carp, and partridge with red cabbage. We drank French champagne and we talked to the strains of the Czardasfuerstin played by Pan Blaške's orchestra. It was the cautious kind of talk one expects from the best English bankers. Did I intend to remain a civil servant all my life? In the event of there being a job for me in the new organisation would I be prepared to consider an offer? Rather hastily perhaps I replied that I was in the market for a job and intimated, if not in the exact words, that I was prepared to sell myself to the highest bidder. Spencer-Smith promised to write to me after he had discussed the whole position with his colleagues in London, and on this understanding we said goodnight.

In due course the letter arrived. It was a long letter. It stressed the difficulties of the new bank. It intimated clearly that in the event of my proving a failure the bank would take no responsibility for my future. It underlined the high moral tone which was expected from everyone engaged in banking, and it hinted in euphemistic language that, while champagne might smooth the wheels of diplomacy, banking ran more efficiently and more unobtrusively on water. There was a rider on the dangers of enthusiasms, and a final warning that, if I decided to join the bank, the risk was my own and no one else's. Then came the offer itself. It was, of course, not so good as I had expected. It guaranteed me a minimum salary equal to the salary and allowances which I was receiving at the Legation. I was to be a kind of industrial watch-dog for the bank in Prague and was to represent it on the boards of the numerous industrial companies which it controlled. My real income was to come from my fees as a director.

Although I was prepared to take a gamble on those directors' fees, I showed my letter to Sir George Clerk and asked his advice before I came to a final decision. He was kind enough to give me the benefit of his ripe experience and shrewd critical faculties, and we had many discussions about the matter. On the whole his advice was "don't." He had not formed a very favourable impression of the new organisation. He did not like the manner in which the gentlemen from London and Vienna had handled the original negotiations. He was more than doubtful whether London business methods could be co-ordinated with Central European methods. He pointed out that, while as an official of the British Government I could render great services to the new bank, I might easily become a cipher as soon as I abandoned that vantage ground.

The advice was sound. It put a damper on my first enthusiasms. But I did not take it. And yet my refusal to bow to superior wisdom was not due entirely to lack of judgment. Comically enough, this was not the first offer which had been made to me by a British bank. In 1920 I had received by Foreign Office bag a letter from the British Trade Corporation informing me that it had decided "to considerably extend its activities in the new Trans-Caucasian Republics of Georgia and Azerbaidjan" and stating its desire to put its "interests in Trans-Caucasia under the control of a senior official." The bank had already opened a branch at Batoum and agencies at Baku and Tiflis. The post of senior official was offered to me.

I had taken a week's leave and gone home to consult the directors of the British Trade Corporation. I had seen Lord Faringdon, Mr. Babington Smith and Mr. A. S. M. Dickson at 13, Austin Friars. The discussions were amicable but brief. They were terminated long before we reached the point of discussing financial terms. Lord Faringdon had asked my opinion of the political situation in South Russia and I had given it succinctly. "Gentlemen," I said, "in three months' time there will be no British banks and no foreign Banks in Trans-Caucasia or in any other part of Russia." My time estimate erred on the side of optimism. All that I collected from this visit was an attack of mumps.

Now, however, my position was different, and there was little opportunity for the exercise either of my own or of Sir George's judgment. My debts were such that they could never be paid out of my salary as a civil servant. The new bank offered both a vague hope of wealth and a possibility of re-establishing my financial position without the aid of my relations. Moreover, if the worst happened and I had to fall back on them as a second line of financial defence, my change of profession would be an asset. They had helped me generously when I had been Head of a Mission in Russia. My knowledge of human nature told me that they would be more indulgent towards a budding banker than towards an insignificant Commercial Secretary of a minor Legation. There was a borrowing asset in that tenuous connection with the Bank of England.

Somewhere, too, in the back of my mind was the feeling that I had exhausted the possibilities of an official career and that in Russia I had already had that hour which inspired Dryden to praise of those who live dangerously. Even stronger was the consciousness that a change was necessary for the salvation of my immortal soul. Like Bruce's spider, I had made several attempts to build a web for myself in the world. It was time to settle down and to insure myself against old age. These were the motives which to the exclusion of all others influenced my mind.

Having made my decision, I sat down and wrote out my resignation. It was forwarded to the Foreign Office with a covering despatch from Sir George Clerk, and by the next Foreign Office bag I received a letter signed by the Under Secretary of State and conveying in the customary official form the appreciation of the Secretary of State for my services to King and country during a period of more than eleven years. Into these eleven years I had crowded more than most officials experience in the full span of their career. In their strenuousness and in their historical importance they had been equal to more than twice their number. They had been exciting and not unpleasant years, and, as I folded up the blue-grey parchment despatch embossed with the royal arms, a fleeting doubt assailed me. Was I making a mistake? The Foreign Office is a tolerant, if not munificent, employer, and it is at once the strength and the weakness of an official career that even the most inefficient are secure from dismissal. Too late I realised that by my resignation I had abandoned eleven years of pension rights.

More satisfying to my self-esteem was the parting letter which I received from Sir George Clerk. Yielding again to my insatiate vanity, I quote one excerpt:

You probably know that I have always considered your work in Moscow under amazing conditions as reflecting the greatest credit on your political sense, courage and readiness to take responsibility, and my experience, during the all too short a time you were my Commercial Secretary in Prague, not only confirmed my belief, but showed me that you were the happy possessor of other invaluable qualities such as a remarkable facility for languages, a grasp of foreign affairs, skill in negotiating with foreigners and a capacity for getting on with them and with your colleagues, and loyalty to your Chief, which would have made you a first-class professional diplomatist."

Such a tribute, I feel, should have been accompanied by a dramatic farewell. Actually, my exit from diplomacy was humdrum and undistinguished. Decency compelled me to remain at my post until the arrival of my successor, and in this case the time factor of decency covered a period of nearly two months.

By this time the minor excitement of my resignation had evaporated. As I was not leaving Prague, I was spared the round of farewell dinners and official leave-takings, which are the concomitants of diplomatic life in small capitals. The only outward change in my life was the transfer of my business activities from the romantic baroque palaces of the old town to the ungainly steel and concrete blocks of the modern business city. Had my monetary difficulties not temporarily submerged my sense of the superstitious, I should have realised the sinister implications of the step which I had taken.

BOOK THREE

☆

FINANCIAL HIGH NOON

"Faites-nous de bonne politique et je vous ferai de bonnes finances."
—Baron Louis, French Finance Minister in 1830.

CHAPTER ONE

I BEGAN my official banking career at the end of 1922 and as the first step I was brought back to the head office in London in order to learn the rudiments of my new profession. It was a pleasant but profitless experience. There is a wide difference between the outlook of the New World and that of Europe. In the United States many of the most successful men have changed their occupation as often as seven times. In Europe and, especially in England, a man who switches more than once is an object of some suspicion. And here at the age of thirty-five I was already making my fourth change.

My new employers were charming men—grave, dispassionate and unemotional, but correct and essentially fair in all their dealings. They included General Sir Herbert Lawrence, our Chairman, Sir Henry Strakosch, the late Sir Ernest Harvey, and M. Peter Bark, the former Tsarist Minister of Finance and the right hand of Mr. Montagu Norman for Central European affairs. They treated me with great kindness and assumed a benevolent tolerance towards my shortcomings. They sent me to a chartered accountant for special instruction in the intricacies of balance sheets. They attached me to an expert in the mysteries of industrial credits. On occasions they consulted me on the vagaries of Central European politics.

But we belonged to two different worlds. In the City of London banking knowledge demands a long and intensive training. It is acquired largely by the accumulation of experience. Its chief props are an instinct which in itself is the result of experience and an imposed attitude of self-restraint and reserve, both of which are foreign to my character. Any departure from orthodoxy is frowned on. Intellect and highbrowism are not encouraged, and bankers, like most English people, reserve most of their thinking for their hobbies. Sometimes the hobbies are pictures, or old furniture, or shrubs. More frequently, they are confined to horses and niblicks.

English banking has proved itself, and the London banker is justly proud of the traditions on which it has been built. Yet the system has certain defects. Knowledge in the City is expert rather than general, and I found almost everywhere an ignorance of geography which seemed strange in the financial centre of a nation whose prosperity has been based for centuries on its export trade. To the vast majority of City magnates Europe, in particular, was a sealed book, and to this day there are heads of big firms—banks, insurance companies, investment trusts—who still have difficulty in distinguishing Czechoslovakia from Yugoslavia. The City, in fact, is the English banker's stronghold. So long as he remains in it, so long as he can bring the foreigner to London, he is impregnable. When he ventures into the wilderness of Central Europe, where a different banking system and different standards of honesty prevail, he is at the same disadvantage as I should be against Tilden or Cochet on the tennis court.

A realisation of this weakness would have saved my bank much money in 1923. But, while the City banker rightly regards banking as an exact science, which demands a long apprenticeship, he is curiously unwilling to apply the same standards of preparation to politics or diplomacy. How far this is a general City failing I am not in a position to state. What is certain is that after the first six months we had a score of new-fledged political experts who, with little or no knowledge of languages and local conditions, were prepared to lay down their own views on the political future of Central Europe and to back their opinion against that of the British diplomatic representatives on the spot.

From these limitations I except, of course, M. Bark, who is the most punctual Russian I have ever met and whose charming manners and diplomatic tact would have made him an admirable Ambassador. A protégé of the great Count Witte, he had served his banking apprenticeship in Berlin, spoke Russian, English, French and German with equal facility, and, understanding the

Continental mentality, was indispensable as a negotiator in our numerous dealings with the various Central European Governments. More than any other individual he was responsible for the successful flotation of the Austrian, Hungarian, and Bulgarian Reconstruction Loans.

From the first moment I was drawn to this cultured and attractive Russian, and the fact that our views on Russia were at variance in no way diminished my respect for his abilities. He treated me with great consideration, consulted me frequently on such political matters in which my local knowledge could be of service, and did his best to help me in banking matters. I think that he realised from the beginning that my new appointment was a mistake and that by accepting it I had placed myself in a false position. It was, indeed, true, and Sir George Clerk's forecast was soon to prove itself remarkably accurate. Apart from other deficiencies I was too old to become a professional banker. As a servant of the bank I had far less influence on the bank's policy abroad than I should have had as a government official.

On the other hand, my three months' apprenticeship in London was not without its compensations. It enabled me to learn something about London, which, having spent practically all my life abroad, I hardly knew, and to make new friends in England. Chief of these was "Tommy" Rosslyn, the wife of the amiable and extravagantly open-hearted Lord Rosslyn. "Tommy," a dark diminutive with the courage of a lion and an optimism which has stood the test of many disappointments and much ill-health, is the friend and spiritual adviser of all lame-dogs both biped and quadruped. A devout Catholic. she is afflicted with no doubts and in her own conduct draws the line between right and wrong with more firmness than almost any one I know. At the same time there is nothing priggish or intolerant in her attitude towards the conduct of others. She is a strangely unworldly figure living in a very worldly world.

Ridiculously enough, we met in a London night-club, which is hardly her milieu, and, always amused by the incongruous in life, I spent most of the evening in talking to her. A common dislike of city life and a common passion for fishing created a bond of sympathy between us, and we became firm friends. It has been and still is a fortunate friendship for me, and fatefully fortunate at that particular moment. For "Tommy" has one unfailing remedy for all worldly ills—mortification of the flesh, and, my own flesh being in sad need of mortification, I began to take a pull at myself with excellent results to my physical and moral well-being. The system resolves itself into a kind of spiritual golf which you play against yourself. All forms of self-indulgence —alcohol, over-eating, extravagance—are personal enemies who have to be fought and circumvented at every hour of the day. No matter how often you fail, you start off all square with your opponents the next morning. The system is more humane and tolerant than the rigid austerity of the Presbyterians. In spite of many lapses it has worked fairly well in my own case.

This was perhaps just as well, for at that moment I was called on to face a serious crisis. I had become a banker, but I had not paid all my debts. During my three years at the Legation I had been recklessly extravagant. My extravagance had increased in progressive ratio to the length of my stay. In my first year, during which the krone price of a bottle of champagne represented only a few shillings, I had lived more or less within my means. During my second year the gradual rise in the exchange value of the krone had more than halved the purchasing power of my sterling salary. With these changed circumstances I should have altered my mode of living. I should have put a severe check on the extravagant habits which nearly everyone, including, of course, myself, had formed during that unsettled period of depreciated currencies and unsettled exchanges. I should have given up my car and my chauffeur. I should have cut down my entertaining in restaurants and I should have eschewed night-life. I did none of these things, and, as my financial worries increased, my visits to Nachtlokals became more frequent. When my wife went back to live in England in the autumn of 1922, partly as the result of ill-health and partly because I had not pulled my weight in a rather difficult reunion, this thing called night-life became almost a habit. I had had very little to show for my extravagance. I had not squandered my money on gambling. I neither played cards nor went in for racing. I had dined and danced with a succession of Ilses, Kitties, and Martinas and other international ladies. But none of them had engaged my heart or even my affections. I had poured my money out of a hole in my pocket, and the hole was the most ridiculous form of vanity. In this new capital I had acquired a reputation for going one better than anyone else in recklessness. It flattered my vanity to be told that we gave the best gipsy parties in Prague and to know that when Jack Cecil and I came into a restaurant or a Nachtlokal the manager and the head-waiter would leave whatever they were doing and whomever they were attending in order to bow and scrape before their best customers. It amused me when the chief restaurant owner had special cut brandy glasses made with our name on them. It gave me what the Americans call a "kick" to have always at my table the prettiest girl who was appearing at the various night-shows. In that court of Momus where the loyalty of the subjects is sold to the highest bidder I was a kind of king. True, it was not a difficult or very expensive throne to conquer, for in those days in Prague there were few large fortunes and no such foolish bidders.

I do not know what my expenditure was. There was no outstanding performance in the programme of my recklessness. It was the accumulation of fifty pounds here for a gipsy party and fifty pounds there for a night with Wolff that had undermined my position. My Prague debts came, I suppose, to approximately £10,000. Some of my friends have risked more on a single stock-exchange flutter or a night's gambling.

Yet for one in my position I have been incredibly foolish. But I had been a thousand times more foolish in not clearing up my financial position before taking up my new appointment. Unfortunately, I have one characteristic which some people are unwise enough to consider an advantage. I never anticipate a crisis. I have a strange knack, probably due to an inborn lazy disposition, of putting all trouble out of my mind until it is actually on my door-step. So it had been with my overdrafts. I had had three in three different banks. Two I had paid off. The third which was least likely to worry me I had left unpaid.

Then, one morning in the bank, Spencer-Smith sent for me. I went into his private room. He had a letter in his hand, and I could see from his expression that the matter was grave. Through an investigation into the affairs of the Prague bank, in which I had my overdraft, its existence and its amount had become known to the Viennese directors of our own bank. They had reported the matter by private letter to Spencer-Smith.

This was bad enough. But there was worse to come. In the protracted negotiations between the Czechs and the Viennese over the splitting up of the branches of the old Anglo-Oesterreichische Bank into two new independent Anglo-Austrian and Anglo-Czech banks, the Viennese had naturally tried to retain as much control as possible in Prague. As the complete independence of the new Anglo-Czech bank had been the chief inducement in persuading the Czechs to settle the matter of the Treasury bonds in our favour and as I personally had little faith in the rapid recovery of Vienna, I had thrown such influence as I had with my English directors on the side of the Czechs. This had made me an object of suspicion to the Viennese, who were now hinting more or less openly that my overdraft was a natural explanation of my pro-Czech sympathies. They had overdone the effect by a detailed account of my night-life in Prague and by a lurid description of my driving down the main street of the city surrounded by naked houris. Spencer-Smith, who had been to my parties and who knew that I was no Sultan, treated me with amazing kindness. He explained the insinuations to me quite frankly, pooh-poohed them, and said that of course he would pay no attention to them. The overdraft, however, must be paid off within a week. The sum, swollen by the rise in the exchange value of the Czech crown, was just under £1500—in those days a largish sum in Viennese eyes.

Raising the money was not quite so easy. My father and mother, who had already come to my aid so often, were not in a position to help me. Most of their investments were in rubber, and rubber was then in a bad way. I was determined not to approach them. My uncle had already paid some of my Prague debts. I had told him that they represented the sum total of my liabilities and had promised reform and repentance. I did not choose to put his good nature to a third or was it a fourth test. I therefore took the easiest and the most disastrous way out. I went back to the moneylender whom I had approached a year before. In fact, I went to two moneylenders. And, strangely enough, for, in spite of their once popular advertisements to advance any sum from £50 to £50,000 "on note of hand alone", moneylenders do not lend without tolerably good security, I received my cash.

For two cheques of £750 each I signed two almost identical agreements, undertaking in each case to repay in monthly instalments of £50 with the main repayment at the end of nine months. The interest on the two loans was about eighty per cent. When the nine months were up, one moneylender pressed me hard and would not agree to any postponement. I paid him and never saw him again. The other, who had been in Russia and who liked discussing European politics, treated me with some consideration and renewed my bill on not more onerous terms than the original deal. To him I went back several times. He took me on my face value and was rewarded, for all his loans were paid in full. He has since gone out of the moneylending business and is now a director of several prosperous industrial companies. The whole transaction was the most disastrous that I have ever made. For an overdraft which had yielded me in actual sterling a spending value of about £400 I repaid eventually just over £4000.

Even if they only postponed my troubles, these loans gave me a respite, and the temporary relief was exhilarating. After repaying my overdraft I had a balance of about fifteen pounds. I spent it the same evening on a dinner to two friends and on a visit to a night-club, where I had my first meeting with the late Mrs. Meyrick. The evening gave me no thrills. With the exception of New York, London has the dullest night-life in the world.

Before I left London there was one more disturbance in the volcanic atmosphere of my banking life. With the collapse of the economic situation in Austria, the Viennese branch of our bank, which had rather foolishly indulged in a policy of industrial expansion, had suffered heavy losses, and one afternoon we were shocked to receive a telegram informing us that Dr. Rosenberg, our chief representative in Vienna, had committed suicide. Rosenberg, who had been Finance Minister of Austria, had enjoyed the full confidence of the English directors. The reasons for his suicide will never be known with any exactitude. I imagine, however, that he had come to the conclusion that his policy had broken down and that to a man of his pride and ambition failure was unbearable. His death impressed one fact upon me. There was no short road to recovery in Central Europe. Without recovery there could be no prosperity for our bank, which controlled scores and scores of industrial concerns in Austria, Czechoslovakia, Hungary, Yugoslavia, and Rumania. And with the fading of this dream there vanished my own hopes of restoring my shattered fortunes.

Apart from my financial worries my life in London had run along easy lines. This period of comparative tranquillity was now to end. At Easter Spencer-Smith sent for me and informed me that he wished me to return to Central Europe. I was to go, not to Prague, but to Vienna. The change, he informed me, would be beneficial to my training as a banker. In banking the dispassionate view was all-important, and in Prague I had seen only one side of the Central European problem. It was necessary for me to absorb the Austrian atmosphere. Above all, it was essential that I should establish good relations with the Viennese directors. They were men of ripe experience, and from them I could learn much.

He made no attempt to conceal the difficulties of the position in general and of my own position in particular. There was a prejudice against me in Vienna. My own tact should be able to overcome it. I was to continue to report to him with complete freedom. He would give me his full support. He was as good as his word and wrote to Vienna saying that I was to be well treated and given every opportunity of studying every section of the bank's activities. Indeed, as far as my personal relations with him were concerned, he was the ideal chief, scrupulously fair and straightforward in all his dealings.

I was given a week's leave which I spent very pleasantly in fishing on Dartmoor. Then, slightly apprehensive, but full of good resolutions, I packed my trunks and took my ticket for Vienna.

CHAPTER TWO

IN the minds of most Englishmen Vienna is associated with gaiety and easy romance. I was no stranger to the city. I had visited it several times from Prague, had stayed with the Lindleys at our Legation, and had seen something of its diplomatic and social world. In those days plenty and starvation lived side by side. The middle-class Austrians starved; the financiers and the foreigners lived luxuriously, and British typists, provided by a generous government with a special subsistence allowance in addition to their salary, flourished like society queens. On Sundays a small army of British diplomats, officers, and Reparations officials flocked to the Legation church to see and hear the immaculate and Byronesque Reggie Bridgeman read the lessons. Alas! he has now abandoned frilled shirts and diplomacy for Socialism and slum work. The British Military Mission ran a canteen where whisky and the best Havana cigars were to be had at nominal prices. Owing to the fall in the Austrian exchange fabulous bargains in the form of cigarette cases, cuff links, and pearl studs were to be found in the best Viennese shops.

I had visited the city for amusement and had found it without difficulty. I was on friendly terms with the redoubtable Madame Sacher, the proprietress of the world's most exclusive hotel. If you were a beggar with good manners and the old lady liked you, you had the best of everything and a nominal bill. If you were as rich as Rockefeller and she disliked your face, not all the gold of Alaska would procure for you a garret. I had drunk cocktails with Count "Ludi" Salm, to-day more famous as a tennis-player but then the hero of Vienna because he had slapped the face of Count Karolyi, the Prime Minister of the first revolutionary government in Hungary and, although not more advanced in his political views than an English Liberal or a member of the American Brain Trust, the most hated man by the combined aristocracy of Central Europe. In the company of young aristocrats I had sampled the night-life of Vienna. After the nth bottle I had heard them make a feeble attempt to raise the old pre-war cry of "H'raus mit den Juden" (out with the Jews!). True, it was no longer efficacious, the proprietors, some of the performers, and most of the clients of the Nachtlokals now being Jewish. It was, however, a link with the past and a curious reminder of the fact that the ideology of anti-Semitism had its birth in Vienna. In a minor way I was an authority on the glories of Grinzing, that suburb of Vienna, where one consumes new wine in open-air restaurants, listens to rusty-voiced singers, and, between drinks, strives to recapture the atmosphere which surrounded Schubert. The effort requires a deal of imagination. Grinzing is distinctly petit-bourgeois. I liked the Viennese and found in them a certain resemblance to the Russians.

Nothing seemed more probable than that this charming city would assert its domination over the frivolous side of my character and lead me into further extravagances. It is a curious yet incontrovertible fact that my five months' stay in Vienna was the most ascetic period of my post-war life. During those five months I was a rigid teetotaller, gave up cigarette smoking, and was only once in a Nachtlokal. After a short stay at Sacher's and the Hotel Astoria I took rooms in the Rathausstrasse near the Parliament buildings, installed a grand piano, devoted my scanty leisure hours to music and art, and spent the rest of the day in strenuous work at the bank. So virtuous was I that, in order to perfect my Czech, I even took lessons from the second secretary of the Czech Legation.

Some may see in my reformation the divine influence of the feminine. My cynic friends ascribed it to the repentance of repletion. The truth was quite different. My pride had received a rude buffet. I felt that my début as a banker had been inglorious. I was determined to prove to these banking johnnies, who despised diplomats and politicians, that I could make myself into as serious and as respectable a banker as the stiffest shirt-front in Threadneedle Street.

It was a case of over-toppled ambition. On this occasion fate and my own inability to retain any figures in my head for more than five minutes were against me. My start was inauspicious. The bank, a huge barracks in the Strauchgasse, was so big that it took me a fortnight before I mastered the intricate route to my room. During that fortnight I was left severely alone and in consequence felt lost. There were other wanderers in this maze. There was the new English Kindergarten composed of admirable young men straight from Eton and Harrow and Oxford and Cambridge. They were part of the Montagu Norman-Spencer-Smith dream. They were to learn Continental banking and German. They were to form the vanguard of the noble army of British bankers who were to purify Central European banking and, incidentally, to extend the sphere of British banking influence. The idea was excellently conceived. Unfortunately, the Viennese, anxious about their own future, did not take very kindly to this foreign invasion. They had views of their own. They wanted British capital and British credits. But they wished to employ them in their own time-honoured way. They had little faith in conservative British banking methods. Certainly, they saw little profit to themselves in training young Englishmen who, if they made good, would one day be their masters. In any case, they had no time. Up to 1923, whatever sufferings the rest of the Austrian population may have endured, the Viennese bankers had prospered by speculating on the fall of the Austrian krone. It had been a profitable if unpatriotic business. Now, with the stabilisation of the krone, this prosperous side-line had been closed down, and the managers, harassed by a perturbed London, had their hands and their minds full in trying to save something from the wreckage of the frozen credits. In most cases the remedy was more British capital to assist the unfreezing. As far as the young Englishmen were concerned, they were left at the post in this banking Grand National. It says much for their character that the experience did them no harm. Most of them have since done well in other businesses—not, of course, in Vienna. As far as I was concerned, they provided me with excellent tennis-partners and at least one charming angling companion.

After my first fortnight I had a humiliating and unpleasant experience. By this time I had been put on to study one or two of the industries which were controlled by our bank. This meant visiting the factories and talking to the managers. At one of these concerns I made friends with a director, who was a keen angler. I had fished in Austria before, and, when Whitsun approached, I had little wish to spend the three-day holiday alone in Vienna. My thoughts naturally turned to fishing, and I asked my charming new friend (all Viennese are charming) how I could arrange some fishing. A car would be necessary. Where could I hire one? My friend was all graciousness. There was nothing simpler. There was a delectable stream at Edlitz-Grimmenstein about thirty miles away. He had a car. He would drive me out himself.

The arrangement seemed ideal, and I spent three thoroughly satisfactory days catching lots of plump trout in glorious sylvan surroundings. I returned to Vienna late on the Monday night, and the next morning I found a message asking me to see Ralph Hamlyn, a partner in Binder and Hamlyn, the well-known chartered accountants, who was at that time in charge of British interests in our bank in Vienna. I was blown up as I have not been blown up since my schoolboy days. I had committed a whole enormity of offences. I had taken an official car to go fishing. This was a bad example to the Austrians and exactly the kind of extravagance which he, Ralph Hamlyn, was determined to stop. Worse still, I had spoilt my Viennese director-friend's holiday by dragging him off to my wretched stream when anyone with the tact of a rhinoceros must have known that he wanted to do something else. Diplomatists led a sheltered easy life. They took things too much for granted. Their egotism was stupendous and their manners were atrocious. Banking was a serious profession. I should learn to take it seriously.

There was more in the same strain, for I was too speechless with amazement to launch any counter-attack. My belief in my own virtue and in the innocence of my intentions was complete. I always prefer to be alone when fishing. I had no idea that the car belonged to the factory (which of course belonged to the bank). I was quite prepared to pay for my own car. All I had asked for was information, and, when the charming Viennese had suggested himself as my companion, I had been too shy or too polite to refuse. Amazement giving way to indignation, I blurted out my own account of the affair. The effect was good. Hamlyn saw that he had been a little unjust. I realised that I had been more than usually witless, and that bank officials, especially British bank officials, do not accept favours of any kind from directors of industrial concerns which are financed by the bank. In future, I learned to be less susceptible to Viennese charm.

This breezy passage of words made a great change in my life. From that moment Hamlyn took me into his confidence, smoothed out all the misunderstandings between the Viennese directors and myself, and did his best—and it was a real man's best—to make me into a useful member of the bank. Tall and slim with glossy black hair brushed back over his forehead, good features, a small black moustache and piercing black eyes, whose penetrative power was accentuated by powerful glasses, he was a complete contrast with the accepted type of English business man. He was a tremendous worker, an ascetic, and an idealist, who believed in team-work. His team was a grandiose conception. In the bank it meant loyal co-operation between the Viennese and the British and loyal service to the bank itself.

At the same time he carried his idea into international politics. There was to be team-work between the nations of Central Europe and team-work between the different classes of Austrians. Occasionally this passion for team-work led him into errors of over-enthusiasm, and there was a story current in the bank that on Easter Sunday he had sent Easter lilies to all the Viennese managers and heads of departments the overwheming majority of whom was Jewish! Outside of business hours he could be eloquently intense over subjects not even remotely connected with finance, and more than once I have heard him argue the case for the British Israelite conception of the world with a heat which seemed to burn with the oil of genuine conviction. In business, however, he was a different person, never sparing himself, caring nothing for money for its own sake and showing a marvellous patience in explaining his case to those who differed from him. The bank was child and mistress to him, and he served it with a devotion which was whole-hearted. If disinterestedness, self-sacrifice, and hard work could have wrought the miracle that they should work in this world, our bank would have gone from success to success and Mr. Montagu Norman's dream would have been realised. As it was, a Europe still idling in the false glamour of the glory of victory and the eternal greed of man were too much for him. He was a man whom few could know without respecting, and at that time he had a considerable and wholly beneficial influence over my life.

In addition to Hamlyn and the Kindergarten there were several other Englishmen in the bank, two of whom deserve some mention. One was Bernard Hooper, a chartered accountant and at that time a partner in Binder and Hamlyn. Hooper, a Londoner with a lightning mind and a photographic brain for figures, was an amusing companion. He was always good-humoured, was always ready to meet the foreigner on his own pitch and in a battle of wits generally held his own even with the Viennese Jews. Self-confidence, combined with a deal of innate and acquired ability, was his strong suit. He had few illusions about the grandiose schemes of our bank and saw little hope of success for a concern which sought to mingle English banking methods with Viennese. About my own position in the bank he had no illusions whatsoever. "You have made a mistake," he told me. "You have certain linguistic assets and a knowledge of Europe which must be rare among Englishmen. They are assets which ought to yield a substantial profit. But not in banking. My tip to you is to attach yourself to some millionaire and make yourself indispensable to him." I shall tell later how I tried to take his advice.

The other Englishman was R. H. Porters, who was then in charge of the organisation department. Actually, he was a Scot married to a Frenchwoman. He was a professional banker and had been at one time private secretary to Sir Edward Holden in the Midland Bank. During the war he had been military secretary to General Sir John Hanbury-Williams at the Tsar's headquarters, spoke French fluently and had a working knowledge of Russian. He had some of the best Scottish qualities: a capacity for clear thinking, an eye for the main chance, and a healthy mistrust of all enthusiasms. He was the one British subject in the bank who did not suffer from its comparative lack of success and who rose on the stepping stones of his own shrewdness to greater heights. To-day, he basks in the favour of Mr. Montagu Norman and is employed by that great man as one of his European watch-dogs. I liked him from the first. He had a pawky sense of humour and an American knack of coining wisecracks which I found amusing. Moreover, he was fond of music, played the piano fairly well and was patient enough to allow me to help him to massacre Wagner, Mozart and Delibes in duets. I have kept in touch with him ever since those Viennese days. But we have dropped the duets.

There was yet one more Englishman whom perhaps I should mention. This was George Young, a former official of the Board of Education, who had been secretary to Mr. Arthur Henderson when that gentleman was a member of the War Cabinet. He had accompanied Mr. Henderson on his famous trip to Russia during the Kerensky revolution. There he had met Sir Francis Lindley, who was then Counsellor of our Embassy at St. Petersburg. Lindley had taken him with him on his ill-fated expedition to Archangel. Later, when Lindley had gone to Vienna as Minister, Young had gone with him as a temporary secretary in the diplomatic service and had been employed by the British Treasury in administrating a special relief fund for Austria. In Vienna he had met Spencer-Smith, and Spencer-Smith made him a director of the new bank.

Hamlyn, Hooper, Porters and I were much of an age, but Young was some ten years older. He was a curious, anaemic-looking man; shy in his approaches and rather antagonistic until one had penetrated his armour of reserve. When one knew him better, one realised his worth. He was a great scholar with a wide range of knowledge and a wonderful command of the English language. His conversation, when he could be induced to speak, was first-class. As a writer he should have made a name for himself. Hitherto, all that he has given to the world is a little masterpiece on Gibbon. A fellow of All Souls, he would have made an admirable don. As it was, he was misplaced in our bank, partly because of his own repressions, which made him a poor "mixer" with foreigners, but mainly because the professional bankers and accountants, who were rather contemptuous of us amateurs, did not appreciate his talents or put them to the best use. As ex-government officials, pitchforked into a totally different kind of farmyard, we had a common bond of sympathy and self-pity. If the professionals tore us to bits in private and sometimes in public, we gave as good as we received and saw and criticised their defects as clearly and as vigorously as they saw and criticised ours.

My working hours in the bank were long and rather wearisome. It is quite a mistake to imagine that the Viennese do not work. They may not work efficiently, but they start early and remain late. They regarded the English as a privileged race who through former conquests and accumulated wealth could afford to be ignorant and lazy. Hamlyn being Hamlyn, we had to do in Vienna as the Viennese did. This meant being in the bank at nine A.M. and remaining frequently until nine P.M. It may be doubted if anyone can produce good work on a twelve-hour day. Schopenhauer used to consider four hours the limit of a man's capacity for intellectual work, and I find his prescription both soothing to my well-being and flattering to my vanity. But in our bank both English and Viennese vied with each other in working as long hours as possible. It seemed the proper way to favour and to promotion.

We received a rude shock when General Sir Herbert Lawrence, our Chairman, came out from London to visit us. The Viennese managers sought to impress him by telling him that they were rarely able to sit down to dinner before ten o'clock. As a banker, the General who had been Lord Haig's Chief of Staff during the war, had many of the soldierly qualities; neatness, organising ability, punctuality, and economy of words. "There must be something wrong with your organisation," was his sole comment. Obviously he was not impressed. And here, too, I found myself in agreement with another great man.

In spite of my laborious days I succeeded in finding time for recreation. On my previous visits to Vienna I had wasted my substance in sampling its night life. Now that I was living more or less permanently in the city, I set about to study it for my mental improvement. On Sundays, if I was not fishing, I rose early and went to Mass at St. Stephen's or at the beautiful Votivkirche. Then, for the rest of the morning, I did my round of the museums and in the afternoon I went out to Kobenzl, Hinterbrühl, the Wiener Wald, or one of the other charming suburbs of Vienna and lay on the grass and read Viennese history. I found a melancholy pleasure in resuscitating the ghosts of the past and on week days I would slip in for a few minutes to the Hofburg and try to visualise Metternich, Castlereagh, the Tsar Alexander, Talleyrand, and the other delegates to the Congress of Vienna. In the streets were real ghosts: generals, who had fought in the Great War and whose threadbare clothes and pinched faces told their own story of pensions and savings reduced to a few pence by the collapse of the Austrian krone. The delegates at the Congress of Vienna had made a bad peace but not so cruel or so foolish as the delegates at the Paris Peace Conference.

My favourite pilgrimage, however, was to the Convent of the Capuchins on the New Market. Here is the crypt where the Emperors of Austria repose in their eternal sleep. Here, too, with all his score of titles including even King of Jerusalem, lies the late Emperor Franz Josef, the man who lived too long and whose earlier demise might have saved Austria from the calamity which has stricken her. But it was not the dead Habsburgs who stirred the chords of my sympathy. On my first visit to Paris nearly twenty years before my father had taken me to see Sarah Bernhardt in "L'Aiglon." It was the first time that I had heard a great actress declaim Rostand's verses, and, like most impressionable young men, I went Napoleon-mad. The Napoleon-mania soon left me, but the charm of Rostand's romanticism remained. And here in this musty semi-darkness, at the feet of his grandfather Franz II and by his mother Marie-Louise, lies the coffin of the pale young man who for an hour or two reigned as Napoleon II. He is the only foreigner in this family mausoleum, for, however fanciful may be the historical conception of Rostand's "L'Aiglon," he is a bold historian who would deny that the son of Napoleon considered himself a Frenchman even although there was no drop of French blood in his veins. To-day official France and official Austria have forgotten the King of Rome, and Rostand spoke more truly perhaps than he realised when he wrote:

"Des touristes anglais trainent là leurs talons,
Puis ils vont voir, plus loin, ton coeur, dans une Eglise.
Dors, tu fus ce Jeune homme et ce Fils, quoiqu'on dise.
Dors, tu fus ce martyr; du moins, nous le voulons."

Was not I here making one of the army of English-speaking tourists from both sides of the Atlantic who drag their heels every year across the stone flagstones which support the last resting-place of the man who shares pride of place with Bonnie Prince Charlie in the romantic affections of the Anglo-Saxon world?

Another of my favourite excursions was to Schoenbrunn, the Austrian Versailles and the summer residence of the Emperor Franz Josef. After the heat of the day I used to run out there in an open car, dine in a little open-air restaurant, and then stroll in the magnificent park. The palace itself I shunned. I had "done" it once with a guide and had felt like an intruder. There were too many ghosts of recent times, and, although I am no admirer of the Habsburgs, there was something indecent in the attitude of the tourists who prodded the simple iron bedstead in which Franz Josef died, and fingered the Chinese wall-paper in the Blue Room in which the Emperor Karl abdicated in 1918.

Schoenbrunn, too, looked like a mausoleum. Only the flowers and the grass bore any sign of life. Close by was a little house with yellow shutters. It was and, for all I know, still is the home of Frau Schratt, the former Viennese actress who for twenty-five years was the companion, confidante, and comforter of Franz Josef. Every morning she breakfasted with the Emperor at five A.M. Doubtless, the little yellow house was handy, but it must have been a hard life. She held sway over the proudest of all monarchs by her capacity to hold her tongue. To her credit she has kept silent to this day in spite of tempting offers from nearly every publisher in the world.

Only once was she lacking in discretion, and then she learnt her lesson. Franz Josef was a great formalist. He discussed foreign affairs only with his Foreign Minister, military affairs only with his Minister of War. He applied this principle to everyone including Kings and Kaisers and even Frau Schratt. In 1908, however, King Edward came to visit the Emperor at Ischl. It was the year of the Morocco crisis. As usual, the scaremongers were busily prophesying war, and on this occasion even Frau Schratt was roused from her customary nonchalance. The two monarchs went for a walk alone. They were absent for a long time. At last Franz Josef came back to his hotel, and Frau Schratt, who had hardly been able to curb her impatience, ran to meet him.

"Well, Sir?" she said, "how did it go off?"

The Emperor looked surprised. Then he replied slowly:

"At the beginning, very well, but gradually I drew my horns in. You see, the King, too, asked me a lot of questions which did not concern him."

In the evenings on an average about once a week there were Hamlyn's parties which generally consisted of a couple of boxes at the opera and supper at Sacher's afterwards. Ultra-respectable, they were, in one sense, marvels of audacity, for Hamlyn insisted on carrying his passion for team-work even into his social life, and a successful party in his eyes had to include at least two members of the old Austrian aristocracy, the British Minister and his wife, a member or two of the Austrian Government, a tame Socialist, and three or four Jewish bankers. In the light of the political upheaval which had taken place in Vienna since the war it was a risky experiment, but Hamlyn, quite fearless where his ideals were concerned, pulled it off with complete success. It was a tribute both to his sincerity and to his personal magnetism and was recognised as such by the great Madame Sacher who took the English banker to her heart. And the old lady was a shrewd judge of character.

There was, too, a pleasant English atmosphere about our Legation, and Akers-Douglas, our Minister (now Lord Chilston and British Ambassador in Moscow), and his talented wife were very kind to all the Englishmen in the bank. At the Legation I met Monsignor Seipel, the priest-Chancellor of Austria and perhaps the shrewdest diplomatist in Central Europe. He was a queer ascetic figure with the inspiring calm and sangfroid of an Englishman. His shaven head and his glasses and rather prominent nose gave a strangely bird-like appearance to his face.

He bore a striking resemblance to Dr. Buchman, the founder and leader of the Oxford movement, and, when some years later I met that business-like Crusader, seated between Mrs. Baldwin and Lady Snowden in a London restaurant, I was on the point of addressing him in German, convinced that I had seen a ghost. Seipel was the victim of an assassin's bullet. In 1924 a Communist workman called Jaworek fired two shots at him at the Vienna South-Western Station. Although he lived for seven years, he never recovered from the effects of a wound which had not healed properly. His death was the greatest individual loss which Austria has suffered since the war.

Another Austrian whom I met—but not at the Legation—was Friedrich Adler, the son of the founder of the Austrian Social-Democratic Party. Friedrich, an excitable ascetic, who was almost the only Austrian Socialist to take a firm stand against the war, is one of the few political murderers who are to-day at liberty. In October, 1916, he shot dead Count Stürkgh, the Austrian Chancellor, in the restaurant of the Meissl and Schadn hotel in Vienna. The police saved him from being lynched. He was tried and condemned to death. The kind-hearted Emperor Karl commuted his sentence to one of eighteen years' imprisonment. He had served less than two years of his sentence when the Austrian collapse raised the Social-Democrats to the supreme power, and in the ensuing armistice he was set at liberty. When I met him, he seemed as gentle and as harmless as a tame pigeon. There was, however, a melancholic look in his eyes, and I imagine that he must have been a victim to nerves from his childhood days. There was a neurasthenic strain in his family and at that time he had a sister who was in a mental home. In his youth he had married a Russian, and I still wonder how far contact with the Slavs was responsible for his genuine but somewhat theatrical fanaticism. I was glad to meet him if only for the macabre sensation of adding one more to the number of political assassins whom I have met and talked to face to face.

In spite of the hopelessness of the political situation life in Vienna was full of interest. The city was a problem in itself quite apart from Austria. The Austrian peasant is a German. The Viennese are a nationality of their own, a conglomeration of Germans, Czechs, Poles, Jews, Hungarians, Rumanians, Croats, and of all the races of Central Europe. They have their own culture and their own outlook on life. It is the greatest tragedy of the Peace Treaty that it has deprived the Viennese of their chance of living.

CHAPTER THREE

AFTER my first months in Vienna my work in the bank began to become more interesting and, as Hamlyn's confidence in me increased, I was employed more and more on semi-political jobs which were more congenial to me personally and more suitable to such talents as I possessed. On account of its connection with the Bank of England our Bank was regarded by the Governments of Central Europe as an excellent approach to the London money market. M. Bark had played an important part in the negotiations of the Austrian Reconstruction Loan, which was floated that summer. Now the Czechs were seeking to float a second loan and, as London desired to see a closer economic co-operation between Czechoslovakia and Austria, I was delegated by Hamlyn to seek a rapprochement between Dr. Beneš and Dr. Simon, a former Austrian Treasury official and since Dr. Rosenberg's death the chief Viennese director of our bank. My mission was not a purely disinterested one. The new Anglo-Czechoslovakian Bank, which had been created out of the Czech branches of the old Anglo-Oesterreichische Bank, was now an independent bank, but London was the chief shareholder, and we naturally wished to make the co-operation between the two banks as close as possible.

All through that summer of 1923 I travelled backwards and forwards between Vienna and Prague, frequently going up the one night, doing my business by day, and returning to Vienna the next night. It was a rather strenuous experience, partly because the summer was very hot and there were no single sleepers and my Czech or Austrian companion nearly always refused to have the window open, and partly because in the middle of the night the customs and passport officials made everyone turn out with all the zeal of officials new to their job. My business was mainly with Dr. Beneš, with whom my personal relations were very friendly. At my request he consented to see Dr. Simon. The interview, which lasted nearly two hours, made a very favourable impression on the Viennese, and, as far as the co-operation between our Prague and Viennese banks was concerned, there was a real improvement.

But there was little change in the general political attitude of the Czechs towards Austria. Nor did the negotiations for the Czech loan in England prosper. I arrived at an unpropitious moment, for the London financial house—a world-famous firm—which was interested in the loan had gone out of its way to write to Dr. Beneš a political lecture on the evils of the Czech administration. Among other things mentioned as undesirable was the Czech Land Reform Law which sanctions the expropriation of big landed estates at a price fixed by the Government. The letter was unhappily worded and, the City of London being, at that time at any rate, not very strong on Central European politics, many of the facts were wrong. The letter gave me the impression that the writer—a banker peer—had been got at by some disgruntled but titled Bohemian land-owner. The effect was unfortunate. The Czechs, whose finances were in excellent order and whose "dispossessed" land-owners were probably better off than most of the heavily taxed English landowners, were hurt in their national pride, and even Dr. Beneš showed signs of serious disgruntlement. In the end the Czechs received their loan—this time in the form of a revolving credit—from America.

In spite of these failures I must pay my tribute to the good intentions both of British diplomacy and of British banking in Central Europe. From the beginning our diplomatists and our bankers and men like Sir William Goode, the Head of the Reparations Commission in Vienna, worked sincerely and disinterestedly for pacification and reconciliation, striving to guide the flow of Central European trade back into its natural channels, without infringing the political independence of the newly-liberated states. True, there was a certain diversity of outlook among the British experts, and a considerable difficulty in differentiating between the lions and the lambs. The recommendations of Sir George Clerk in Prague were not quite the same as the panaceas of Mr. Akers Douglas in Vienna or the nostrums of Sir Thomas Hohler in Budapest. All three, in turn, differed from the remedies put forward by our bank or by Sir William Goode. But the general effect was good and, given firmer backing and less subservience to France by the British Cabinet, would have produced better results. As it was, everyone was afraid of action, and the situation drifted steadily from bad to worse.

All the Succession States must bear their share of responsibility for the misfortunes of Central Europe: Austria for the culpably light-hearted administration of her public and private finances, feudal Hungary for a characteristic intolerance and intransigence which have been intensified rather than curbed by the war, and Czechoslovakia, Yugoslavia, and Rumania for an egotism which one day they may have cause to regret. But the most malevolent influence was the influence of France who, having got Germany down, was determined to keep her there and who, by building up a system of military alliances in Central Europe, encouraged the Czechs, the Rumanians, and the Yugoslavs to adopt a similar policy towards Austria and Hungary. The time to make concessions to nations is when they are weak and not when they are strong. Unfortunately, France was the only nation which knew what it wanted in Central Europe, and an unrivalled opportunity of winning the acquiescence at any rate of Austria to the new order of things and of assuring the economic existence of the Austrian Republic was sacrificed on the altar of a policy which, as the French flatter themselves on their logic, can best be described as the logic of fear.

If my politico-economical peregrinations were unfruitful of results, they afforded me an admirable opportunity of seeing many new places. Dr. Beneš, in particular, I had to chase all over the country and had to travel long distances by motor-car in the process. On one occasion, when I had to see him urgently, he asked me to come to Topolčiansky, President Masaryk's summer residence in Slovakia. It was an idyllic day spent in idyllic surroundings. Topolčiansky itself is an old shooting-seat of the Archduke Josef. It is an ugly house and the interior is spoilt by the same abundance of shooting trophies which characterises the house of the late Archduke Franz Ferdinand at Konopišt. But it stands in an English park where the haphazard lay-out of the trees made me think of home.

When I arrived in the early morning at the little station not far from the village where President Masaryk once worked in the local blacksmith's shop, the sun was shining from a clear blue sky. The heat was almost tropical, and a procession of Slovaks dressed in their picturesque national costume, the men in quaint top hats and the women in masses of petticoats covered by a skirt of bright red, was trudging its way to church in roads ankle-deep in dust. As the President's car drove me to the house, the whole panorama of Slovakia, with its cornfields shimmering in the plain and the rugged line of the Tatra Mountains forming a glorious background, unrolled itself before my eyes. When I drew up at the door, there was a long silence. The house seemed deserted, and it was some time before the servant came to take my hat and despatch-case. The President and Dr. Beneš were out riding. Dr. Alice, the President's daughter, and Madame Beneš were walking in the woods. Would I wait inside or in the park? I went out into the park and sat down on a seat under a huge oak.

Presently a bearded figure on horseback came cantering down a steep path through the woods. He managed his horse with consummate ease. His seat was firm and his back as straight as a ramrod. It was the President. He cantered up to my tree, jumped off his horse with an agility which would have done credit to a man thirty years his junior, and shook hands. "Welcome to Topolčiansky," he said in his slow, measured English. "Beneš and Osusky will be coming soon. I seem to have lost them." He sat down and began to tell me how he was looking forward to his approaching visit to England in the autumn. As we talked, another horseman made his way through the woods but at a more sedate pace than the President. He, too, came up and shook hands. It was Osusky, the Czech Minister in Paris.

He retired almost immediately to the house. He seemed stiff. Five minutes later yet another horse appeared down the same steep path. He carried a little man in an English cap and riding-breeches. The man looked strangely ill at ease. As he drew near, I saw the sweat standing out in beads on his face. It was Dr. Beneš, admirable example of physical fitness in a politician, ex-footballer, and agile tennis-player, but no horseman. He was very stiff and made no attempt to conceal it.

Luncheon, although a teetotal meal, was a gay affair. We sat on plain chairs, and the thoughtful President had provided cushions for Beneš and Osusky. He enjoyed his joke as much as, doubtless, Beneš and Osusky were grateful for their cushions.

In the afternoon we discussed the future of Central Europe and foreshadowed a brighter future in which the Succession States, whom nature had made economically interdependent, would co-operate wholeheartedly for their common good.

That night, as I drove back to the station, I was filled with a new hope. The setting sun, still flooding the mountain crests until they assumed an almost ethereal appearance, had left the plain, in which the tiny villages with their white churches stood out with remarkable clearness in the soft, grey light. The whole scene gave me that peculiar feeling of infinity which I have felt only in Russia. Once again my incurable romanticism banished my imperfectly acquired cynicism. Why should the tolerance of President Masaryk not triumph over the hates of his own countrymen and of their next-door neighbours? Was not the way of peace and reconciliation the way of common-sense? In the morning the cold barrack-like walls of my bank seemed more repulsive than ever, and the peaceful mood of the previous evening had vanished.

Another pleasant excursion was my trip to Bratislava where I had to see Jan Masaryk with a view to arranging an interview for M. Bark with M. Antonin Svehla, the Czechoslovak Prime Minister. Bratislava, the bridgehead of the new Czechoslovak-Hungarian frontier, is one of those racially mosaic towns, which make President Wilson's famous self-determination clause look silly. The city, which is pleasantly situated on a broad, flat stretch of the Danube, has three names: Bratislava, which is the Czechoslovak name, Pressburg, which is the German name, and Pozsony, which is the Hungarian name. It belonged to Hungary for over a thousand years. For two hundred and fifty years it was the Hungarian capital. At the Peace Conference it was transferred to Czechoslovakia. Its population of 120,000 is divided more or less equally into Czechs, Slovaks, Hungarians and Germans. But even to-day the Germans still persist in calling it Pressburg, the Hungarians Pozsony, and the Czechs and Slovaks Bratislava. Three languages are in daily use.

It was an appropriate place for my rendezvous with Jan, who is one of the best "mixers" and best linguists that I have ever met. I know no one who is quite so clever in adapting himself to the psychology of a foreign nation. He can cap a Frenchman's *bon mot* in French. He is one of the few foreigners who is at home in Hungarian, and his imitation of a Hungarian talking German is equalled only by his mimicry of a New York Russian Jew talking Russo-Yiddish-American. He speaks all the Slav languages. His German is perfect, and he talks English with all the breezy picturesqueness of an American, for much of his early manhood was spent in the States. He is at home in every class of society. Slovak peasants gather round him while he plays his Slovak reed. And when he sits down at the piano and sings his Slovak songs, not only Slavs, but chilled Anglo-Saxons, feel a lump in their throats.

Jan, who is now Czechoslovak Minister in London, was then Dr. Beneš's right-hand man and a well-known figure at Geneva, where his charm of manner made him *persona grata* with every one. To every Englishman and every American who come to Prague he has been a warm and loyal friend, and I know of no occasion where he has failed to carry out his promise when once it is given.

He is, of course, the son of President Masaryk, and in one sense this has been a handicap to him especially with his own countrymen. For he is something much more than the President's son. He has inherited much of his father's tolerance and breadth of vision, and, if lacking his father's scholarship, he has a practical knowledge of the modern world which the Sage of Prague has never known at first-hand.

Although no man loves his country better, he is no chauvinist. Behind an exterior of cultivated cynicism he is a great humanitarian with a profound sympathy for the under-dog and a wonderful sense of fair-play. These qualities have made him a first-class negotiator. I always used to say that, if one could find a Hungarian Jan, an Austrian Jan, a Rumanian Jan, a Bulgarian Jan, a Yugoslav Jan, and Jan himself and lock them up in a lonely castle until they settled the Central European question, a solution, satisfactory to all parties, would be forthcoming by the next morning. It is a plan which may yet have to be tried.

There are countless stories about Jan, nearly all of them to his credit. In one of the best I myself was concerned. A year or two later I was dining in Prague at the house of Fred Pearson, the First Secretary of the American Legation. The dinner was in honour of a new foreign diplomatist and his wife, who had just arrived. There were about ten guests including Jan Masaryk. The new arrival, who had come to Prague armed with letters of introduction to the old Austrian aristocracy, was a young man with more social ambitions than brains. Taking Jan's impeccable dress-coat and faultless English as the attributes of a rich American, who had his clothes made in London, he began to expatiate with some pungency on the social defects of the Czechs. What was one to do in this God-forsaken hole where peasants were ministers and where even the richer people were boors without any manners? It was a dreary prospect, but, after all, what could one expect in a country where the President was a peasant's son. There was more in the same strain, for from where we sat neither Pearson nor I could kick him under the table and, presumably, the women who sat next him were too embarrassed to do anything. The only person who was not uncomfortable in the room was Jan himself. He made no attempt either to snub the foolish fellow or to lead him into further tactlessness as many another man would have done.

Almost any other Czech or, indeed, any other Central European would have made an incident out of an affair which might have had serious consequences for a diplomatist. But Jan took no action, never repeated the story, and never showed and, I firmly believe, never bore the slightest grudge against the blundering diplomatist. Instead, he went on with us to Zavrel's, the leading Prague restaurant, where he danced with all the women including the new arrival's wife and was his usual cheerful self until the party broke up. It was a lesson in manners, tolerance, and self-control to all of us. In any case the young man was sufficiently punished, for the story of course leaked out—trust diplomatists never to miss a scrap of scandal—and went the round of the diplomatic corps.

As a reward for the travelling and running about which I did that summer, Hamlyn sent me off on a fortnight's holiday in July. Like most unexpected pleasures, I used that holiday to the best advantage. I rushed back to my rooms, bought a map on the way, and after ten minutes' reflection decided on a circular motor-tour through the Tyrol, Bavaria, Thuringia, Saxony, and home by Prague. I hired a car, packed some clothes and my fishing gear, and left the same evening for Innsbruck.

My start was inauspicious. When I arrived at Innsbruck, the dawn was bitterly cold, and the mountains were covered with snow. My heart sank, and after a profitable morning during which I visited the Hofkirche and saw the monument to Andreas Hofer, the Tyrolese patriot who was shot at Mantua in 1810, and the magnificent statue—the finest of the German Renaissance period—of King Arthur of England, I spent the rest of a rather miserable day in my hotel. The next day, in spite of the weather, I determined to motor to the Brenner Pass. My resoluteness was rewarded. By eleven o'clock the weather changed, the clouds rolled away as if by magic, and the sun shone with a warmth which presently sent silver threads of water streaming down the rocky precipices from the melted snow.

My chauffeur was a Tyrolese and in 1918 had driven the Emperor Karl. He was a magnificent specimen of a man and the champion "skier" of his district. What was more important, he was a mountaineer and had therefore a love and a profound respect for Nature which are rarely found among city-dwellers, and he knew the history of every stone and every slope. I was glad to be alone. Rarely have I spent a happier day. At the foot of the Brenner itself there was even a small lake where the trout were rising as, doubtless, they rose when Roman legionaries passed on their way into Germany.

The next day I motored from Innsbruck through the Bavarian Alps to Munich, stopping for an hour at Mittenwald at the summit of the road and lunching at the little inn where Goethe rested on his famous Italienische Reise. And as I ate my truite au bleu, taken straight from one of those fish-tanks which every Bavarian restaurant possesses, and drank my cool Bavarian beer, the landlord told me the history and local gossip of his village. Here Richard Strauss used to spend his summers. Here, too, was a family of craftsmen who had made violins for fifteen generations. I listened fitfully. My eyes and half my mind were fixed on the spotless whitewashed Bavarian houses with their green shutters and their carved gables. Nearly every house had a text or a homely proverb painted high on the wall above the entrance: "The Lord loveth a cheerful Giver." Since the war these honest villagers had had little to receive and less to give. But the children looked clean and healthy, and both about the men and the women there was something which denoted self-reliance and self-respect even in adversity. The winter here must be as severe as in Russia, but in the summer sunshine it was as fair a scene as any in Europe. From the grassy slopes of the plateau came the intermittent tinkle of cowbells and the singing larks, and in the peaceful atmosphere the sense of impending tragedy which had enveloped me ever since I left diplomacy was blotted out of my mind.

I left Mittenwald with a regret which did not pass until I reached Munich. The city looked a little shabbier than on the occasion of my previous visit the year before. My friends were a little more dejected. Although the mark had not started on its final mad plunge into the abyss of inflation, it had depreciated heavily, and many of them had been ruined. There was a monotonous similarity about their attitude towards reparations which were then at their acutest stage. Germany, they said, must pay and is willing to pay but France wants to impose on us a sum which we cannot pay in order that, once having got us down, she may hold us there. They seemed convinced that the French militarists did not really want Germany to pay. There was at that time no hate in their hearts. They accepted their fate with stoical calm as a consequence of the Peace Treaty which had to be borne until sanity returned to the world. They were as kind and as hospitable as ever, lavished entertainment on me, and took me to the opera.

But I had come to fish and, escaping as politely as I could, I spent four glorious days on my old dry-fly stream in the happy valley of the Semt. It was too late in the summer and too hot for day fishing, but the evening rise was famous. On the first three nights a cold wind rose from the Alps as soon as the sun went down, and the rise never materialised. On my last night the conditions were perfect, and for ninety minutes I scarcely needed to move a yard. All the big fish of which I had heard so much but which I had never seen seemed to have assembled in the one big pool. They fed steadily and eagerly and very rarely did they refuse my fly. Of course I lost the really big one—and trout of twelve pounds have been taken from the stream on a worm or a miller's thumb. After a tremendous fight more thrilling than any struggle with a salmon he broke me on a bridge pile. But why try to guess his weight or mourn a tragedy which leaves no sting? Perfection in anything is the acme of monotony.

The rest of my trip was something of an anti-climax. The journey from Munich to Dresden was disappointing. Dresden itself, which I had known in my student days and had frequently visited since, had lost much of its former charm, and the drive home along the Elbe through the pine and birch-clad scenery of the Saxon-German-Switzerland was spoilt, partly, by the dislike of going back to work and, still more, by that sense of dread which always assails me whenever I have to return to city life.

On my arrival in Vienna I found a new mission awaiting me. Owing to the French occupation, the Austrian motor-industry, which was dependent on the Ruhr for its supplies, had run short of aluminum. All attempts to obtain permits from the French had failed, and the industry was threatened with a stoppage. In the precarious state of Austrian finances the prospect of several thousand men being thrown out of work was alarming, and, as our bank was financing the largest motor firm in Austria, Simon suggested that I should go to Coblenz, the seat of the Rhineland Commission, and, if necessary, to Essen, the headquarters of the French Occupation, to see if I could achieve by diplomatic intervention what the companies themselves had been unable to do in the ordinary commercial way.

I jumped at the offer. My preparations were quickly made, and armed with letters of recommendation stressing the urgency of my business both from our own Minister and from the French Minister, and with papers from the Austrian Government, I set out on one of the most interesting missions that I have ever undertaken.

CHAPTER FOUR

I HAVE travelled so much in European trains that the retention of individual railway journeys defeats my memory. My journey to the Rhineland, however, remains very clearly in my mind, partly because of the torrid heat and partly because of the unusual circumstances in which it was accomplished.

Owing to the closing of the frontiers between the occupied and unoccupied parts of Germany, I had to travel via Switzerland and Luxembourg. On this part of my journey I had as carriage companions two Hungarian bankers. Both were Jews and self-made men. I had never seen them before, but in that pleasant semi-Oriental manner which is characteristic of Central Europe conversation became intimate, and in an hour or two I knew most of their life-history. They were taking shares and Hungarian pengoe, which they had successfully smuggled out of Hungary, to Zurich and were highly pleased with themselves. They talked glibly of the new dynasty of Raubritter or robber barons which had grown up in Central Europe since the war and to which, on their own confession, they obviously belonged. They seemed to think that anyone who did not look after himself in these distressing times and who did not take the gifts which the gods and the exchange offered him was little better than a fool. After they had left the train, the Wagon-Lit conductor came up to me: "Excuse me, Sir," he said. "Those friends of yours were rich men or poor men?" "I do not know them," I replied, "but they said they were bankers and from the contents of their portfolios they seemed to be rich." The conductor grunted. "I thought so," he said. Then he pulled out his purse and took out two Hungarian notes. "There's their tip, and they gave me more trouble than half-a-dozen American millionaires." He threw the money down on the seat in a passion of disgust. The equivalent in English money was about threepence. It was a curious sidelight on Raubritter psychology.

At Luxembourg I had to change and take the French military train, which supplied the main service between Paris and Coblenz. The train was clean and the food excellent, but it ran very slowly and never exceeded twenty miles an hour. There were no Germans on board and very few civilians. The stations and railway crossings were guarded by black troops. I discovered afterwards that very few people would take the risk of travelling on a French train in the occupied territory, as "accidents" were of daily occurrence. The French officers, who comprised ninety per cent of the passengers, were quiet and correct in their demeanour and infinitely less aggressive than Prussian officers would have been in similar circumstances. But they made no attempt to enter into conversation with me and were, in fact, as silent and as uncommunicative as the most frigid Englishman. I had to show my papers on half-a-dozen occasions. The atmosphere of hostility was unmistakable. The French, in fact, were sore with the English because we had refused to participate in their occupation of the Ruhr.

I ought to have enjoyed that journey. For miles on end the railway ran alongside the Rhine through parts of Germany which were new to me. The weather was superb, and the succession of castles and vineyards was a pleasant enough vista. I tried hard to recapture the spirit of my first youthful romance of nearly twenty years before when I had entered into a boy and girl engagement with the daughter of a German naval captain. Heine's "Ich weiss nicht was soll es bedeuten," I remembered, had been the first poem which I had ever learnt off by heart in German, and here was the very rock which had inspired the Lorelei. Yet I was not impressed. Perhaps it was the fault of the scenery. Certainly, its grandeur has been grossly exaggerated both by the poets and by the guidebooks. It is more probable, however, that the actualities of the moment dominated every other thought in my mind. In Prague and in Vienna I had seen some of the evil consequences of the Peace

Treaties. I had taken a keen interest in the solution of the economic problems of the Succession States and had written innumerable memoranda on the subject. I had revisited Germany several times since the war and I had lost all traces of the war hate which had animated me in 1918. But I had been too thoughtless and too bent on pleasure to realise the unnecessary sufferings of others, too intent on drinking the champagne of victory to think very much about any one except myself. Although subconsciously my sympathy with the under-dog was not wholly dormant, I should have been indignant if any one had labelled me a pro-German. Here, however, in the occupied territory I was face to face with realities which seemed to belong more to the war itself than to the peace. It was a depressing thought that nearly five years after the war the state of Europe should be so chaotic that a journey, which in peace time occupied fifteen hours, took on this occasion over forty.

On arriving in Coblenz I found myself completely shut off from the outside world. I could obtain no money from the banks. I could neither telegraph nor telephone. As I sipped my coffee on the hotel verandah overlooking the river, I felt more miserably lonely than I have ever felt before or since. My instinct told me then that my mission was bound to fail. Coblenz, the headquarters of the Inter-Allied High Commission, seemed to be almost entirely a French town. French troops were everywhere. Every second building was commandeered for barracks. The French influence seemed and, indeed, was supreme. The local population was sullen and dejected. Even the troops were tense and humourless. There were blue uniforms and a blue sky, but the town itself was grey and strangely silent.

My first duty was to call on the High Commission and present my letters of recommendation to the British and French High Commissioners. Lord Kilmarnock, the British representative, was a charming man, gentle, cultured, and literary in his inclinations. He had written several plays and a volume of ghost stories. He listened with patience while I told him of the seriousness of the Austrian situation and of the political importance of meeting the demands of the Austrian heavy industry. No one could have called him a strong man. Indeed, even then he looked tired and ill. But it is difficult to see how any one else could have done much better. To have taken an anti-French line would have been against the policy of the British Foreign Office, and any government servant who anticipates official opinion generally suffers for his prescience. We had already had strong men in the Rhineland who had protested against the prevailing policy and who had been transferred to quieter and more distant parts. In any case there was no question of "a strong British line" locally, for the High Commission was entirely dominated by M. Tirard, the French High Commissioner. The High Commission was composed of three members: the British, the French and the Belgian, and the Belgian voted as a matter of course with the French. Occasionally the British representative registered a formal vote of dissent, but, as he was always outvoted, the part which he played was neither dignified nor effective.

Lord Kilmarnock, having listened, promised to do his best and passed me on to the head of his economic section. This gentleman was an efficient official, was on good terms with the French, and strongly recommended conciliatory methods. More flies, he said, were caught with honey than with vinegar. He went to some pains in denying the stories then current among British business men that the French administration was cruel and brutal and that the French were wilfully obstructing British attempts to trade with the occupied territories. As regards the administration I think his statement was substantially correct. But in the matter of trading the fact remained that no goods could be exported from the occupied territories without an export licence and that the granting of an export licence was attended with an immense amount of red tape and irritating delays.

M. Tirard I never saw. I handed in my letter of recommendation and was referred to one of his assistants who, as I became more intimate with him, was refreshingly frank—and pessimistic. I gathered that one of the chief stumbling blocks to the granting of licences was the difference of opinion, amounting sometimes to tension, between the French civil power and the military power, who did not always see eye to eye. The civil authorities were inclined to be lenient but dared not be so for fear of being reported to Paris by the military authorities, who were then all-powerful. One specific instance was quoted to me of an attempt by the civil power to get rid of a certain French customs official who had on several occasions been grossly rude to British business men and who had coined the notorious phrase: "I shall receive the French and the Belgians first, the Germans and the British afterwards." The request for his removal had been blocked by General Degoutte, the French Commander-in-Chief in the Ruhr.

Doubtless, the French were irritated beyond measure by the campaign of passive resistance which the local population had organised with German thoroughness. But things were done which disgusted every Englishman, notably, the expulsion of 100,000 German railwaymen with their families for no other reason than that they, as servants of the German Government, had obeyed the orders of Berlin not to work for the French authorities.

One of the serio-comic performances which I witnessed in Coblenz was a meeting organised by Dr. Dorten, the leader of the Rhineland Separatist movement. At that time the idea of a separate Rhineland Republic loomed large in the plans of the French military, and substantial subsidies and every other encouragement had been given to Dr. Dorten and his handful of followers. The meeting, which I attended, was a curious open-air affair. The square on which it was held was lined with French troops, and, without their presence, Dr. Dorten would not have dared to show himself. As it was, there were not more than a hundred or two persons present. Most of them were curious sightseers. I do not think that the French expected any great local enthusiasm for this wild project, but they believed that they would be obeyed and that, by bringing home to the local population the advantages and comforts of life in the Rhineland Republic as compared with the discomforts of life in Germany proper, they would meet with little resistance. The prize of course from the French point of view was the control of the vast German industry in the Rhineland and in the Ruhr.

The whole affair made a painful impression on me. I tried to picture to myself a French occupation in England and what we should have thought of a Devonian Doctor Dorten getting up and suggesting the separation of Devon and Cornwall from England. It was a project which took no account of national psychology and which could have been conceived only in a certain type of military brain. Yet at the time there were many Frenchmen who believed that the project was feasible. There are Frenchmen to-day who still think that it should have been put into effect. Altogether Coblenz made on me very much the same impression as the Ambassadors' retreat at Vologda during the Russian revolution—a little backwater where one was far removed from the heart of actuality and where one saw and heard only what was unreal. It was a dead city strangled by a military garrotte.

Having delivered my letters of recommendation and applied officially for my export licences, I left Coblenz and went to Cologne, which was about two hours away by car and which I made my headquarters. The British officials on the High Commission very kindly allowed me to travel in the Commission car. Otherwise, I should have been hard put to it to find a means of transport. For the railway service was chaotic—how chaotic may be gauged from the fact that in the French zone the sale of the German time-table was forbidden—and there were no private cars.

It was a strange journey, and, as I made it backwards and forwards some ten or twelve times in all, its memory is firmly embedded in my mind. The road and the railway run side by side along the Rhine, and from my car I could see the broken-down trucks and railway engines which the French had damaged and had been unable to repair. The contrast between the French zone and the British zone was startling. In the French zone the control was severe. Black troops guarded every bridge and every railway crossing, and every few miles my car would be stopped in spite of the British flag mounted on its radiator. A Senegalese corporal with rifle and fixed bayonet would poke his head through the door and unceremoniously grunt out a snarling "passpor." I am even-tempered and easy-going to the point of laxity. Long years of residence abroad have made me, I hope, impartial and objective. I was prepared to believe then, and still believe to-day, the evidence of the High Commission officials that during the occupation the Senegalese troops conducted themselves with admirable restraint. But their presence in a European country and the powers given to them over a white race depressed me and filled me with forebodings. In the British zone there were, thank God, no black troops. The control was scarcely noticeable, and during the whole duration of my visit I was never asked to show my passport.

There was another contrast which illustrated the attitude of the Germans towards the two occupations. When I was in Essen in the Ruhr itself, the town was plastered one night with leaflets giving the names of four or five German girls who had been seen walking out with Frenchmen. Below the names was this text: "Fellow-citizens, who have so much to suffer from the tyranny of the invader, keep these shameful names in your memory lest they be forgotten when the day of reckoning comes." In Cologne British Tommies were to be seen with German girls at every hour of the day, and the fraternisation between the British military and the German civil population was almost complete.

I had been told in Coblenz that the British garrison and the Consulate-General in Cologne were anti-French, but their attitude came as a surprise. In the British officers' club "those damned Frogs" was the Alpha and Omega of almost all conversation, and from our senior military and consular officials I heard grim stories of the truculence of the French, tales of Englishmen insulted and even imprisoned, descriptions of women in childbirth in Duisburg and Essen who had died because no doctor was allowed out of his house after eight o'clock, and lurid accounts of the horrors of the French expulsions of German families. Doubtless, some of the stories were exaggerated. When feeling runs high, propaganda has a habit of outrunning truth. Doubtless, too, British feeling was more anti-French than pro-German. For, if the truth must be told, our position at Cologne was in some respects ridiculous and undignified. The British zone was completely encircled by French and Belgian troops, and nothing could come in or go out except with the permission of the French Customs authorities. A typical story, which went the round of the officers' club, was an alleged conversation between General Degoutte, the French commander in the Ruhr, and General Godley, the British commander-in-chief.

In reply to a complaint of the Englishman, General Degoutte was reported to have said: "You English like sitting on an island. Well we've put you on one." The story was, of course, an invention, but an officer of General Godley's staff gave me chapter and verse for an incident, reported in the British press at the time, in which the British general was turned out of his sleeping-car while the Belgian authorities examined his papers.

Altogether Cologne made a shattering impression on me. The mark was tumbling at the rate of a hundred thousand or so every few hours. Profiteers and "Schiebers" were reaping a speculator's harvest, and in the more expensive restaurants like Wiesel's the price of a meal in sterling was as high as the most expensive restaurant in New York in the heyday of prosperity. But the middle class, with all their savings wiped out, were destitute, and the distress of the workers, whose wages became worthless almost as soon as they were paid, was pitiful to behold. The shadow of a winter famine hung heavily over the land, and in this atmosphere the characteristic English sympathy with the under-dog ran high. Certainly, the British in Cologne, including officials and business men, were almost unanimous in their condemnation of the methods of the French and even then seemed to realise that a peace without reconciliation could not be a lasting peace. Their attitude was the first evidence of pro-Germanism which I had met with, and it was an encouraging sign that its first manifestation should come from soldiers, nearly all of whom had fought in the war.

Unfortunately, British opinion in Cologne was far ahead of public opinion in England. Just how far ahead I was able to realise for myself. For, taking advantage of a lull in my negotiations, I flew over to London for the week-end. On the Saturday night in my club I recounted my adventures to my friends and told them of the strange change in British feeling in the occupied territories. The next day the Secretary took me aside and gave me a hint that in future I should confine conversations of this sort to my bedroom or my own flat. Some of the old colonels had complained of my disgusting pro-Germanism. They themselves were still living in the glory period and were not yet ripe for the change which was later to transform the attitude of the man in the street. This, indeed, was the tragedy of the whole post-war period and of the peace itself. Public opinion gradually took the right view, but it moved slowly. When a crisis arose, the Allied politicians, depending for their ministerial position on the suffrages of the masses, waited on public opinion. The result was that, when it at last swung round, the crisis had passed and had been replaced by another which demanded different treatment and a further advance of public opinion. German diplomacy was always too early. French diplomacy was always too late, and in the absence of a strong man to shape it British diplomacy wobbled ineffectually between the two.

In spite of these rather gloomy reflections my stay in Cologne and Coblenz was neither idle nor uninstructive. I had friends in the city: Paget-Thurston, the Consul-General, and Colonel Allen, the uncle of G. O. Allen, the English cricketer. I visited the Cathedral and made excursions on the Rhine steamers. My headquarters were the old Dom Hotel where ten years before I had met my wife on my first leave home from Russia. The impression that remained with me from those days was of a dining-room thronged with fat-necked and prosperous merchants and stiff-cuffed, rosy-cheeked officers who drank innumerable bottles of Berncasteler and smoked cigars in white paper-holders. They were neither unfriendly nor aggressive, but their Kultur was very military and filled me with a vague feeling of uneasiness. Now the same dining-room was packed with red-tabbed English officers whose every word was law to these once proud Germans and who were looked up to by the whole population with a respect which was at once a compliment to their sense of fair-play and a tribute to their excellent behaviour. If any one had told me on the occasion of my first visit that in ten years time British officers and British troops would be in command of the town, controlling the traffic, maintaining order, dispensing justice, and running things with less noise and greater smoothness than the Germans had ever done, I should have laughed in derision. Now that the thing was an accomplished fact I felt no exultation. An occupation, even one as mildly executed as the British occupation in Cologne, is never a very pleasant affair either for the occupiers or the occupied, and most soldiers, I fancy, dislike the rôle of a policeman.

Let it not be thought, however, that I was in Cologne for pleasure and merely because I found Coblenz unsympathetic. Every second day or so I motored to Coblenz in order to worry the High Commission with my presence and to stir them to greater activity. In Cologne itself I had another string to my bow. Here were the headquarters of the regular agents of the Austrian motor-companies and heavy industries on whose behalf I had undertaken my mission. They, too, were still trying to obtain supplies of the sorely-needed aluminum in their own way. They did not bother themselves about the High Commission or about export licences. They favoured the direct method—the same method as, doubtless, scores of bootleggers employed in the United States in their relations with the American customs officials. It was a form of approach which I did not like and did not understand, and from the start I told my Austrian friends that I would have nothing to do with graft. We met, however, every day in order to exchange views, and after several fruitless visits to Coblenz I arranged with them that they should go ahead in their own way, while I pursued the straight and narrow diplomatic path. They smiled. They were not very confident of their own success. They were quite certain of my failure. British officials, whom I consulted in Cologne, were of the same opinion. Finally, after three weeks of fruitless negotiations during which I went over the same ground over and over again, of fluctuating hopes and fears, of expensive cables to Vienna and London, and of countless instructions and counter-instructions, I hauled down my flag and confessed myself beaten. Irritated by my failure—a doubly depressing one because, when I left Vienna, I had been so confident of success, I set out on the tedious journey back to Austria. On arriving in the bank, I was met with smiles and congratulations. A telegram had just come in from our agent in Cologne. Six truck-loads of aluminum had been released from the Ruhr and were already out of the occupied territory. The Viennese directors naturally attributed this gratifying result to my efforts and patted both themselves and me on the back—me for the efficacy of my diplomacy and themselves for their prescience in sending me to Coblenz. I did not enlighten them. But in my heart I knew very well that my presence had not affected the issue in one way or the other. The direct method had triumphed. In this case I imagine the graft had been applied to and accepted by the Belgians. My mission had been a complete failure, and the consciousness of it was a severe blow to my pride.

This was my final effort for the Viennese bank. A month or so after my return I began to develop a sub-normal temperature accompanied by fits of giddiness and an extreme lassitude. Perhaps it was the reaction of my Coblenz failure on my mercurial temperament or perhaps the strain of those reckless post-war years in Prague on a system which, while still robust, was not so resilient as before. Perhaps even the sudden change from self-indulgence to complete asceticism had played the deuce with my metabolism. At any rate Simon and the other directors were sympathetic. They sent me to the best doctor in Vienna. He shook his head, diagnosed low blood-pressure and war-strain, and prescribed injections and immediate rest. He communicated his views not only to me but to Simon, and Simon packed me off to England.

As I left Vienna, the first wind of autumn set the grey-dusty leaves of the lime-trees swirling through the streets. There was a coldness in the air which lent a finality to my departure. Whatever the future might hold in store for me as a banker, my instinct told me unerringly that the grim grey barracks in the Strauchgasse would know me no more.

CHAPTER FIVE

I HAVE few pleasant recollections of that autumn of 1923 which I spent in London. I possess a fairly robust constitution and chafe under the restraints of ill-health. I visited an eminent specialist in Harley Street, who gave me an incredible number of injections and ordered me three months' rest. The chief difficulty lay in the resting. For the first time in my life I could not conquer my depression. There was perhaps some excuse for it. When I took stock of myself, the showing was far from satisfactory. Even the front window was almost barren. My official career in Russia had been meteoric and hectic. My romance with Moura had been flung in the face of the world. Nevertheless, it had been excused and glossed over on the score of youth and of the revolutionary atmosphere of Russia. In Prague, by an assiduous attention to my duties and by taking up some such special subject as the influence of ethnography on frontiers or the divergences of Eastern and Western Communist philosophy—subjects for which I was admirably qualified by knowledge if not by temperament, I might have staged an official comeback. But I had done none of these things. My four years at our Prague Legation had been wasted, and I had just pulled myself back in time from the precipice of financial disaster. At that moment the arrival of Spencer-Smith and the creation of the new bank had seemed to offer a loophole of escape. Now, although I was no banker, it required little perspicacity to see that the bank itself was unlikely to achieve the success for which its promoters had hoped. Moreover, I had undertaken heavy obligations in the shape of life insurance policies in order to satisfy my creditors, and to misgivings about my future was added the burden of financial worry. At the end of the three months, in spite of a needle-pierced posterior, my blood pressure remained obstinately low.

It was at this point that Spencer-Smith intervened. He sent me with a note to his own doctor, J. L. Birley. I imagine that if Birley's report had been adverse my banking career would have terminated there and then with the payment of a year's salary. As it was, everything was for the best with this best of doctors.

Birley, who, incidentally, brought Lord Northcliffe back from Evian to England during his last illness, was a grand fellow. He prescribed neither medicine nor injections. Instead he pumped some optimism into me, diagnosed that for years I had been masquerading as a man of action (which was true), informed me that so far from being a man of action I possessed a purely reflective mind (which I found flattering), and then asked me what I liked best in the world. I replied: "Country life in general and fishing in particular." He smiled. "Go away and do some salmon fishing. Get out of London and don't let me see you for three months. I'll square Spencer-Smith, and, if you're not as fit as ever you were, I'll eat my hat." He was even better than his word. I told him that I had no money for salmon-fishing, but a rich uncle. He wrote to my uncle, who most generously took a little house for me at Kelso and put his boat on the Tweed at my disposal.

The experiment was a complete success. For three months I lived on the water and for the water. I caught all the salmon that I wanted. I had a gillie who was nearly eighty and whose palsied hands shook so that he could hardly raise a glass of whiskey to his lips. Yet he could hold his boat against the Tweed in flood and carry me across the fords on his back. And as for the whiskey it reached its destination by a series of jerks and without the spilling of a single drop.

When I tired of fishing, I studied the bird life, which is extraordinarily varied in the early spring. But, above all, I steeped myself in Border history. There was all Tweed and Teviot—most beautiful of Scottish rivers—, where every stone had its part in the history of the clashes between my countrymen and the English enemy. When I fished the Teviot, my back-cast nearly touched the trees which surround the ruins of Roxburgh Castle, where James II of

Scotland was killed in the moment of victory by the bursting of one of his own siege guns. I made the pilgrimage to Ancrum to see the grave of Maid Lilliard, the Scottish Joan of Arc. It lies in an admirable setting in a fir-wood, and the stone bears the following inspiring inscription:

"*Fair Maiden Lilliard,
Lies under this stane;
Mickle in stature
But muckle in fame.
Upon the English loons,
She laid monie thumps,
An' when her legs were cuttit off,
She fought upon her stumps.*"

Above all, there was the whole of the Scott country almost at my door, and both by my grandfather and my father I had been brought up as a Scott worshipper. Now I was prepared to worship without any prompting. I owed a debt of gratitude to the great man. Fifteen years before, when I was living far from any white man in the Malay States, I had read every one of the Waverley Novels, and I firmly believe that they saved me from the boredom which drives most lonely men in the East to drink or drugs and sometimes to both. I visited Melrose both by day and by pale moonlight, stood where Bruce's heart is buried, and with American inventiveness convinced myself of my direct descent, with the spider thrown in, from the greatest of Scotland's Kings. During those three months I must have been the most constant visitor that Abbotsford has ever had. I sighed over the lock of Bonnie Prince Charlie's hair. I gazed in admiration at the gun, claymore, dirk, sporran and skene dhu of Rob Roy. I gently touched the sword-hilt of the gallant Montrose. But my chief joy was the study with Sir Walter's desk and with its little stair leading up to the book gallery and to his bedroom. I think that it was the circular stair which attracted me most. Whenever I looked at it, a vision of Sir Walter coming down at five in the morning, to light his own fire and then to take his place day after day at his desk, projected itself before my eyes. Modestly I traced a parallel between Sir Walter and myself. His debts had been over £100,000 and he had paid them off with his pen. My own debts were a nought less. Why should I not pay them off by the same method? And in making my resolution I did not forget either the cold of those early winter mornings or the fact that Sir Walter had killed himself in the process of repayment.

I have been a hero-worshipper all my life. If it will give any satisfaction to my enemies, I am even willing to admit that at one time or another Lenin and even Trotsky have figured among my idols. They are, in truth, an incongruous lot ranging from "Ranji" to Pierre Loti. But Sir Walter stands unassailable on a pedestal of his own—the greatest of them all and, in spite of his Scottish snobbishness, the most inspiring example of courage and industry in adversity that the world has ever known. In my own case the inspiration has lasted. To-day, whenever my habitual laziness threatens to find some excuse for idleness, I think at once of that staircase and of the stocky, slippered figure descending to its daily task. Strangely enough, the trick works. My debts have been reduced, and they have been paid off with the pen. Moreover, I began to put my resolution into effect during my stay in Kelso.

A year or two before, I had signed a contract with a firm of London publishers to write a book on Czechoslovakia. My uncle provided me with a typist, a buxom Highland girl from Sutherland, whose attempts to take down Czech names from my dictation were a source of endless merriment to us both. I worked hard on that book. I finished nearly two-thirds of it including a 40,000 word epitome of Czech history from the days of Krok to the return of Masaryk. It was, I feel sure, a vastly erudite performance. At any rate, it increased my own knowledge, and for a few months I was an authority on the true story of good King Wenceslaus. But the book was never finished—a lapse for which the publishers should have praised the soundness of my commercial instinct rather than have blamed my indolence. To do them justice they made little complaint about the loss of this unfinished masterpiece.

I have no wish to give the impression that my life at Kelso was entirely misanthropic. From time to time my uncle sent down guests for a few days' fishing. They stayed at my house, and for a day or two there was a break in the strict routine of my life. I enjoyed these interludes and, more particularly, the visit of Charlie Gilroy and his son, who came for a week at Easter. Charlie, a jute king, who had captained Harrow at football and had been a great athlete in his day, was an incorrigible wag, who required only an audience to draw him out. We fished all day, and in the evening we explored the amenities of the local cinema, a crude affair in those days frequented only by the "locals." One night the film roll broke in the middle of a rather lurid picture, just when the villain had enticed the heroine into his bedroom. The packed hall was plunged into complete darkness. This, I felt, was Charlie's opportunity, and, sure enough, his voice rang through the room like a rusty fog-horn: "Damn it, that's just my luck. Every time I go into a cinema the film breaks just when the picture's getting interesting." There was a slight guffaw, which changed into a general roar, when in a voice even more audible because of its strident tone a buxom farmer's wife shouted out from five rows behind: "You've missed naething, ser-r-r. A've seen the picture twice already, and the next scene doesna' star-rt till the mor-r-ning."

Otherwise, my life was one of monotonous virtue. During the week I took any amount of exercise, ate like a horse, and went to bed early with excellent benefits to my health. On Sundays I went to mass in the little Catholic Church. For some time I had been meditating a return to the original faith of my forebears. In London I had established contact with Father Vincent McNab, who is one of the modern saints of this world. The peacefulness of Kelso supplied the necessary atmosphere for the stifling of all my doubts, and that summer I was received into the Church by Father Vincent at St. Dominic's Priory in London.

In Kelso itself I had only one fall in grace. Towards the end of March my uncle proposed to me that I should accompany him to London to see the rugby football international between Scotland and England at Twickenham. As it was nearly time for me to see Birley again, I thought it would be a good plan to kill two birds with one stone. Scotland lost—a fact which to Scots at any rate will explain the break-down of my teetotalism and my participation in the national consolation for defeat. I sat up late and drank and smoked, not to excess, but far too much for a man who had been an invalid. The match was on a Saturday, and I had to see Birley on the Monday morning. I went with the trepidation of a guilty conscience, fearful less my dietary errors should be detected and condemned. But I passed my test with the fullest measure of success. My reflexes were perfect, and, when the pump was put on my arm, it registered the normal pressure prescribed by the text-books for a man of my age. Full of elation I went off to report to the bank.

My instinct about Vienna had been right. I was not to return there. I was to go back to the job for which I had been originally selected. I was to return to Prague, to take up my directorships on the local industrial companies controlled by our bank, and to keep an eye on the credits which we had advanced. This time my instinct filled me with forebodings. How would my newly-found asceticism stand up to the temptations of a city which had proved a pitfall not only to myself but to most of my colleagues?

CHAPTER SIX

ALTHOUGH I had been away only a year, I found many changes in Prague. The period of hectic glory and extravagant expenditure had come to an end, and life had now entered a calmer channel. Many of my old friends in the diplomatic corps had left, and at our own Legation there was, with the exception of Sir George Clerk himself, an entirely new personnel. Jack Cecil was in Washington, where he had just married Miss Cornelia Vanderbilt, and his place as First Secretary had been taken by Maurice Peterson, now head of the Egyptian Department in the Foreign Office. I had made enquiries about Maurice in London and had been told that he was silent, reserved, very serious, and not at all my affair. I found him reserved and not over-talkative. In every other respect he was a most agreeable companion, cool and reliable in a crisis and thoroughly sane in his outlook. Of all the diplomatic secretaries whom I have met he was the most efficient, combining great courage with the proper mixture of Scottish caution and running his chancery with a self-reliance which should carry him far in his diplomatic career. I liked him at first sight, and we became great friends, eventually sharing my old flat which he had leased during my absence in Vienna.

It was in the bank itself that I found the greatest change. Although we had earned an indirect kudos from the part played by M. Bark, our director, in the floating of the Austrian and Hungarian Reparations Loans, things were not going too well, and the general atmosphere was unpleasant. In the composition of its personnel, the bank was a miniature League of Nations. Before its establishment as an independent Czech institution, the managers and the staff had been mainly Jews. Most of them had been taken over by the new concern. But the Jewish element had been liberally mixed with a compound of British, Czechs, and German-Bohemians. Kuneš Sonntag, our President, was a Czech. He had been Finance Minister a year or two before and was, in my opinion, the ablest man in the whole of our new Central European organisation. Tall, with high forehead, small mouth, rather closely set eyes, and a ragged moustache and small, tufted imperial, he was, when one knew him well, a clear, level-headed thinker with an outlook much wider than that of most of his countrymen. He had a shrewd knowledge both of men and of affairs and posed as a cynic. His cynicism, however, was relieved by a keen and wholly delicious sense of humour. Having been a politician himself, he had the lowest possible opinion of politicians in general and of Central European politicians in particular. I remember taking him one Sunday, when we were over in London on business, to Windsor. On the way back I stopped our car opposite Runnymede and waved an arm towards the island where Magna Charta was signed. "There," I said with more sense of the dramatic than of historical accuracy, "is where the Mother of Parliaments was born." Sonntag, who had been silent throughout the drive, took his cigar from his mouth. "She was not a mother," he said drily, "but a painted old harlot who has led many young men astray."

He always reminded me of one of those Malayan elephants which draw the timber in Perak. Like them he was very wise, and capable of tackling any problem if properly handled, but full of suspicious reserve towards strangers. He had, in fact, certain limitations. He never quite succeeded in understanding the English, and, like many foreigners, suffered from an inferiority complex in their presence. Admittedly, the English are difficult to understand. He had, too, an almost feminine sensitiveness, and his worst defect was that, when he himself was misunderstood, he nursed his grievance in silence instead of airing it at once.

Another Czech, who had received a post in the new bank, was my old friend Ctibor Bubela, who had been our Czech secretary at the Legation. Bubela belonged to the very best type of Czech and had done invaluable work for Sir George Clerk. He had married my own lady secretary, and in him at any rate I knew that I had a loyal friend.

In addition to Sonntag we had an English managing director, T. H. Darton, who as London's representative was the real boss of the whole concern. Tommy Darton had nearly all the qualities which make for success. He had charming manners and a very high sense of duty. He was as conscientious in his work as a Prussian professor. He was popular, and deservedly so, with the government officials and with the diplomatic corps. He was hospitable and generous and extraordinarily kind. He regarded himself rightly as the watch-dog of British interests and in his rigid conception of his duty he had all the typical Englishman's suspicion of the foreigner. Once again it was a case of British banking methods and foreign banking methods not assimilating, and, as can be readily guessed, Sonntag and he never quite hit it off together.

Apart from Darton and myself there was George Young, who, as a kind of travelling director at large, came frequently to Prague. We had, too, other English watch-dogs in the various departments, and, in addition to the periodical visits of Spencer-Smith and M. Bark, other English employees were always being sent out from Head Office in London on some mission or other. And, to add to their number, there was always at least one of Binder and Hamlyn's accountants on duty in the bank. The English, in fact, were always falling over each other's legs, and in the British Legations in Central Europe we came to be known rather sarcastically as the "travelling circus."

The Jews, who filled most of the minor managerial posts in the bank, were hard and, in their own way, efficient workers. But their ways were not British ways. The two first principles of British banking are the safe custody of deposits and the maintenance of a high standard of liquidity. Foreign banks are more adventurous. They take part in promoting and directing industries. When trade is good, they make large paper profits. When trade languishes, the banks languish with it. It is a system which provides rich plums for the managers, some of whom, in good times, received as much as £50,000 a year in directors' fees and tantièmes. In Prague the local managers resented the superimposition of English directors and managers, whose efficiency they were inclined to mistrust.

It was not a very happy atmosphere. It was a particularly unhappy atmosphere as far as I was concerned. For the post of industrial director, which I had been led to expect in London, never materialised. The simple truth was that there was no real job for me in the bank, where I was as much out of place as a sparrow in a cats' home. True, I was put on the board of several industrial companies. But I had an associate, a local expert called Geduldiger, who did all the work. He was a kind of pleasant man, very easy to get on with and scrupulously conscientious. We shared a room together, and for several hours daily I listened to fierce wrangles between our industrial debtors, who wanted to borrow more English money, and my honest Geduldiger, who was doing his best to adapt himself to the English standards of liquidity. Once or twice a week we rose at some unearthly hour of the early morning and set out by car to inspect a factory or to attend a board meeting. Once a month I wrote a long report for London on the state of the various leather, porcelain, textile, sanitary ware, and kitchen utensil companies which we were supposed to control.

From Geduldiger I learned a great deal about Central European life, but very little about Czechoslovak industry. The fault was, of course, mine and not his. When I am hard driven, I can work as long hours as most men. But here I had no initiative, and, indeed, very little to do. Moreover, I was, I confess, more interested in the processes of manufacture than in the infinitely more important question of costing. When I went to inspect our leather factory, I wanted to know what chemicals were used for the curing, what parts of the skins were used for shoe leather, and, above all, why the skins stank so overpoweringly. My real job was to ascertain why the company was spending so much money and where the leakage was. Geduldiger could ferret out the shortcomings of the personnel almost by instinct. I was more interested in the men than in the managers.

The committee meetings, too, I found overwhelmingly tedious.

They were just like a Central European Parliament—all tattle and no action. And, gradually, I began to find a more pleasant outlet in outside interests. When we went to Eger to attend a local board meeting, I would steal away for an hour after luncheon to inspect the castle where Wallenstein was murdered and to ponder over the fate of my compatriot, John Gordon, incidentally an ancestor of Byron, who, as one of the three foreign assassins, was hanged for the crime. Why, I wondered, was it necessary to employ Irish and Scottish mercenaries for this dirty job? Were the Austrians too squeamish or did they prefer the talking and the bribing to the action? I do not imagine that Central Europeans have ever been strong where action is concerned. At any rate, when I returned to the board meeting, the directors were still discussing the same point at which I had left them.

When Spencer-Smith and M. Bark came out on one of their periodical visits, I re-entered for a short space into the limelight. There were interviews to arrange with Beneš and with the Finance Minister of the moment, and to official circles I was still the medium of approach. There was a certain amount of official entertaining to be done, and on all questions of international etiquette I was the official arbiter. There was the provision of suitable relaxation, and, as the night king of Prague, I was the last word on Central European relaxation. Occasionally, too, an American banker would call on us. When he had discussed his business, he would be passed on to me for instruction in the elementary geography, history, and politics of the new Central Europe.

It was an unsettling life. For six days in the week I sat dutifully in the bank, doing my best to keep my end up and praying silently for the Sunday when I could play golf with the Ringhoffers or go fishing with Sir George Clerk or shooting with Maurice Peterson and Fred Pearson, the American Secretary, with whom I shared a shoot near Brünn. In the evenings I went to bed early or worked fitfully at my book on Czechoslovakia. For I still stuck rigidly to my asceticism and studiously avoided my old night-life haunts. For ten weeks I led the life of a saint.

It was at this moment—on July 29th, 1924, to be precise—that I was rung up on the telephone from Vienna. Will Hicks, who had been my assistant in Russia and who was now head of the Cunard office in Vienna, was at the other end. We exchanged one or two rather pointless remarks. Then, just as I was beginning to wonder why he was wasting his money on a long-distance call, he broke off with a sudden "there's some one here who wants to speak to you" and passed the receiver to some one else.

It was Moura. Her voice sounded as if it came from another world. It was slow and musical and very controlled. She had escaped from Russia. She was in Vienna, staying with the Hickses. For four years she had heard no word from me, almost no news from the outside world. The receiver shook in my hands, as I asked a few idiotic questions: "How are you, my dear?" and "Are you all right?" Geduldiger was in the room. His presence unnerved me. I have always hated the telephone. Yet, in that moment, I remembered like a flash how during those days of crisis in July, 1918, when she had gone to Esthonia and it seemed unlikely that we should ever meet again, I had rung up her flat in St. Petersburg from Moscow seven or eight times every day to ask if there was any news of her. She had come back at great risk to herself, walking across the frontier in the night. She had joined me in Moscow and had remained with me to the end through my imprisonment by the Bolsheviks until that last farewell at the railway station when I was sent out of Russia under a Bolshevik escort. Now after a separation of six years I was speaking to her again—and on an accursed telephone. "Let me speak to 'Hickie,' " I stammered at last. Quickly I shot my questions at him. "May I come for the week-end? Can you put me up?"

When everything was arranged, I walked out of the bank and went home in a stupor of uncertainty.

That night I had to dine with Fred Pearson. Fate willed, of course, that there should be a Russian present—Wirin, the son of the Admiral of the Baltic fleet. The father had been in Kronstadt when the Bolshevik revolution broke out. The sailors had disembowelled him, filled his stomach with petrol, and set fire to him on the Anchor Square. The son had escaped to America, where he was trying to start a Russian university on Anglo-Saxon lines in order to foster and encourage leadership. He talked so dispassionately about the past and with such hope about the future that I marvelled at his courage. In spite of all that he had suffered, he seemed to have mastered life much more successfully than I had done. His self-reliance impressed me with the necessity of coming to some decision. Whatever that decision was, there must be no more drifting. Entirely owing to my selfishness and self-indulgence my married life had not been exactly a success. My job in the bank was unpleasant and precarious. I was heavily in debt, and for a moment I clutched rather desperately at the idea of cutting myself loose from England and making a new start. It had been done before. It might be done again. But... there were several buts. I was six years older and much nearer forty than thirty. My prospects of earning a living for myself were far from bright, and there were my wife and my boy, a post-war child, to consider. Finally, I had just become a Catholic, and divorce would mean a complete break with my new resolutions.

The next night I left for Vienna, my mind still not made up. I arrived at 6.30 and went straight to Mass at St. Stephen's. After Mass I walked to my hotel. I was to meet "Hickie" at his office at eleven. I did not know if Moura was to be there or not. We were to go out to "Hickie's" villa in the country for the week-end. I sat in the hotel, drank my morning coffee, smoked a chain of cigarettes, and tried to read a newspaper. At half-past ten, I began to walk slowly down the Kaertnerstrasse. The sky was cloudless, and the sun beat down fiercely on the pavement, turning the asphalt into a soft putty. I looked into the shop-windows to pass the time. Then, as the clock struck eleven, I turned into the Graben, where above a large bookshop the Cunard Company had its office on the first floor.

Moura was standing at the foot of the steps. She was alone. She looked older. Her face was more serious and she had a few grey hairs. She was not dressed as in the old days, but she had not changed. The change was in me—and not for the better. In that moment I admired her above all other women. Her mind, her genius, her control were wonderful. We walked up the stairs to the office where "Hickie" and his wife were waiting for us. "Well," said Moura, "here we are." It was just like old times.

We collected our suit-cases and took the little electric railway out to Hinterbrühl, which lies in the beautiful Brühlertal, flanked with rugged rocks and hills and pine-forests, and bedecked with vineyards and ruined castles, about twelve miles to the South of Vienna. We all talked at once and laughed at every word. Yet it was rather a nervous laughter. "Hickie," good, gentle, and very English, was, I knew, a little uneasy. As we were leaving the office, he had mumbled something about being careful and I knew exactly what he had meant.

Liuba Hicks led the conversation, talked very quickly, and jumped from subject to subject, recalling episodes from the revolution and picnics in the country and games of rounders at the Yusupoff's country house at Archangelskoe. Moura was the only person who seemed completely self-possessed. For myself I was tongue-tied with that dread of anticipation, which is so much worse than the actual ordeal. I knew—we all knew—that this thing had to be talked out, and after luncheon Liuba and "Hickie" left us alone, and Moura and I walked out to the hills behind the villa. Climbing up in the warm sunshine until the sweat ran down my face, we reached a crag where we sat down and rested.

Below us a mountain stream splashed noisily through the ravine. Behind us a grove of silver birches softened the gloomy darkness of a pine forest. Away to the right lay Gumpoldkirchen with its smiling vineyards. For a few minutes we sat in silence. Then I began to ask her about her life since our separation, and in a calm, matter-of-fact way she filled in the gaps. She had been in prison and had tried to escape. She had been released and had tried to flee from Russia across the ice of the Gulf of Finland. Then she had met Gorki, and he had befriended her, given her literary work to do and made her in some sort his secretary and literary agent. Finally, she had obtained a foreign passport and she had gone back to her old home in Esthonia. The land had been confiscated, but the house remained. It was a home for her two children whom she had to educate. She was paying for her own and her children's keep by translating Russian books into English. She translated six books a year and wrote 3000 words daily. She had translated most of Gorki.

It was an amazing record of fortitude in adversity and of the Russian genius for adaptability. Here was a woman who only a few years before had been a child of fortune, gay, attractive, fond of the pleasures of life and without a care in the world. The revolution, which had weighed so many of her compatriots in the balance and found them wanting, had put her to the test, and she had emerged triumphant. During those six years her mind had developed in a remarkable manner. Her tolerance was equalled only by her complete mastery of herself. She had a new attitude towards life, which I found wholly admirable and which I myself was incapable of imitating.

When it came to my turn, I stumbled miserably. What was there for me to say? When I looked back on those six years in Prague and Vienna, they seemed to stand out starkly sterile in the barrenness of their achievement. I had lost even my old impudent self-reliance. She had heard that after the war a son had been born to me. She did not know, until I told her, that I had become a Catholic. Clumsily, stammeringly, like a schoolboy pleading guilty to his housemaster, I blundered through the record of my debts and my follies.

"Oh God!" she whispered softly, and I winced as the words left her lips. For a moment I expected reproaches either of words or looks. But she remained silent, her brows knitted, her chin resting on her hand, and her eyes fixed on the valley below half-hidden by the heat haze. Then she turned to me and said gently: "You will be thirty-seven on the 2nd of September—the anniversary of Sedan and Omdurman? You see I remember the date. At thirty-seven one is not the same, men are not the same, as at twenty-seven. Don't let us spoil something—perhaps, the one thing in both our lives—that has been perfect. It would be a mistake, would it not?"

There was a mist before my eyes, and my temples throbbed violently. I knew that she was right, that she had gauged my character exactly. I saw myself again in Moscow. I heard again the voice of Peters, my amiable Bolshevik gaoler, who had been strangely fascinated by our romance and who had given me every encouragement to remain behind and deny my country and marry Moura. "Lockhart," he had said, "will always choose the golden mean." It was true at that moment, but, although I said nothing, made no protestations, I half hoped that she would take her words back and beg me to take my courage in my hands and start a new life with her.

She stood up and took both my hands. "Yes," she said, "it would be a mistake." This time there was a firmness about the words which denoted finality. Then in the fading sunlight she began to pick her way down the narrow mountain path.

That night we all sat up very late talking of the past and of the future. The present had brought little satisfaction to any of us. There was none of us who had not been influenced by the Russian revolution, and we looked on the state of Europe with profound pessimism. Certainly, there was nothing noble or generous in the conduct of European affairs. Everywhere speculation and self-seeking were rampant, and in the new states the spectacle of honest peasants converting themselves as rapidly as possible into dishonest bourgeois was nauseating. Individual selfishness vied with national selfishness in a common effort to hold and add to its gains. Only one law prevailed—brute force, and it was used unsparingly to make the weak weaker and the strong stronger. The idealists had failed, because they had not the necessary will-power to translate their ideals into action.

We wondered how long this madness could last and talked of the inevitability of revolution.

Moura prophesied that the economic system of the world would alter so rapidly that within twenty years it would be closer to Leninism than to the old pre-war capitalism. It might be a selective compromise combining the best feature of both systems, but the historians would give the credit for it to Lenin. If the capitalists were wise enough, it would come about without revolution.

I countered with Sorel's statement that no government has

ever been overthrown by a revolution. Revolutions occur, when government breaks down. Already government in Europe was morally bankrupt. At the best it lent an illusion of order to what were really the workings of chance and chaos. Yet capitalism would not go down without a struggle. For, while a man will abandon his wife, his mistress, his mother and even his children, he will never give up his possessions.

"Hickie," who had kept his pre-war ideals, talked eloquently of a transformed League of Nations, which would no longer be a judgment seat of the victors and a prisoner's dock for the vanquished.

On one point we were in agreement. Our generation would not remake the world. Although we were not responsible for a war, which had been made by our fathers, unborn youth would blame us for post-war effeteness.

It was a typically Russian conversation and rather more ineffectual than most Russian conversations.

The next day we made a feeble attempt to play rounders. Moura, however, was no longer the Atalanta of our Moscow days. "Hickie" already bore the traces of the disease which was to end his life a few years later. Night-life in Prague had ruined both my figure and my wind. We sat down and had a good laugh at ourselves.

That night I had to return to Prague. At the last moment Moura decided to come with me. As we left, it began to rain, and we made the long drive to the station in an antiquated hooded victoria which kept us in a cramped position with our heads almost touching our knees. There were no sleepers in the train, and we sat up all night in a crowded first-class carriage. We made no attempt to sleep and, in order that we might converse freely, we spoke Russian. Moura has a great sense of the fitness of things. She has a theory that everything in life depends upon the time-factor. Given the proper surroundings and the opportunity, anything may happen. An Austrian railway-carriage provided neither the time nor the place for sentimentality, and we both made a gallant effort to maintain our conversation on a gay note. It was, of course, mainly reminiscent—a long series of "do-you-remembers." We recounted all our personal experiences with the Bolsheviks: Trotsky's tantrums, Radek's brilliant witticisms, Kollontai's love-affairs, Peters's English wife and Chicherin's sex complexes. We discussed the probabilities of the Reilly plot and of his alleged proposal to frog-march Lenin and Trotsky in their shirts through the streets of Moscow. We discoursed eloquently on the pomposity of the French Ambassador. It was a gloriously unguarded conversation, and we laughed immoderately. When we reached Gmünd, there was the usual irritating customs and passport examination. When the passport officer came in, he had some difficulty in deciphering the passport of a short, little man with dark hair and a sallow face who was sitting next to me. In order to see better, the official bent down under the lamp beside me, and I could read the passport clearly. It bore the name of Ovsenko, the Soviet Trade Commissioner to Czechoslovakia. As he was not a member of the diplomatic corps, I had never met him. Throughout the journey he had remained as immobile as a Siamese cat before a rabbit hole. I imagine he must have enjoyed our conversation almost as much as we did.

At six o'clock in the morning I said good-bye to Moura at the Masaryk Station in Prague. She was going on to Berlin and to Reval. I had to be in my bank at nine o'clock. As I drove home to have a bath and change, the sun shone down on the silent, deserted streets. On the river by the Palacky Bridge a few immobile fishermen sat in anchored punts and watched their floats. I felt nervous and ill at ease. All my life seemed to be behind me. Had I made a mistake in throwing away this opportunity of going back to it? Ten years before I should not have hesitated. Was my indecision due to lack of courage or had the flame of our romance burnt itself out? On mature reflection I think that Moura's time-factor was chiefly to blame. We had met again at one of those rare moments when the ascetic in my nature was in the ascendant.

CHAPTER SEVEN

AFTER Moura's departure my work—or rather the lack of it—in the bank seemed grimmer and more irksome than ever, and gradually I began to slip back into my old Prague ways. My first lapse was my abandonment of teetotalism. It was a particularly stupid performance. One week-end I went to Marienbad with Maurice Peterson and two young honorary attachés. We played golf all day and in the evening we did a round of the night-places. Eventually we settled down in Max's Bar, a small dance-hall with a stage at one end and a row of boxes at the other. We took a box and sat down to watch the show. I drank black coffee. The cabaret performance was dreary, but among the guests was a fair-haired girl of remarkable beauty. She was sitting with an opulent-looking Jew who was old enough to be her father. Probably she was his unofficial wife for the duration of the season.

One of our young attachés wanted to dance with her but was too shy to risk a rebuff. He sought my advice. I told him that all he had to do was to walk up to their table, click his heels, introduce himself, and ask her for a dance. All would be well. It was the custom of the country. Only half-believing me, our young stalwart rose from his seat several times but never got beyond the door of the box. We began to chaff him and finally he lost his temper. "It's all very well for you to talk, but I'll bet you a hundred crowns you wouldn't do it yourself." A bet was a bet, and this one was a certainty. But a greater incentive was the challenge to my reputation for recklessness. I rang the bell, ordered a bottle of champagne, gulped down a bumper, and, walking boldly across the room, carried out my own advice to the letter.

The blonde was delighted. She danced once with me. For the rest of the evening, much to the amusement of the opulent Jew, she danced with the young attaché.

Those hundred crowns which I won were the most expensive bet that I have ever made. It led me back to the doubtful allures of Central European night-life. The next week-end I went to Marienbad with Sir George Clerk. We had arranged a golfing blood-match against the Dutch Minister and Baron Ringhoffer—an encounter which my old chief, with a proper pride in the superiority of the British race, took seriously. When we arrived on the Saturday evening, the hotels were crowded, and I had to sleep in a dressing room off Sir George's room. On retiring to bed after a serious game of bridge, I felt restless, and, as soon as Sir George was sound asleep, I got up, dressed again, and, shoes in hand, crawled out of the hotel and made my way to Max's Bar. The next day my golf suffered from lack of sleep, and we were heavily defeated. Sir George was not pleased.

I do not mean to imply that I became a drunkard. My constant companion at this time was Maurice Peterson, and Maurice was as firm as granite. But we entered fully into what was then the normal life of the foreigner in Prague, and in my own case I could plead that night-life was a buffer to the engine of a superfluous energy which found no outlet in my work. I did everything that was asked of me, and this was not very much. I attended my board meetings. When our London directors came to Prague on their periodical visits, I trotted them round faithfully to see President Masaryk and Dr. Beneš. I acted as cicerone to important foreign visitors. All this meant a vast deal of entertaining and an expenditure which I could ill afford. It developed, too, habits of laziness which come from self-indulgence. In the leading restaurant a double cognac was known as a Lockhart. An unfortunate propensity for over-tipping combined with a dislike of walking made me the favourite client of every taxi-driver in Prague.

To this unenviable popularity I ascribe my one important contribution to diplomacy during my Prague career. One night I was driving down the Graben with Maurice Peterson, when an open car, driven by a Czech chauffeur, passed us on the wrong side at terrific speed. To add insult to injury the chauffeur jeered at us as he passed. Maurice, who was driving his own car, is a nervous driver, and the shock to his system provoked a grave departure from his usual inarticulate stolidity. His face went livid. "Schweinehund" (pig-dog) he roared in a voice like a train going over a railway bridge. It was an insult doubly serious because it was made in German, and in those days German was not a popular language in Prague. When we came to the end of the street, we found the chauffeur's car drawn up across the road and a policeman holding up his hand. We stopped and got out. There was no means of concealing our identity. Maurice's car flew a British flag. In vain he sought to explain the enormity of the chauffeur's provocation. In vain he referred to his position as First Secretary of the British Legation. He was no linguist, and the policeman, who knew nothing of diplomatic privilege, had already heard the whole story from his brother Czech.

The situation began to look serious. The usual crowd, which always assembles on such occasions, took the Czech's side, and for a moment it looked as if we might have to go to the police station. Yet in the end it was the crowd that saved us. Fortunately, we had been pulled up just opposite the Obečny Dum or Municipal House outside whose doors is the largest taxi-rank in Prague. And in the crowd which surrounded us were some fourteen or fifteen chauffeurs. When I began to take part in the argument, they spotted me. A big burly fellow, who had driven me often, drew me aside, and in a moment I gave my own version in my best Czech to the little circle of chauffeurs. Headed by my brawny Sandow, the chauffeurs advanced en bloc on the policeman. "Did he know what he was doing? He had better be very careful. The chauffeur who had made the complaint was a notorious liar. He *was* a Schweinehund. He had knocked down an old woman the week before with his furious driving. The English gentlemen was Pan Lockhart's friend, and Pan Lockhart was the man who had helped the Czechs in Russia. Above all, Pan Lockhart was the best payer in Prague.

Sandow's eloquence was magnificent. It worked, too, like

magic. The policeman's face made two lightning changes. He smiled politely as he apologised to us for the inconvenience to which we had been put. Then he turned savagely on our would-be prosecutor and cursed him soundly for wasting his valuable time. As we drove away, he was still giving him a metaphorical kick in the pants.

When Maurice is Ambassador in Paris or Berlin, as he assuredly will be one day, I hope he will remember with gratitude the Scottish "Pan" who saved him from what might have been an ineradicable blot on an otherwise brilliant career.

It was at this period, too, that I was present at the rescue of a more distinguished diplomatist from even greater peril. Taking advantage of one of the numerous bank holidays, I arranged a long week-end's fishing with Sir George Clerk in the Bohemian Forest. Our destination was Anatal, a small village with a world-famous glass factory on the upper reaches of the Otava. The weather was superb. The mountain scenery, softer and more restful than that of Canada and Scotland, was the perfect antidote to the noise and dust of Prague. True, the trout were scarce, but the catching of fish is only one of the charms of angling, and the sight of a huge salmon lying at the end of a long pool whose dark waters swirled majestically against the wall of a huge limestone precipice was more than sufficient compensation for my own lack of success. I lay on the rich mountain grass and was well content to live for a few hours instead of being merely alive.

In the evening we dined with M. Novotny, the glass manufacturer. He was a fine old type of Czech with four sons and four strapping daughters. While we ate, a tame fox ambled gently round the room and took scraps of meat from his mistress with the neatness of a stage-trained poodle. The next morning we rose at six and went to see the factory where the glass is cut on a kind of sand-stone wheel over which drips a mixture of sand and water. The glass, all hand-cut, is the finest in the world. Then we set out in Sir George's high-powered open Austro-Daimler for Mader, a tiny mountain village which lies over 3000 feet above the sea. For eight months in the year the village is under snow, but in summer the scenery is magnificent, and the view over the

Boehmerwald plateau is as wide a panorama as any I have seen. At Mader the Otava splits up into several smaller streams not very much larger than a Highland burn. Sir George and I took a stream apiece and during the whole day we never saw a living soul. In the evening we set out on the thirty-mile return journey to Anatal.

The road, narrow, precipitous, and with numerous hair-pin bends, forced us to a slow speed. We had that rare combination of a clear sky, a harvest moon, and the pink afterglow of a perfect sunset. Well-content, I lay back in the car to enjoy the scenery. Sir George smoked his pipe in silence. Never, I thought, had I known such peace. It was to be rudely disturbed. As we turned a sharp corner, a high-powered car, driven by some madman, was bounding up the hill at forty or fifty miles an hour. It was not a road for cars. There was no room to pass and no time for either car to pull up. We were on the outside with two hundred feet of sheer precipice below us. Nobilis, our chauffeur, never hesitated. He swung over to the left, skirted the precipice to the last blade of grass, and with our left rear-wheel suspended in mid-air, we passed with an inch to spare. The whole adventure happened in a flash, but in that second I lived an eternity of fear.

In helpless rage I stood up and shook my fist at the other car. Nobilis pulled up and jumped out of his seat. His eyes were gleaming. His moustache bristled more fiercely than ever. "One inch," he said to Sir George in his comic Czech-German, "one inch—otherwise..." He waved his arms expansively towards the precipice, then drew himself up proudly to his full height and laughed. He was a magnificent driver and a swashbuckler who feared neither God nor man. For myself I could have kissed him on the spot. Not even in 1918, when Krylenko was shrieking for my blood, had I looked death so closely in the face.

My escape, which should have brought me to my senses, made little difference to my mode of living. Every day I grew more dissatisfied with my position in the bank and saw no issue out of what was indeed a hopeless cul-de-sac. Although I knew nothing about finance, my instinct told me that sooner or later a crisis was inevitable. Over-industrialisation, which has been the curse of all the Succession States, was beginning to show its effect in increased difficulties among the individual companies which we controlled. The only remedy proposed by the local experts was to throw good money after bad. The English, already alarmed by the extent of their commitments, were bent on retrenchment and improved liquidity. The clash of systems bred personal jealousies and mistrust. There was, too, no outlet for me in my politico-economical work. The remedies for the situation were easy enough to suggest: a more enlightened policy on the part of the victors towards the vanquished and a realisation by all the Succession States that their economic salvation lay in closer economic co-operation. So long as each state continued to shut itself off into a water-tight compartment, it was obvious that neither our bank nor any other form of business could prosper and that the loans, contributed by Englishmen and Americans, were just so much wasted money or, at the best, palliatives destined merely to postpone the day of reckoning. Like every other impartial observer, I had pointed out these truisms in numerous memoranda. Like the despatches of our diplomatic representatives, they bore no effect. In the face of France's ruthless determination to keep Germany where the Treaty of Versailles had put her, England had no policy either in the City or in the Foreign Office. France's allies in Central Europe aped the same policy with regard to Hungary and Austria, and, although every one prated glibly about reconciliation and reconstruction, these pious expressions of good-will were unsupported by any practical measures. In the Succession States the inter-racial hate of centuries, so far from being quenched, was fanned by the flames of a new resentment. Unlike the war-crisis, to which an end was always in view, the peace-crisis was one of helpless drift.

I drifted with it, living for the day with little thought of tomorrow. My lack of foresight took its most reckless form in my personal extravagance. True, the professional Russian gipsies had long since abandoned Prague for Paris. At this time, however, I received a visit from a consumptive Russian ex-officer. He had formed a private gipsy troupe from Russian refugees. Would I give him a trial? Would I help to find rich clients for him among the members of the Prague diplomatic corps.

Partly from natural desire and partly from an insane ambition to pose as a kind of gipsy master of ceremonies, I took him up with ardour. The troupe were first-rate and not so rapacious as the professional gipsies. I brought them to the British Legation, dressed up as a gipsy myself, sang a solo, and derived a childish pleasure from fooling both my own Minister and his guests. I gave several private parties in my own house. They were enjoyable but very expensive. Once again I was plunging rapidly into debt.

My greatest extravaganza, however, was the St. Andrew's Day celebration which I staged in Prague. We had had a small Scottish dinner two years before, but this was a more elaborate affair and should go down to history as probably the first St. Andrew's Day celebration held in Prague since the days of Elizabeth Stuart, the Winter Queen of Bohemia, and Prince Rupert. We Scots in Prague were six strong: Sir George Clerk, Maurice Peterson, Taylor, our Vice-Consul, McKechnie, the honorary attaché, and Douglas, a son of Norman Douglas, the author. We invited the five leading Englishmen and Jan Masaryk, the President's son, as our guests and then we set about to give a lesson in Scottish hospitality both to the English and to the Czechs. We obtained a Waugh haggis from Scotland. The Cameron Highlanders lent us their champion piper from Cologne. We had a freshly killed Rhine salmon and oysters brought by aeroplane from Paris. Through the foresight of Taylor we had even a thistle for our button-holes. Prague gave us all it could offer in the way of vodka, champagne, and old brandy. We made only one mistake. We left the making of the Athole brose to Oldfield, our military attaché, who claimed to be an expert. He was an Englishman.

The dinner was held in the private room of Zavřel, and, as we were piped to our places, a large crowd assembled in the market-place outside. It remained there for the rest of the evening. The first part of the dinner was a huge success. Maurice Peterson sang a Vive-la which he and I had composed for the occasion. I read an ode which I had written in honour of Jan Masaryk. All the hosts and all the guests made speeches. Then the Athole brose was brought in. It was served in a huge silver bowl as big as a bath tub and was drunk in loving cup fashion with a man standing on each side of the drinker. The precaution was a wise one. I do not know how Oldfield had prepared his concoction (he confessed afterwards that the ingredients were a pot of honey, four bottles of whiskey and two bottles of slivowitz), but the fumes alone were strong enough to fell a giant. The piper blew his brawest, and solemnly the cup was passed round until it had been drained to the last drop. Then the table was cleared away, and we danced an eightsome reel. It was not a success. McKechnie, a man of brawn, thought that he was playing rugby football and attempted to tackle His Majesty's Minister. One of the Englishmen received a kick on the knee which kept him on crutches for three weeks. The "heuchs," however, were "whooped" in the best Scottish manner and were echoed sympathetically by the crowd in the street outside. After the reel Sir George beat a dignified retreat, and then Taylor, Maurice Peterson, Jan Masaryk and I proceeded to collect the casualties and to send them home. The sorting out was rather a complicated task. Some of the younger men did not remember their address. All had private cars and wanted to drive them, and we had only one chauffeur. In the end, however, all were safely berthed. The next day the piper, who had drunk no Athole brose, was asked to pipe before President Masaryk on the castle square of the Hrad. The Prague garrison turned out in full force to receive him, and the Czechs, who had never seen a Scottish piper in the flesh and liked him when they did see him, gave him a rousing welcome. Alas! only one of his compatriots was up in time to witness this historic performance. Somehow I feel that the chief honours of this St. Andrew's Day celebration belonged to the piper.

The only serious casualty of the celebration was I myself. Two days before the dinner a tiny abscess, caused presumably by an insect bite, had formed on my lip. I had pricked it with a needle and had already a temperature of 100 on the afternoon before the dinner. The next day my lip swelled up like a cricket ball, and for nine days I lay between life and death with blood-poisoning. I was attended by Dr. Lenz, the Legation doctor and a Czech. He must have had a very trying time, for my German-Bohemian friends, with the best intentions in the world, tried to persuade Sir George and Maurice Peterson that I would surely die unless they called in Schloffer, the famous German surgeon. I was too ill and too delirious to realise what was happening, or to care whether I lived or died. Fortunately, Lenz, who was determined not to have an operation if it could possibly be avoided, kept his head. Nevertheless, on the ninth evening, when my temperature was 106, he gave way and made arrangements for me to be operated on the next morning by Schloffer. When Lenz came round with Maurice Peterson in the morning to take me away, the poison had come to a head and, inserting a pair of tweezers into the opening, he extracted a lump of solid matter as large as an army colt revolver bullet. The relief was almost instantaneous, but my convalescence was a long one, and it was a month before I was fit to go back to work.

CHAPTER EIGHT

BOTH morally and materially 1924 had been a year of backsliding for me. The year 1925 was to see a change in my fortunes. Yet its opening could hardly have been less auspicious. My blood-poisoning had left me in a very depressed state. My finances were in a hopeless tangle. Already there were well-founded rumours that our English directors were planning to reduce their commitments both in Prague and in Vienna and even to sell a part of their holdings to local interests. This could mean only a decline of British influence in both banks and a reduction of the British staff. I had no illusions about myself. As the bank's most superfluous luxury I was prepared to be the first to submit my head to the inevitable axe. Worse still, Maurice Peterson was transferred to Tokio early in the year, and, in spite of my own evidence to the contrary, Maurice had been a steadying influence on my life. His departure was followed by an amusing incident which illustrates better than any detailed psychological analysis the difficulties of social life in a small capital where diplomatists see too much of each other.

The friendly rival of Sir George Clerk in diplomatic hospitality was Mr. Lewis Einstein, who had succeeded Richard Crane as American Minister in 1921. An erudite Republican with a scholar's knowledge of Italian art, he and his charming wife, the mother of the present Lady Tweeddale, kept open house for the whole diplomatic corps, and dinner and bridge parties and dances in their Legation, the former Schoenborn Palace, were weekly affairs.

In order to relieve the monotony of the Prague winter they decided or perhaps were persuaded to launch a more ambitious kind of party—an amateur cabaret in which the artists were to be chosen from the ranks of the diplomatic corps. In addition to the various turns there was to be a conférencier, and the close of the performance was to be a personal skit on the corps written in the form of musical couplets by the secretary of the French Legation.

The show was vigorously rehearsed, and on the night of the party all social Prague was present in full force to see the finished production. A stage had been set up in the far end of the ball-room. In the front seats sat the Czech ministers and the heads of the diplomatic Missions with their wives. Then followed in order of precedence the nobility, the leading Czech officials, the military attachés, and the junior secretaries of the Legations. The bankers and the thirsty stood in the back row close to the buffet. Never before or perhaps since has Prague witnessed such a cosmopolitan array of starch and powder. The first part of the programme passed without a hitch. The applause was of the correct warmth. Madame Einstein smiled benignly. The show was going with a swing.

Then came the cue for the skit which had been rehearsed in private and the words of which had been kept secret even from the hosts of the evening. The verses were sung by Pepi Carcer, the Spanish secretary, who combined good looks and a natural talent as an actor with a perfect French accent. Cosme, the French author, had a pretty if caustic wit, and the first verse, a reference to the American Minister and to the bemonocled elegance of Sir George Clerk, drew a round of applause which put the self-confident Pepi entirely at his ease. The buffet emptied, and the stragglers, eager for more, trooped back into the room. The rest was not so good. The next couplet was a dig at the diplomatic penchant for scandal-mongering with a slightly unkind reference to one of the American secretaries. It was followed hotly by a sarcastic comment on the ancestry of the Belgian Minister, who was punctiliously insistent on the inclusion of the "de" which preceded his name. This produced titters from the ladies and uproarious applause from the more unruly secretaries at the back. From my point of vantage I saw a red patch rise above the white collar of the Belgian. I predicted trouble, but Pepi, stimulated by the applause, went from strength to strength. The climax came with his reference to Mynheer Mueller, the Dutch Minister, a dignified and broad-beamed figure, who had been in numerous posts and had amassed a whole chest-front of orders in the process. I cannot remember Pepi's exact words, but their purport was unmistakable. It was to the effect that if the Dutchman collected any more stars he would have only one place to put them and then he would be unable to sit down.

The words sounded less crude in French. An Englishman or an American might have accepted them with a laugh. But not so the honest Dutchman whose sensitiveness was affected in its most vulnerable spot. His grey beard bristled. His face went white. With the fall of the curtain he left the building. Long before the party was over, the scandal-mongers were busy with rumours of diplomatic incidents, of handshakes proffered and refused; in short, of an unholy row.

And for once scandal was not far removed from truth. The Belgian and the Dutchman were furious. They took official cognisance of the alleged insult, and for weeks afterwards Sir George Clerk, as doyen of the diplomatic corps, had to listen to demands for an official apology, and even to suggestions of a duel. Sir George used all his tact and all his flattery in order to effect a reconciliation. He succeeded finally in making formal peace between the Belgian Minister and Cosme. But the injured dignity of the Dutch Minister demanded nothing less than a public humiliation of the American Minister—a demand which Sir George turned down with some emphasis, and to the end of his stay in Prague the Dutchman at any rate refused to be comforted. My sympathies were entirely with Mr. Einstein, who had been rather unfairly let down and who had done everything that man could do to repair an incident for which he had been only indirectly responsible. The whole affair, however, was a lesson in internationalism. Without an international sense of humour there will never be a satisfactory League of Nations.

In the spring I had a pleasant diversion in the form of a business journey to Budapest and Belgrade, where I interviewed various ministers, made my first personal acquaintance with Sir William Goode, and wrote a report for my directors on the economic situation in both capitals. In June I came over to London on a barley deal which our bank was trying to put through with the English brewers. Rarely, if ever, have I been so reluctant to return home. I was now at the end of my financial tether. I was ashamed to approach my relations and would willingly have remained in Prague. Nevertheless, as my means were exhausted, some kind of explanation and assistance was necessary. With that fatal habit of postponing trouble which has always been my undoing, I did nothing, and my visit was nearly ended when once again, as it has done so often before, Fate knocked at my front door. The knock came in the form of a telephone ring from my old Prague colleague, Frank Aveling, who was then an assistant in the Central European department of the Foreign Office.

"Do you remember the Baron de Forest case?" he asked. "Well, we can do nothing more with it. We have suggested to the Baron that he should negotiate privately with the Czechoslovak Government, and I have recommended you as the most suitable person to employ for the negotiations. Rigby, the Baron's agent, will be coming to see you in half-an-hour."

At first I did not appreciate the importance of this conversation nor did it convey to me any particular message of hope. For six years Baron de Forest's case had been a plague spot in the tranquillity of our Legation. The Baron's estate at Rossitz in Moravia had a glorious castle, excellent shooting, and rich farm-lands.

In 1914 it must have been worth over a million pounds sterling. The estate, too, had a history. It had belonged to the ancient family of Trauttmannsdorff. The last Trauttmannsdorff owner had been a great gambler. In return for moneys borrowed for his gambling he had mortgaged his place to Baron Hirsch, the Jewish financier, who afterwards became the friend of King Edward and settled in England. Baron de Forest had inherited the estate.

After the war the Czechoslovak Republic passed a Land Reform Bill which entitled the Government to confiscate the large estates at a compensation fixed by themselves at a considerably lower rate than the pre-war value. The law applied to all estates whether held by Czechoslovak nationals or by foreigners.

Baron de Forest, a British subject and a former member of Parliament, was not prepared to sacrifice his property in this manner. A good-looking man with charming manners, he could be bafflingly obstinate when he thought that some one was trying to get the better of him. He had been fighting the Czechs over their right to apply the law to his estate ever since 1919. He had enlisted the help of the Foreign Office. He had had questions asked in the British House of Commons. He had taken the matter up with the Ambassadors' Conference. He had come himself to Prague, and his bitterness against the Czechoslovak Government had been vitriolic.

Of course, I remembered the case. The Legation files were full of it. Various schemes had been suggested for a compromise, but the Baron had turned them down or had hesitated so long that the opportunity had been lost. Now the Foreign Office had given it up as a bad job or rather as a case in which they could properly do no more. What hope was there that I could succeed where official diplomacy had abandoned the field? Frank Aveling's suggestion sounded like a bad joke.

When Rigby arrived, I was prepared to listen and to shake my head. He told me that this time the Baron meant business and was ready to sell his place lock, stock and barrel, provided he could obtain a fair price. He would be willing to pay a large commission for a rapid deal and for cash down.

The size of the suggested commission struck a chord of hope in my heart. It was only a faint clang, but I was not in a position to hesitate. I did some rapid thinking. Sending Rigby away with a promise to give him a definite answer within a week, I sat down and wrote out a long letter to Sir George Clerk to ask his advice. I begged him to send me a telegraphic answer. He replied immediately to the effect that, provided I had a full power of attorney and a free hand and came alone, there was a reasonable prospect of a settlement. Sir George's telegram made up my mind for me. Interpreting the "reasonable prospect" of a shrewd

British diplomat as a damned good chance, I told Rigby that I was prepared to undertake the mission.

This was the beginning of a whole series of almost insurmountable difficulties. Rigby had already committed himself to another agent, a tactful, white-haired old gentleman called Walter Scott Leefe. He suggested that the three of us should proceed to Prague together and that we should share the commission. This was straining the "alone" in Sir George's telegram to the utmost. Even a third of the commission, however, would be sufficient to pay my debts. So, after extracting a promise from Rigby and Leefe that the actual negotiations would be left entirely in my hands, I agreed to these conditions.

The next job was to obtain the necessary leave from my bank directors. Fortunately, my chance presence in London enabled me to approach Spencer-Smith personally. He listened to me sympathetically. I showed him Sir George's telegram, and, although he considered the venture in the light of a hundred to one chance, he gave me a fortnight's leave in which to try my luck. Perhaps he remembered my deal with the Treasury bonds or perhaps he was sorry that my career in the bank had gone wrong. At any rate, it was a very magnanimous decision on the part of a London banker.

There remained one more obstacle, and it was the greatest. The negotiations would entail a certain amount of personal expenditure. When one plays for a big stake, one must play high, and I was down to my last shilling. I went back to the moneylender who had treated me best and, putting all my cards on the table, asked him to back my chance. He gave me £500 on a three months' bill for £700. I was grateful. I have known men in less desperate circumstances than myself, who have gone to moneylenders and been sent away with a flea in their lug. Yet, barring the exorbitant rates of interest which in the circumstances are perhaps not unjustifiable from a purely monetary point of view, I have only once had a raw deal from a moneylender. I am not vain enough to attribute this qualified success to any special persuasive talents of my own. Rather I think must it be ascribed to my Russo-Scottish upbringing. All my moneylenders had Scottish names and all came from Odessa.

Armed with my £500 and accompanied by my two colleagues, I set out at the beginning of July for Paris where we had to see Baron de Forest and to receive our power of attorney. The Baron, a picturesque figure in an open tennis shirt without a tie, was amiable but stubborn. He cut down the percentage of the commission which had been suggested originally. Having declared in advance that I was not prepared to undertake the mission purely on a gambler's chance, I had to abandon £1500 of my problematical commission in return for a cheque for £200 for my expenses. I made the sacrifice willingly. The £200 would pay the interest on my moneylender's loan.

Let it be said at once that the Baron's offer was a handsome one. The proposal was that we were to sell the estate for the best price that we could obtain. There was a reservation of £250,000— a very large sum for any Central European state at that time. If we were successful, we were to receive a commission of ten per cent. The power of attorney, which was the all-important factor, was short and clear. It had no ambiguous limitations. It seemed eminently satisfactory.

On our arrival in Prague I went at once to see Sir George Clerk. I found the situation more hopeful than I had expected. The Czechs were thoroughly tired of the case and, provided that we could make a final and binding settlement, were glad to have this opportunity of liquidating the whole affair. The price would be the big stumbling-block. Sir George undertook to use all his powerful influence in the proper quarters.

The next day we began our official negotiations. They were conducted with the President of the Land Office and took place in a dingy old building on the Wenceslaus Place. The room in which we met was like the court of a justice of the peace in a provincial Russian town. Voženilek, the President of the Land Office, sat at a table with his back to the wall. He was attended by his legal experts and other officials. We sat opposite him on three wooden chairs, ridiculously small for Leefe and Rigby, who both were big men. I felt a strong inclination to giggle.

The proceedings opened on a friendly note. Voženilek made a long preamble in which he insisted that the deal must be kept within the framework of the Czech Land Reform Act. It had little bearing on the deal and was of no interest to me or to my colleagues. When at last he got down to hard facts, the atmosphere became electric. When he mentioned the price which the Czechoslovak Government was prepared to pay, Rigby, whose experiences with the Czechs had been unhappy, stood up to the full height of his commanding figure and nearly exploded. Fortunately, the Czech negotiators understood no English. My colleagues knew no Czech and very little German and, as on these occasions the interpreter is nearly always master of the situation, I was able to avert a major catastrophe. The outlook, however, seemed hopeless. The price mentioned by Voženilek as his maximum was nearly £200,000 short of our minimum! And after two hours of persuasive argument we were unable to make him budge an inch from his position.

In the circumstances there was only one thing to do—to "lobby" my political friends in the Government with all the skill and tact that I could command. I concentrated on obtaining the support of Dr. Beneš and my old friend, Jan Masaryk. I spent my days in the Czechoslovak Government offices and my evenings with Sir George Clerk, whose advice, guidance and active help were invaluable. Meanwhile, Rigby had enlisted the co-operation of Dr. Dolansky, the Baron's lawyer and a former Minister of Justice.

It was an exciting situation every minute of which I enjoyed. But, although every Czech official promised his support and obviously wished to reach a settlement, the days passed without much progress, and my fortnight was slipping away all too quickly. Three days before I was due to return to work, Voženilek's bid was still £75,000 below our minimum. After a preliminary consultation with Sir George, I decided to bring the whole matter to a head and to risk my commission and my future solvency on a definite yes or no. I went straight to Beneš. Knowing that the Land Office officials thought that I was bluffing about my fortnight's time limit, I put all my cards on the table. I gave him my word of honour that I should have to abandon the negotiations in two days' time and that there was no hope of an extension. I told him that never again would the Czechs have such an opportunity of ridding themselves of a rich and hostile critic. If the present negotiations broke down, the Baron would lay the case before the Hague Tribunal. This would mean anti-Czech propaganda in the foreign Press. It might affect even the financial credit of the Republic on the London and New York money markets. And then I played my last trump. I told him that I had a minimum price below which I was not empowered to go. I told him approximately how far the Czech offer fell below our minimum and I explained that I could not accept the bare minimum, because otherwise the Baron might think that we had made no effort to obtain a larger sum.

Dr. Beneš listened to my arguments with great attention. With head on one side and with the outstretched fingers of both hands pressed tightly against each other in an arch he remained silent for several seconds which seemed to me like eternity. I knew what he was thinking. He was whole-heartedly in favour of settling a matter which had been a thorn in the flesh of his own department. But how could he justify the purchase price in the Czechoslovak Parliament? I waited without moving a muscle while the clock on the wall struck five. My temples were throbbing in the July heat. Would the man never speak? His face was an enigma. At last he nodded twice and stood up. "I'll see what can be done," he said quietly. As we shook hands, he smiled. He went off to see Jan Masaryk. Jan saw M. Švehla, the Prime Minister. That night the deal was settled for £272,000. The money would be paid immediately.

And then in the hour of triumph Fate played me a scurvy trick. The next morning, when we went to the Land Office, everything was in order on the Czech side. The protocol was ready for signature. The cheque for £272,000 was made out. All that we had to do was to deposit our power of attorney and collect the cash. But when we handed over the power of attorney there was an ominous hitch. Voženilek called an interpreter to translate it to him. The interpreter summoned the legal expert. There was some rapid whispering among the Czechs. Then Voženilek launched his bombshell. "Gentlemen," he said, "your power is not in order. It has not been witnessed by the Czechoslovak Consul-General in Paris or London. You must take it back and have it properly attested."

I could have kicked myself for my folly. As a former Consular Officer I knew everything about powers of attorney. But in Paris I had been too busy to attend to the matter myself. My heart sank. And not without reason. For the Baron, so far from being satisfied with the price which we had obtained for him, began to regret his previous decision to sell and took advantage of the flaw in the power to raise all kinds of side-issues. For ten days or more he refused to execute a new power, and, at one moment, it seemed as if all my work were to go unrewarded. In the end the Czechs did the wisest thing possible. They informed us that, if the power were not deposited within a week, the deal would be cancelled. This had the desired effect. The Baron issued a new power. The Czechs paid promptly, and the whole sum was transferred by telegraph to the Baron's bank in London. This, however, was not the end of all my troubles. Although the price was the highest ever paid for any estate in Central Europe since the war and although the deal itself was strongly attacked in the Czechoslovak Parliament both by the Socialists and by other landowners who had suffered the full rigours of the Land Reform Act, the Baron was not, or pretended not to be, pleased. I was involved, too, in two senseless lawsuits over the commission. Long before the matter was finally disposed of, all my initial exultation over a difficult task successfully performed had left me. Firmly and irrevocably I resolved that never again would I mix myself up with big business interests.

Let the reader not think I was ungrateful. I *was* grateful: first, to Providence which had miraculously rescued me from an almost hopeless position and, secondly, to Sir George Clerk and Jan Masaryk, without whose help my own efforts would have been fruitless. Very grateful was I, too, for my commission of £7400. True, it was £1500 less than the commission paid to my two colleagues both of whom had played a more or less passive rôle in the negotiations. True it is, too, that, as there was a minor rubber boom at the time, I might have profited by my special connections with the rubber industry to have a gamble with my money and to have increased my capital by fifty per cent within six weeks. Instead, I liquidated my overdrafts, paid my debts, and gave some presents to my friends. When all my bills were paid, there was little left. But I could breathe freely, and the sense of relief which my freedom brought me was a better tonic to my self-respect than the fattest bank balance in the world.

This was my last "giddy parergon" in Prague. In the autumn of 1925 I made a new arrangement with my directors. I gave up my position in the Anglo-Czechoslovakian Bank in Prague and accepted a new post as Manager of the Intelligence Department of the Anglo-International Bank in London. The Anglo-International Bank was the new name of the old Anglo-Austrian Bank, and the change in my position meant merely that I should be working in closer contact with our English directors. It also involved a smaller salary, but, as my new duties were defined as six months in London and six months abroad to be spent in touring all the States of Central Europe in which we had interests, I accepted with alacrity. It was a job which I realised would lead me nowhere, as far as my banking career was concerned. But it was a job much nearer to my heart than routine banking. It would titillate very pleasantly my capacity for Continental experience.

I gave up my house and packed my belongings. I spent the best part of a fortnight in paying calls and saying good-bye to my friends. I presented the bank with my German Boxer, the bravest, most faithful and most feared dog in Prague. I was fiercely glad to be leaving. For my own self-respect I had every reason to rejoice. I could look back on my Prague career with little satisfaction. I had frittered away my chances with a recklessness for which the post-war glory period is an unsatisfactory excuse. During my last two years I had lost all faith in myself and had resigned myself to a kind of composed despair. It was no consolation to reflect that others had gone through the same shattering post-war process. Yet when I look back to-day on the fate of my British and American colleagues I realise that there must have been something baleful in the atmosphere of those years or in this medieval city itself. Coulson, our Military Attaché, crashed financially. Norman, our Passport Control Officer, and Alan Winslow, most gallant of American diplomatists, ended their own lives. Neilson, another American, had died in tragic circumstances in Japan. These were men of my own age or younger. In 1919 they had been full of the zest of life.

Now I, the last of the immediate post-war batch, was leaving. I had suffered from a surfeit of sameness. It was high time to go. Yet when the actual moment came for my departure, I was sorry to leave. The beauty of the old city had always fascinated me, and the autumn tints of the trees intensified the haunting nature of its appeal. There was no city in the world in which I knew, and was known to, so many people. I had assisted at the birth of a new nation. I had seen its growing pains. I had watched it develop into a strong, sturdy child, fully capable of striking out on a path of its own. Czechoslovakia had been the one unqualified success of the new states of Europe, and with all their faults the peace-makers had never justified themselves better than by granting full independence and recognition to this Czech people who during three hundred years of oppression had preserved their own culture and their own language. The Czechs themselves had been extraordinarily kind to me, extraordinarily forbearing towards all my shortcomings. And now I was going right away out of their lives. During my last three nights my thoughts were tinged with a melancholy which was half regret and half remorse.

The day before I left, I had my first meeting with Mr. Ramsay MacDonald, who came to Prague with Lord Arnold to spend a few days as the guest of President Masaryk. He lunched and dined at the Legation one day, and I was present on both occasions. As Sir George Clerk introduced me, Mr. MacDonald drew himself up and, in the manner of Stanley to Livingstone, said very graciously: "Mr. Lockhart of Moscow, I presume."

Idiotically enough, the phrase stuck in my memory. It flattered me that after eight years my Moscow adventure should be remembered by one of the unco great. And it was with this Stanleyesque greeting singing in my ears and with a case of glass, presented by the Czechoslovak Government to the first Labour Prime Minister of Britain, under my arm that I steamed out of the city in which I had spent or wasted the six most important years of a man's life.

BOOK FOUR

☆

RETREAT FROM GLORY

"Ya perežil svoi želania;
Ya razliubil svoi mechty;
Ostalis mnye odni stradania,
Plody serdechnoy pustoty."
—Pushkin.

"I've lived to bury my desires;
To see my dreams corrode in rust;
Now all that's left are fruitless fires
That burn my empty heart to dust."
—Translation by Maurice Baring.

CHAPTER ONE

MY new job lasted almost exactly three years. On the whole it was a period fruitful in experience, if not in material rewards. My life in London was pleasant enough. My duties were to keep my directors posted about economic and political developments in Central Europe. I supplied them with a daily news bulletin. Once a month I compiled and edited a more ambitious monthly review which was sent to our friends and clients all over the world. I read all the Central European Press. I maintained a close contact with the Central European Legations in London. I conducted a regular correspondence with my business and political friends in the various Central European capitals. I ran all the bank's advertising. I had regular hours and ample opportunity for recreation.

True, my salary was all too small, and London alone would not have satisfied my ambition or my pocket. But there were compensations. There was still the lure of the Continent, and after a few weeks in the City I was longing to go abroad again. I was given frequent opportunities of satisfying my desire. The range of countries, too was extended, and in turn I visited Germany, Czechoslovakia, Hungary, Austria, Yugoslavia, and Italy at regular intervals on the bank's business.

Being now in daily contact with the London directors, I had a closer connection with the general policy of the bank. This now consisted in a cautious retreat from our Central European commitments and in an attempt to sell a part of our holdings abroad to local interests. The first step in this policy of contraction was the sale of our Italian branches to the Banca Italo-Britannica, and my first error as an editor was when I included the branches, after they had been sold, in an advertisement of our own bank. M. Manzi Fé, the managing director of the Banca Italo-Britannica, was annoyed, and I was requested by our directors to call on him in order to apologize for my mistake. I did not enjoy the interview, nor did M. Manzi Fé make it easy for me. He was pompous where a bigger man would have been gracious, and, although I am a poor hater, I disliked him. I had met him previously at the gaming-tables in Le Touquet and was not surprised when, later, his affairs became involved and he incurred the personal wrath of Signor Mussolini.

Another form of business, in which I played some part, was our attempt to raise minor loans in London for various Central European enterprises. We received numerous proposals of this sort, and my personal acquaintance with the various Central European Finance Ministers brought me into most of the negotiations. I enjoyed this kind of work, and soon after my transfer to London I made a very agreeable trip to Prague and Vienna with Sir Ernest Harvey, the senior partner of Allen, Harvey and Ross, the well-known bill-brokers, to investigate the prospects of two loans: one for a Czechoslovak power station and the other for the Wienerwald Railway. Harvey was a charming companion, who understood how to handle foreigners better than most Englishmen.

During that trip I learnt more from him about financial negotiations than I had acquired during my three years' banking experience in Central Europe. When we came back to London, we decided to recommend the loan for the Czech concern and to turn down the Austrian proposal.

Harvey then sent me off on an attempt to place the loan with various London banks and insurance companies. This was my first experience of direct dealing with the magnates of the City, and rather nervously I called in turn on Sir Henry Hambling, Lord Bethel, Sir Alexander Kleinwort, Sir Arthur Worsley, Lord Lawrence, and Mr. Cobb, the Treasurer of Lloyd's Bank. I was impressed by the rapidity with which these men made up their minds. Without any waste of words they turned down the proposition or they agreed to underwrite so much. As soon as the amount was agreed, no confirmatory letter was required. Their word was sufficient. It was an impressive contrast with the long palavers and legal documents to which I had been accustomed in Central Europe. Naturally, I met with many refusals, but Sir Henry Hambling of Barclay's Bank and Sir Alexander Kleinwort were kind, and with two good names on my list I had little difficulty in persuading others to complete it. We placed the loan, which was only a small one, in two days, but in the end the Czechs, who found the rate of interest combined with the 2% British stamp duty too high, backed out.

I was disappointed, but Harvey laughed. "You'll have lots of other opportunities," he said. "In business you must never show emotion over either a success or a failure. Come down to Aldeburgh for the week-end. We'll play some golf and forget all about loans." He was a fine type of English businessman and, when he died a year later, I felt that I had lost both a friend and perhaps an opportunity of bettering my own position. After his death I succeeded him as Austrian Consul-General in London, a post which in the past had been held by rich City magnates including Lord Rothschild, whose main duty was to subscribe largely to Austrian charities. In me the Austrians found a poor representative in the literal sense of the adjective. I filled this post, which imposed no burdens on me and which brought me no reward, from 1927 to 1929.

Later, I had several other loan ventures, notably, an attempt to raise a million pound loan for the city of Leipzig in conjunction with an Anglo-German syndicate of which Sir Robert (now Lord) Hutchison and Commander Kenworthy were the sponsors. Fortunately, as events have turned out, these ventures came to nothing. At the time there were too many American firms offering money in Europe for London to have much chance.

When the loan business petered out, I returned to my normal duties, which in any case were becoming more exciting. The bank's liquidation policy was beginning to take a definite form. Various proposals were on foot for the transfer of our Viennese branches to the Credit-Anstalt, for the sale of a block of our Czech shares to the Czechoslovak Government, and for the amalgamation of our own bank with the British Trade Corporation, a bank started by the British Government during the war and at this time mainly interested in Yugoslavia. In the spring of 1926 Spencer-Smith sent me off on an extended tour of Central Europe.

I left London on the third day of the general strike, and, as the railways were not running, I motored to Folkestone. It was a cheerless beginning to what was to prove a distressing tour, at least as far as business was concerned. My first visit was to Prague, where I arrived on a Friday morning and stayed with Sir George Clerk at the Legation. I had my old room with its windows looking out on to the Legation garden and on the Hradčany. The garden was then at the height of its glory, and I awoke every morning to the song of a hundred blackbirds and thrushes. On the Saturday we watched the Czechs beat the Indians at tennis in the Davis Cup and then in the late afternoon we went across to the Slavia ground to see the Arsenal, the famous English League team, play the leading Czech side at "soccer." For once the Englishmen won a clear-cut victory by five goals to one, and Sir George was well-pleased. On the Sunday we had a day's fishing in the Bohemian Forest.

During that week-end I met for the first time a young Russian girl, whom I shall call Jenia. She was then only nineteen, tall, fair, self-reliant and very beautiful. She was a cousin of the young officer who murdered Uritsky, the Head of the Petrograd Cheka, on August 30th, 1918. This murder had been followed by the attempt on Lenin's life in Moscow the next day. These outrages had provoked the still greater outrage of the Bolshevik raid on the British Embassy in which Captain Cromie, the British Naval Attaché, was shot down by the Red Guards. The raid had been followed by my own arrest and imprisonment in the Kremlin. And here in Prague I was now meeting the charming cousin of the young man whose rash act had nearly cost me my life. We became firm friends, and our Prague meeting was the beginning of an innocent attachment which has lasted to this day. Jenia's name will occur again in these pages. To-day, she is one of the best known actresses in Germany.

As far as my own enjoyment was concerned, there was everything in my surroundings to make me happy. Yet I was ill-at-ease. The truth was that I had arrived in the middle of several crises. The strike in England and Pilsudski's coup d'état in Warsaw had unsettled the Czechs. Worse still, the story of the proposed sale of our Austrian branches to the Credit-Anstalt had leaked out prematurely in Prague. The Austrian and Czech shareholders had been alarmed. There had been hostile criticism in the Press and even a small run on the bank. In Prague I had long talks with Beneš, Engliš, the Finance Minister, and Sonntag, the President of our Czech bank. Beneš, as usual, was unperturbed. We discussed my favourite topic of closer co-operation between the Succession States as the only preventive of economic disaster in Central Europe, and I suggested that as a first step the Succession States should appoint permanent Transport and Tariff Commissions to prepare the way for a freer exchange of goods. There should be no interference by the Great Powers. With certain reservations Dr. Beneš expressed himself in agreement with this proposal. As I was to visit Belgrade later, he gave me some very useful letters of introduction to the Yugoslav ministers. His kindness and his confidence reassured me considerably.

It was a different matter when I talked to Sonntag. This shrewd and far-seeing Czech had built great hopes on British financial co-operation in Central Europe. He had seen a great future for the Anglo-Czechoslovakian Bank. To him, as to all other Central Europeans, the name of the Bank of England was an open Sesame to unlimited credits. With experience of London banking methods had come a gradual disillusionment which was aggravated by the difficulty of his personal relations with the local English managers and staff. The sale of our Austrian branches, now on the verge of completion, appeared to him as a red light both for himself and for the Anglo-Czechoslovakian Bank. He was too shrewd a business man not to realise that the retreat from Vienna would be the forerunner of other retreats. I shared his apprehensions. I was even more depressed by my conversation with Dr. Hotowetz, the former Minister of Commerce, with whose ideas I had always sympathised. Hotowetz was an out-and-out free-trader as far as the Succession States were concerned. He gave me a pamphlet which he had recently written and in which he set out his proposals for the gradual return to free trade between the old component parts of the Austro-Hungarian Monarchy. He predicted with great assurance that the present system must lead to a catastrophe and expressed his fears that only such a catastrophe would teach wisdom to the chauvinists and economic nationalists.

While I was in Prague, the sale of our Viennese branches became an accomplished fact, and I was summoned to Vienna by M. Bark in order to prepare a suitable statement for the Central European Press. M. Bark, a born diplomatist, had conducted the negotiations with great tact and skill, and the sale had a better Press than might have been expected. But the depression among our Austrian staff was painful to witness. The liquidation meant not only the collapse of a rosy dream, but also the shattering of many idols. Directors and managers, who, a year or two before, had enjoyed the full confidence of our London directors, were now stamped with the stigma of failure. Worse still was the plight of the rank and file in a city like Vienna where the chances of re-employment were severely restricted. True, London behaved nobly in the matter of pensions and compensations, but the gloom of the employees was only partially relieved and for several days the long corridors of the bank building were filled with little groups of men who talked in whispers as though they were present in a house where some one had died. They were, in fact, assisting at a funeral—the burial of an idea which, sound enough in itself, had been drowned in a sea of over-optimism and over-expansion. It was my first experience of wholesale distress among men and women who had been my colleagues.

From Vienna I returned to Prague where I said goodbye to Sir George Clerk, who had just been appointed Ambassador to Turkey. His approaching departure left me with a feeling of profound personal loss. I owed him innumerable kindnesses. So long as he remained in Prague, I enjoyed a privileged position which was of the utmost value to me in the bank. Having advised me against accepting the bank's original offer of employment, he continued to take a personal interest in my career and to further my prospects in every legitimate way. I felt that I had lost my best friend in Central Europe. There were many others who shared my feeling, and the Czechs will count themselves fortunate if ever again they are sent a foreign diplomatist so able and so universally respected as Britain's first Minister to the new Czechoslovak Republic.

From Prague I went to Budapest. I had spent several pleasure week-ends there in previous years, but this was my first business visit to the Hungarian capital. During my long residence in Prague, I had naturally heard much about the Hungarians, and in that much there was little that was favourable. Like nearly all Englishmen I found the city enchantingly beautiful and the people warm-hearted and almost excessively hospitable. Society was dominated by the landowners and squires who still maintained a semi-feudal state. They were very different from the Austrian aristocracy, being more virile, more attractive, more Oriental, and more vigorously resentful of the wrongs which they had suffered under the Peace Treaty. They seemed, however, to be singularly indifferent to everything that had happened in the world since 1914. Although charming towards English people, I found their attitude towards the Czechs, the Rumanians, the Slovaks, the Croats and the Serbs, all of whom they professed to regard as a race of servants, distasteful and arrogant. They seemed to labour under the delusion that their pre-war rule had been popular, and, although I was and still am in favour of a fair treaty revision in Central Europe, I have never met a Hungarian who, in his secret heart, if, indeed, he does not demand it openly, does not understand by revision the return to Hungary of all the minority races who once composed the bulk of her pre-war population.

In every Hungarian squire I met I seemed to see the ghost of Tisza, that proud, romantic statesman and hero of a hundred duels, who foresaw the dangers that lay hidden in the reckless Austrian ultimatum to Serbia in July, 1914, and who opposed its despatch not only in the Crown Council in Vienna but in a memorandum addressed to the Emperor Franz Josef.

Since his death Tisza, who in 1918 was almost the first victim of the Hungarian revolution, has received full credit for his stand against the war. He had acted, however, solely in the interests of Hungary. So far from being liberal or broad-minded in his outlook, he was as relentless as any of his aristocratic compatriots in his attitude towards the minority races of his own country. Throughout the war he had continued to put Hungary first. I could never forget the story of Tisza's meeting with Conrad von Hoetzendorff, the one military genius produced by Austria, at Teschen during a critical moment of the war.

"Why," said Hoetzendorff, appealing to Tisza, "cannot you use your great gifts for the common cause and for the whole monarchy instead of for Hungary alone?" Tisza shrugged his shoulders. He was incapable of dishonesty, but he was equally incapable of changing his point of view. His horizon never extended beyond the broad flat plain of Hungary. In this respect his attitude was typical of that of every Hungarian squire. These first impressions of Hungarian intransigence were to be confirmed by subsequent visits to Hungary. They left me with an aggravated sense of the difficulties of the Central European problem.

Budapest itself I found enchanting. Like Prague, a river, the broad yellow Danube, divides it into two towns. Like Prague, too, it has its old town and its new town. Buda, the old town with its ancient citadel and its magnificent hill site, is the historical capital. Here since the beginning of history invading hordes from the East, of whom the Hungarians themselves were one of the first, have been broken on the rampart of European civilisation. Here two hundred years ago the Turkish invader was finally driven out, and Buda itself became a European stronghold. But the Eastern side comes right up to its base. Pest, the commercial capital, is true to the English meaning of its name. It is a creation of the last fifty years and a conglomeration of a hundred different architectural styles. It is as flat as a bowling green. Its buildings are a jazz symphony of ferro-concrete and stucco plaster. And in this semi-modern market-place the Orient holds sway. The business world of Pest is composed almost entirely of Oriental Jews, who bring to the business life of Hungary the financial genius of their race and an ability to save and make money which gives them enormous advantages over the Hungarians proper, who are too proud to trade and who in any case have always been the most lavish spenders among the nations of Europe. During the last fifty years the Jewish population has multiplied with great rapidity. The main physical bridge between the old town and the new was built by an English engineer. The political and racial bridge between the two populations has yet to be made. Its construction will demand greater ingenuity than any Hungarian statesman seems capable of at the present moment.

In spite of these forebodings I enjoyed every minute of my Hungarian visit. I made my first acquaintance with Hungarian gipsy music and found in it the same minor intoxication as Russian gipsy music excites in me. But I was growing older. Perhaps first loves are best. Without wishing to appear discourteous to my hospitable hosts I am bound to confess that the Hungarian gipsies seemed to me to lack something both of the abandon and of the subtlety which characterise the Russian tsiganes. Both, however, succeed in creating that delicious sense of melancholy and infinite longing which seem to spring from boundless plains and wide horizons.

I played golf with Raymond Parr, the First Secretary of our Legation, on a mountain course overlooking Budapest and met a Scottish compatriot in Goodwillie, the local professional. The course was poor, but the view was superb. I lunched with Sir Colville Barclay, our Minister, and dined with Rawlins, our Commercial Secretary. Both were helpful and forthcoming, but mixed their hospitality with some mild sarcasm about the number of Englishmen who were always floating round Central Europe for the bank. I had interviews with Dr. Bud, the Finance Minister, with Dr. Walko, the Acting Minister for Foreign Affairs, and with numerous representatives of Hungarian industry and finance. I did the round of the Budapest cabarets, finishing up in the early hours of the morning at the Admiral Bar, where various sprigs of the Hungarian aristocracy regaled me with sweet champagne, ham and eggs, and a tale of Hungary's woes. I spent an evening with the Hungarian representatives of my own bank on the famous Margaret Island. All the Hungarians were very friendly, very flattering, and very frank. They seemed to assume that every Englishman, including myself, must be Hungary's friend and a champion of Treaty revision in Hungary's favour. I discovered afterwards that their frankness towards myself was the result of a misunderstanding. I had a namesake who was then President of some Anglo-Hungarian Society at Oxford. I was no relation, but several of the Hungarian newspapers assumed that I was. Owing to this mistake, for which I was in no way responsible, I was received with open arms.

My most interesting conversations were not with Hungarians, but with two Englishmen, Sir William Goode and Harry Siepmann. I had met both of them during my previous visit to Budapest, but this was the first occasion on which I had any serious discussion with them. Both were remarkable men. Billy Goode, the son of a missionary in Newfoundland, had had an extraordinary career. As a young man he had gone to sea and had then drifted into journalism. He made his name in the Spanish-American War during which he represented the Associated Press on Admiral Sampson's flag-ship. His work attracted the attention of Sir Arthur Pearson, the British newspaper proprietor, and he came to England. His journalistic posts included the managing editorship of the *Standard* and the news editorship of the *Daily Mail*. During the war he had helped Mr. Hoover to organise relief for Belgium. He had been British Director of Relief at the Peace Conference. In 1920 he had been sent to Vienna as Chairman of the Austrian Section of the Reparation Commission. At that moment he was financial adviser to the Hungarian Government, a post which he has held for over ten years. He was then a man in the early fifties. He had written books and short stories and had knocked about most of the queer corners of the world. His greatest asset was his knowledge of human nature which, backed by a shrewd judgment of affairs, enabled him to handle both men and situations with great adroitness. In Budapest he had established himself in a suite in the Ritz Hotel, where daily he held a minor court. For all foreigners he was the best approach to Count Bethlen, whose confidence he enjoyed in a remarkable degree. Doubtless, he had cultivated it, for Goode was too shrewd a man not to realise that Count Bethlen was by far the ablest of the Hungarian ministers.

A dinner with Billy Goode was an experience not to be missed or forgotten. Better than most men he understood the value of food and drink to the successful prosecution of propaganda. But a private conversation was even more entertaining. Heavily built, clean-shaven, with broad forehead and firm jaw, he looked slightly forbidding until his eyes began to twinkle. As they twinkled often, one's first feeling of awe soon vanished. He had a breezy manner and an infectious laugh.

When I came into his room, he sat me down on a chair. On a table was a row of bottles. "Have a drink? No! Well, what can I do for you?" I began to put a few tentative questions about the financial situation in Hungary and about the prospects of our bank. He cut me short and then in a series of quick, jerky sentences in the manner of Mr. Jingle he began an exposé of the whole Central European situation. As he talked, he walked up and down the room in jerky strides, flicking the ash from an endless chain of cigarettes. "Just off to Geneva with Bethlen to-morrow. No time deal with situation. Government finances good. Commercial situation bad. Like you meet Bethlen. But not possible now. You understand. H'm, great man, Bethlen. Very reasonable. Clear vision. Only Hungarian with patience. H'm. Have a drink? No. Your bank. H'm. These English bankers. They mean well. But they don't understand this part of the world. Never will. Why should they? Bethlen too good to them. Your bank. H'm. Well, they've made a mess of things. They'd better clear out. All wrong Bank of England being mixed up in a private bank. Whom have you seen? Want to see Walko? Miss Vaughan"—a half-right wheel and a sudden jerk towards his secretary—"ring up Dr. Walko and ask him when he can receive Mr. Lockhart. No, stop. Dine with me to-night. I've half-a-dozen Ministers, and Walko's coming. But Bethlen's the man. See Bethlen next time."

There was more in the same strain. At the end I was a little dazed, but, when I began to sort out this conversational jig-saw puzzle, I realised that it contained a mine of valuable information and sound judgment. When I got to know him better, I soon discovered that behind this jerky exterior lay a very penetrative mind and that both his advice and his predictions were rarely wrong. In those days his was a name to conjure with in Hungary, and on my future visits to Budapest his suite in the Ritz was my first port of call. A big-hearted man, he has never promised a favour which he has not fulfilled. He was and is a very loyal friend to the Hungarians, for he has never allowed his job to interfere with his judgment, has never encouraged exaggerated Hungarian ambitions, and has indeed restrained more than one Hungarian minister from committing serious indiscretions. Hungarians, who have a passion for creating statues to English politicians who have helped their cause, owe and will always owe a monument of gratitude to Sir William Goode.

Harry Siepmann was the exact antithesis to Goode. Where Billy talked freely, Harry was like a Sphinx. Even when one won his confidence, he talked in a whisper. But the talk was always very much to the point. I think that he wilfully cultivated a cynical exterior in order to hide the idealism which lay within. A former official of the British Treasury, he was then the Bank of England's representative in the Hungarian National Bank. He took his job very seriously and did it remarkably well. He, too, was very pessimistic about English banking in Central Europe and disliked the Bank of England's connection with our bank. He was then engaged in elaborating Mr. Montagu Norman's latest scheme for closer co-operation between the Central Banks of the world. When, later, this admirable plan came into fruition, Harry was appointed head of the new foreign section of the Bank of England. To-day, this brilliant young man, still an enigma even to his friends and a surer receptacle for secrets than any safe, presides over the coming and going of Mr. Norman's private diplomatic corps.

CHAPTER TWO

MY conversations with Goode and Siepmann left me still very depressed about my own future. Belgrade, which was the next capital on my list, provided an excellent antidote. I like primitive peoples and primitive cities, and both the Serbs and Belgrade were primitive enough to satisfy all my desires. Belgrade was then in a transition stage from a Balkan village to a Middle West American town. After centuries of battling the people were at last free to build. Twelve-storey blocks rose in a night beside a hovel. One part of the street would be paved with asphalt. Two hundred yards ahead was a cobbled wilderness full of ruts and holes. Motoring was possible only with an old-type of Ford and then only in an open car. The dominating note in the architecture was the King's Palace, which looked like a cheaply built German railway station. The city had only three hotels. A night in one dictated an immediate change to one of the others. When one had stayed in all three, a flea-bag in the open air was an obvious choice.

The Serbs, however, were jolly buccaneers with the priceless quality of guts. A nation which in the heat of a Belgrade summer can breakfast off slivowitz is not to be despised in these days. and, if ever Italy makes the mistake of going to war with Yugoslavia, I shall put my money on the Yugoslavs. Admittedly, the country, unripe for democracy, was governed with strangely un-European methods. The Skupština, which I visited, was more like a monkey-house than a Parliament. I heard, too, sinister tales of ministerial corruption, and certainly justice in the commercial courts was non-existent. Nevertheless, the government machine, based on a magnificent army, worked well enough. I could not help feeling that all these defects were merely the infantile diseases of a healthy, virile child. True, from the ministers whom I visited I heard much the same criticism of the English as I had heard in Prague, Vienna and Budapest. Here, however, the criticisms were levelled at the British Trade Corporation, which was accused (1) of not understanding the necessity of giving credits and (2) of having given its industrial advances to the wrong people. Obviously, the British had not understood how to oil the wheels of the ministerial chariots. Indeed, the Finance Minister told me that the bank was in a hopeless situation. As my own bank was shortly to amalgamate with the British Trade Corporation, my apprehensions regarding my own prospects were not dispelled.

In Belgrade I added one rich adventure to my experience of Central European night-life. The city offered little in the way of distraction except the usual string of cabarets of the Viennese style. Here, however, the entertainment was poorer and the interior more sordid. The artistes, too, were older and more jaded than those of Vienna, Prague, and Budapest. Belgrade, in fact, was the magnet for those unfortunates, who were too old or too incompetent to obtain an engagement in more civilised capitals. There was no glamour and no romance about a Belgrade Nachtlokal. To a Serb a woman was a woman and a drink a drink. Both cost money and both had to be bought as cheaply as possible.

Together with an English friend I did the usual tour of the Belgrade cabarets. We finished up at the Luxor, an underground establishment off the Kralja Milana, which with Knez Mihalova forms the main street of Belgrade. In a long narrow room with a bar at one end and tables against the sides a Hungarian orchestra was playing selections from "Zigeunerbaron." There were not more than half-a-dozen guests, and most of them were Serbian officers. Their behaviour was exemplary. In a corner by the bar nine or ten rather jaded and heavily rouged girls sat yawning and smoking cigarettes. They were the Animierdamen or dancing-partners. They looked thoroughly bored. The place reeked of patchouli. The atmosphere, aggravated by the heat of a Belgrade summer night, was stifling. As we came in, there was a buzz of activity. The proprietor, followed by a train of waiters with greasy napkins, advanced to meet us. He bowed obsequiously. The English milords would have champagne and girls. All that was best was at their disposal. For champagne there was real Roederer costing only 500 dinars (about £2) a bottle. As an amusing companion he could recommend Liesl, who had just arrived from the "Parisien" in Vienna. The orchestra was at our command. This servility was a tribute to the stability of the English pound. After the Americans the English were the most delectable guests of any Central European Nachtlokal proprietor.

We surrounded weekly to the French champagne. We invited Liesl to join our table, and Toni, the leader of the orchestra, shuffled across the room to play before us. A swarthy Hungarian Jew with thick, purple lips and Mephistophelian eyebrows, he was one of the ship-wrecks of Central European night-life. His soft dress-shirt was yellow with drink stains. Probably alcohol had brought him down to his present condition. Liesl told us that when he cried his tears were brandy. Until he began to play, he filled me with nausea. The man, however, had music in his soul and could make his violin sob. Liesl sang to us and, indeed, to the whole room. She had only one song: "Jetzt zuende ich mir ein kleines Zigarettchen an." She sang it boldly with arms akimbo, and, when the room applauded, she repeated it. Her voice sounded as if she herself had never stopped smoking since her childhood. Yet there was something essentially Viennese about her performance which made it not unpleasant. The bottle of champagne was followed quickly by another. In turn we danced with her. Liesl had succeeded in creating what the Germans call "Stimmung."

We had been in the place about an hour, when suddenly there was a violent commotion at the entrance, and two huge men swaggered into the room. The first, my friend whispered to me, was a Belgrade police official in mufti. But it was the second man who held my attention. He looked more like a bull than a man. He seemed to have no neck, and his huge shaven head stood out like a cannon ball on his massive shoulders. He had a chest like a stallion's front. His legs were like tree trunks. His eyes flashed with a villainous fire. But it was his hands which fascinated me. They were gnarled, immensely strong, and as large as hams. He was, I think, the most powerful-looking man that I have ever seen.

His arrival created a depressing silence. The waiters deserted us. Toni went back to his orchestra. The girls in the corner whispered and shivered. Liesl became suddenly grave. "Be careful," she said. "That is 'Luna,' the famous Komitaji leader. He comes from the Macedonian frontier and fights against the Bulgarian Macedonians. He is as strong and as brave as a lion. When he's in a good temper, he's not so bad. When he's angry, God help you. He's killed twenty-five men with his own hands and is proud of it." It was more or less true. Fortunately, "Luna" was in a happy mood and already well lit with alcohol. He tossed down two glasses of slivowitz, ordered champagne, brought all the girls to his table, tossed a hundred dinars to Toni and told him to play dance music till he dropped. Obviously, he was a gentleman who took his pleasures grandly.

Reassured by his good humour, my friend took the floor with Liesl. "Luna" followed his example. The proprietor rubbed his hands. An evening which had started badly promised to end with a profitable sunrise. Then came a startling moment. I was dancing a Viennese waltz with Liesl. "Luna" was doing a dance of his own invention—a kind of kitchen lancers in which he swung himself and his partner round in furious circles. Just when the dance was at its height, we collided. I do not know how it happened. I must have caught him off his balance. But, as I was hurled against a pillar by the contact, the eighteen stone of "Luna" crashed to the ground. He picked himself up with an oath and ambered towards me with hands outstretched, head bent low and murder in his eyes. With the speed of a falling star Macaulay's lines flashed through my mind. This was not the stately stride of the "great Lord of Luna" but it was formidable enough. Horatius would have had no chance against this giant, and I was not in Horatian mood. With a yellow fear in my heart and my best smile on my face I advanced to meet him. At that time I knew not a word of Serbian, but a happy instinct inspired me. I bowed gravely and said to him in Russian: "I speak no Serbian. I am English. Please forgive me for my clumsiness." I do not know how much he understood, but he caught the word English. The murderous look transformed itself with a broad grin. "Englez!" he roared. "The Englezi are my country's allies and my friends. You will drink with me." Before I knew where I was, he had embraced me warmly on both cheeks. He dragged me over to his table. He came over to our table. We drank again: toasts to England, to Yugoslavia, to "Luna," and, finally, to the confusion of the "bloody Italians." "Luna" did not like the Italians. We had nothing against them, but we drank the toast all the same. For the rest of the night my one apprehension was how we could get away without offending "Luna." Fortunately, slumber overcame him, and, as the giant slept, we paid our bill and crept out into the daylight.

The story has a sequel. Three years ago "Luna" was travelling down to Nish. As he was leaving the station, a customs officer stopped him. On account of the Macedonian outrages, the Yugoslavs keep a strict lookout for bombs and other engines of terrorist destruction. As a loyal Yugoslav citizen, "Luna" took offence. "You swine," he said. "You don't know me. You ask me, 'Luna,' to open my luggage. I'll show you." Out went the huge hands. Another victim was to be added to the list of the throttled. But before the death-grip closed, the terrified official drew his pistol and by a lucky aim shot "Luna" through the heart. It is perhaps a tribute to the respect and awe in which "Luna" was held that, although the official had acted strictly in self-defence, the Yugoslav Courts condemned him to three years' imprisonment.

After ten days in Belgrade, during which I saw most of the ministers and politicians, I left for Zagreb. I carried away with me one concrete business offer: a polite intimation from M. Perič, the Minister of Finance, that, if the Bank of England cared to make an offer of a loan, the Yugoslav Government would consider it favourably. The attitude was typical and, although it gave me a quiet laugh, it impressed me more favourably than the hat-in-hand method of other money-seeking nations. In their self-reliance and utter indifference to foreign opinion the Serbs stand alone among the nations of Central and South-Eastern Europe.

CHAPTER THREE

AFTER the heat of Belgrade I was glad to escape to the comparative seclusion of Zagreb, the capital of Croatia. The city had grown since I was there in 1922 with the Moscow Art Theatre. It had now a large modern hotel with bathrooms. Halfway between Belgrade and Vienna, it had the culture and civilisation of its geographical position. The Croats, in fact, are a charming people, more cultured than the Serbs but lacking some of the Serbian virility and ruthlessness. In Belgrade I had seen ministers and officials. In varying degrees they supported the existing régime and the domination of the Serbs. Here in Zagreb I met the opposition, including Stepan Radič and other leaders of the Croat Peasants' Party. They were earnest and sincere men, perhaps a little unpractical and difficult to handle. Radič, in particular, was an extraordinary figure, a kind of Slav Gandhi with a corpulent body and a round head. At this time he was almost stone-blind. One of his admirers showed me a photograph of him in bathing-dress. Had I wished to do him a bad turn, I should have circulated that photograph among his followers. Radič in a bathing costume was not an impressive figure.

Nearly all the Croats had grievances against the Belgrade administration. They considered themselves the intellectual and social superiors of the Serbs. They resented the fact that their officers received no high commands in the army and that the best places in the Government offices and in diplomacy were reserved exclusively for Serbs. But they were not then a disloyal opposition. I do not think that they are a disloyal opposition today. Their loyalty to the Yugoslav state is perhaps a matter of necessity determined by their hate and fear of the Italians and by their detestation of their former Hungarian masters. Tactfully handled, they would be excellent and valuable subjects of King Alexander. Tact, however, is not a Serbian characteristic, and it is one of the tragedies of post-war Central Europe that these two fine races, speaking the same language and sharing the same military qualities of courage and endurance, should have drifted farther apart instead of welding together.

In Zagreb I had some banking business to do. My bank had an interest in the Croatian Discount Bank, and here, too, various schemes for amalgamations were under consideration. My job was to ascertain and report on the real attitude of the Croats towards these proposals. These business connections made me several friends including Stanko Sverljuga and his charming wife. Sverljuga, who was then managing director of the Croatian Discount Bank, became later Yugoslav Minister of Finance. His wife, who speaks excellent English, is to-day Lady-in-Waiting to Queen Marie. Cultured and amazingly well-read, they were, I think, the nicest people that I met during my ten years in Central Europe. Both have always been very good friends to England and to Englishmen.

To Sverljuga I owe my introduction to a whole host of charming Croatian friends who took an almost American delight in showing me the glories of their beautiful country. Their hospitality, too, was truly Slav in its lavishness, and I remember for more reasons than one many a pleasant evening in a Croatian orchard, where I was made to sample the new wine, or at the Mandalay Club where Mažuranič, the son of the famous Croat poet, made a speech of welcome to me in ten different languages including old Slavonic and Latin. Sometimes, the hospitality was more than I could stomach, and one luncheon, given by a Croat baron, laid me out for three days. The menu began with caviare followed by a heavy vegetable soup and proceeded through twelve courses, including baked carp, a Croat meat pasty, veal cutlets, roast pigeon, cold meats, salads, a vegetable cheese entrée, a jam tart, strawberries and cream, and Croatian butter cheese, to coffee and brandy. As every dish was prepared in a special Croatian way for my benefit, I had to taste them all. This, too, on a blazing day in mid-June.

There is one more debt which I owe to Stanko Sverljuga—my introduction to the Krka. This delectable Slovene stream runs through a tiny village, almost fairylike in its spotless cleanliness, 1000 feet above sea-level at the foot of the Julian Alps. Although it lies so high up, the countryside was a riot of colour with rich crops and vines on that June day when I first visited it. Except for the local Catholic priest and the village doctor, the villagers were peasants, and friendlier, simpler people I have never met in all my travels. Like most mountaineers they were men of magnificent physique. My gillie, a weather-beaten old warrior, stood as straight as a young birch. Neither summer heat nor winter cold kept him indoors, and at sixty he could still walk his fifteen miles a day. The river itself was a dream water, and, when I grew tired of catching fish, I lay on the bank and read my book, reserving my strength for the evening rise which I had been told was famous. It was as good as it was said to be, and, when I stopped, I was ashamed both of the size and number of my catch.

Supper in the little wooden inn was a glorious meal. My throat was parched, and fresh trout, delicious boiled potatoes, and home-made bread and butter were washed down with copious draughts of local white wine. The meal was accompanied by a marvellous serenade of shepherds' pipes and crooning violins and part-singing. Not even in Russia have I heard more pleasant music than the voices of those Slovene peasants floating through the open windows from the moonlit valley below. Over coffee we joined forces with the village fire brigade which was celebrating its annual dinner. As the wine was passed round, tongues were unloosened, and I heard horrible tales of Slovene persecution by the Italians in Istria and the other parts of Slovenia which Italy had acquired under the rapacious Peace Treaty. Their recital stirred flames in the slumbering eyes of these hardy mountaineers, and in a flash I understood more clearly than from any military text-book how an Austrian army, seemingly torn by racial dissensions, had rolled back the Italians at Caporetto. To-day, Italian imperialism has done more to weld Croats, Slovenes, and Serbs into one Yugoslav nationality than the wisest statesman could have done in fifty years. As we rose to go, the village doctor, an old gentleman of sixty, who had put on an antiquated and very shiny dinner-jacket for the occasion, stood up and raised his glass: "Brothers," he said, "Engleska zivela." "Long live England," came a rousing chorus from the fire-brigade. England was very glad to be alive, but she slept most of the way back to Zagreb, which was perhaps just as well. For, in the dark, the Croat chauffeur took the hair-pin bends with a disregard for human life which was terrifying in its callousness. Since then I have revisited my Slovene retreat on several occasions. Its charm has never palled. I know no place which so fully satisfied in my own heart the sentiment in Byron's words:

> *I live not in myself, but I become*
> *Portion of that around me; and to me*
> *High mountains are a feeling, but the hum*
> *Of human cities torture....*

And here, if ever I can free myself from the bondage of my city existence, I shall come every summer to write my books and to fish in those clean, pellucid Slovene waters. I count myself an impartial witness of the European scene. I am what Mr. Lytton Strachey would have called a frigid observer of the golden mean, but in my affections Slovenia has her place among the lovely, everlasting things, and till I die I shall be a champion of Slovene rights and Slovene culture. I am not the only Scot who has found a second home in this quiet shelter. Colonel James Blair, who won the St. George's Cross in Russia in the Great War and who was the most modest brave man I have ever met, came to Belgrade as Military Attaché after the war. He, too, was a great fisherman, and, when he died, he was buried at his own request in the heart of Slovenia.

From Slovenia I made a tortuous route home via Vienna, Prague, and Berlin. In the German capital I spent a week seeing officials and investigating economic conditions. I made copious notes of my conversations. To-day, in the light of all that has happened, they seem as stale and as dead as the period to which they refer. Berlin had still an air of prosperity and even of extravagant gaiety. Night-life flourished. The Adlon, where I stayed, was packed with foreigners, mostly German-American Jews. Everything was very expensive. Everything, including human life, was to be bought and sold. Vice flourished almost unchecked. Nowhere in the world had I seen such coarse men and such hard women as those who then thronged the roof garden of the Eden and the gaudy haunts of the Kurfuerstendamm. Morality had sunk to its lowest ebb, and the general atmosphere was replete with the same recklessness of the future which heralded the Russian revolution in St. Petersburg in February, 1917. Above all, the new type of financier who then flourished disgusted me. The Bourse seemed chock-full of Emperors Jones: men who shared that hero's view that the world is divided into big stealers and little stealers and that while the little stealers get put in quod the big stealers "are made Emperors and given a place in the Hall of Fame when they croak." Only the permanent officials and the soldiers of the Reichswehr seemed to retain the German characteristics of hard work and self-respect. But the officials, under-paid and over-tired, seemed depressed. Locarno had been signed a year before, yet already Stresemann was sick with hope deferred. Serious people were pessimistic. Their pessimism was no blacker than my own.

Not that I was unhappy in Berlin. Here I found old friends— the Hickses, Colonel Thornhill, Colonel Thelwall, the brilliant commercial Counsellor of our Embassy, and—Jenia. Above all, Jenia. In the evenings, when my work was done, I avoided the usual round of senseless hospitality and went out instead with her. I watched her dance at the Opera House and supped with her afterwards at Foerster's, the Russian restaurant, where we ate seledka and borsh and listened to Gulescu, the Rumanian violinist, an old friend of pre-war Russian days. And while he played to us and for us, Jenia told me the story of her life as a Russian refugee in Berlin, of her first attempts to get a job as a dancer, of her encounters with impresarios and film-directors. They were unpleasant stories. She had begun as a dancer in a cabaret of questionable repute. But her belief in herself and her own sense of self-respect had lifted her out of the ruck, and she had come through unscathed, surer of herself and with her courage undiminished. On many occasions I had admired the amazing pluck and adaptability of Russian women in exile. Jenia was a shining example.

One afternoon we took a car and did a round of all the little restaurants and cafés which I had frequented when I was a student in Berlin more than twenty years before. It was a melancholy resurrection which appealed to my mood of the moment. Many of them had disappeared in the stress of the war. The little café near the Potsdammer Station, where I had once drunk innummerable Krugs of Munich beer with Frederick Wile, the *Daily Mail* correspondent, had been replaced by the giant structure of the Vaterland Café. But Kempinski's was still there. In those days it represented the limit of my extravagance—a place to be visited once a month. Now it seemed shoddy and incredibly middle-class. In the cool of the evening we drove out to Gross-Lichterfelde and stopped at Ringstrasse No. 40, where in pre-war days William Tilly, an Australian professor, assisted by a vast family of sons and daughters, had run a remarkably successful institute for English students of German. It had been the scene of my first calf love. The daughter of a German naval officer, who lived next door, had captured my affections, and for six months I had been her devoted admirer, carrying her shoes to her dancing class and sending her pressed flowers in notes written in my best handwriting and containing youthful poems freely borrowed from Heine. The Institute had been broken up by the war, and the house was now divided into flats. But the little shoemaker's shop in the basement next door was still there, and the shoemaker's wife gave me all the news. The Tilly family had been scattered all over the world. Tilly himself, who had done more for Anglo-German friendship than any man living, had been interned during the war. He is now Professor of Phonetics at Columbia University. My German naval officer was dead, but the daughter was still alive and living in the district with her mother. She had never married. For a moment I examined my conscience. Then I reassured myself. My conduct had been irreproachable. Nevertheless, I broke off the conversation and went quickly back into the car. Jenia laughed: "Are you stolid Englishmen then so romantic?" "No," I said, "it's only our incurable egotism." Perhaps it was true.

On my return to England I wrote a long report on my tour. Doubtless, it was an excellent report, but I have not bothered to resurrect it. There have been thousands of excellent reports on Central Europe. Some are in the archives of the League of Nations and the Foreign Office. Others, like my own, are gathering dust in the filing cabinets of London banks. None has had any influence on Central European policies or has retarded for one instant the process of European disintegration.

After my labours I was given a welcome leave of absence which I spent, first at Sandwich, where I stayed with the Rosslyns and played my first game of golf with the Prince of Wales, and later in Scotland, where I recaptured the memories of my boyhood by fishing again the Speyside burns.

My Scottish holiday was cut short by a telegram from the bank asking me to return. The amalgamation of my bank with the British Trade Corporation had now received the blessing of the Bank of England and was about to become an accomplished fact. My presence was required in order to secure the most favourable notices possible in the British Press. This task accomplished with more success than the venture perhaps deserved, I resigned myself to a long period of humdrum routine in the Intelligence Department of our Head Office in London. It seemed an important moment for taking stock of my own position. Actually, the amalgamation did not affect our staff very much. We, the old Anglo-Austrian Bank, had really taken over the British Trade Corporation, and, although one or two B. T. C. directors joined our board, my own directors remained in full control. Yet my own prospects seemed gloomy. So long as my present job lasted, it was at any rate bread and butter and not unpleasant bread and butter. But I had not very much faith in the future of the bank itself. Leading City bankers with whom I discussed it were of the same opinion.

When I reviewed the assets and liabilities of my own position,

I found it hard to show a favourable balance. I had a wide and practical general knowledge of the politics, geography and general economics of the Central European states. I knew personally and had the entry to a large number of the leading politicians and business men. I spoke half-a-dozen languages with considerable fluency. I had begun to dabble in journalism and had written serious articles on Central European politics and personalities which had appeared in such reputable periodicals as *The Edinburgh Review, The Fortnightly,* and *The New Statesman.* Two or three times a year the leading page of the *Times* was open to my views on some aspect of Central European affairs. For the same newspaper I wrote the stock obituaries of prominent Central European personalities (still living, of course) and had a certain journalistic thrill from enlisting the co-operation of men like Dr. Beneš in the preparation of their own death-notices. For the *Times,* too, I wrote a number of Central European fishing sketches which brought me many interesting letters. My credit was good in almost every restaurant and cabaret in Central Europe. None of these assets in itself provided a golden opening to a new career. On the other side of the ledger were my debts, which were again mounting up with startling rapidity. On the purely human side my situation was not much better. I had been more or less separated from my wife and boy, who were living with my father and mother in Berkshire. This separation was caused, partly by the accident and nature of my work and partly by my own restlessness. My own conduct had wavered with a jazz-like irregularity between rigid asceticism and undisciplined self-indulgence. I was not, I concluded, a very satisfactory person either to myself or to any one else.

My introspective mood was shattered by a bomb-shell which burst unexpectedly over our bank one September morning. The announcement of our amalgamation of the British Trade Corporation had been followed by startling news from Belgrade. The Belgrade branch of the British Trade Corporation had lost about £100,000 through the fraud of their Serbian manager. Without the authority of his head office he had given a guarantee of £100,000 to a Serbian gentleman named Vojnovič. The guarantee had been used almost to the full amount. As this transaction was disclosed after the amalgamation, my bank had to bear the loss. The Serbian manager had tried to blow his brains out and was lying dangerously ill in hospital. His assistant had fled to Greece. On the first examination the affair looked black. The only asset possessed by Vojnovič against this formidable advance was a doubtful title to a timber concession in Montenegro. No one knew for certain if the forest even existed. Some one would have to go out to Belgrade immediately to unravel the mystery. On the same morning I was sent for by my directors. They explained the situation to me. They wanted some one to safeguard their interests in Belgrade and to report on the possibilities of recovering the loss either by acquisition of the forest or by legal action. Could I leave at once?

I could. Here was a cure for the depressing monotony of city life—a concrete battle of wits against government officials and lawyers and the prospect of an exciting adventure in Montenegro, one of the few European countries which I had never visited. Exultantly I packed my bags, and on October 16, 1926, I left for Zagreb. The affaire Vojnovič was to occupy my whole time and attention for the best part of the next twelve months.

CHAPTER FOUR

TO those who have had financial dealings in the Balkans the story which follows will present no novel features. To the less initiated it may serve as a warning. To me it was like a tale from the Arabian Nights—more vivid and more delightful because it was a personal experience.

On my way to Belgrade I stopped at Zagreb in order to consult Sverljuga and the timber experts of the Croatian Discount Bank. Their views were not encouraging. Sverljuga had not a high opinion of the British Trade Corporation. Like every one else in Central Europe he hinted politely that the English did not understand Central European finance. He had heard of Vojnovič before. We should find him a difficult customer. Forests in Montenegro were like castles in Spain, but they were more dangerous. Ulmansky, his timber expert, had just returned from a forest close to Vojnovič's reputed forest. He had been called there suddenly because the forest manager and his three assistants had been attacked by robbers. One had been killed. The other had been severely wounded. In Sverljuga's opinion the whole affair was a black business into which much good money might easily be thrown after bad.

On reaching Belgrade I found his pessimism fully justified. Here I met Dickson, the former general manager of the British Trade Corporation and now a director of the Anglo-International Bank, with whom I had been instructed to co-operate. At the same time I was to report independently to London. In the circumstances our co-operation demanded considerable tact and good-will on both sides. Fortunately, I liked him from the first moment. Then about fifty-four, he had spent most of his life in the

Near East, which he knew intimately. Serious in manner and very hard-working, he had an expert knowledge of the technique of banking. His principles were of the highest. He was scrupulously fair in his judgments. In spite of a somewhat cold exterior he was a kind and generous man who, when drawn out, could expand and talk with learning and understanding on other subjects than banking.

For days on end we negotiated with the lawyers and with Vojnovič himself. This gentleman, whose name in Serbian means "son of a warrior," was just what I expected him to be: a sturdy, bullet-headed Serb who talked big, but was not without brains. I guessed that he had been in many a tight corner before and would fight hard. The surmise was correct. He expressed his amazement that the Serbian manager had given the £100,000 guarantee without the authority of London. He had assumed that it was in order. In any case the English bank had done a splendid deal. His forest in Montenegro was the finest in Europe. It was worth a million pounds, half-a-million pounds—certainly not less than a quarter-of-a-million pounds—. He had spent the £100,000 on developing the concession. Give him another advance of £50,-000, and the English bankers would receive their money back with a hundred per cent profit.

As far as the legality of the guarantee was concerned, he was right. Our lawyers gave their opinion that there was nothing to hope from a law-suit. The bank could not evade responsibility for the illegal act of its manager. Meanwhile, I had seen most of the Yugoslav ministers and had received little satisfaction. They expressed their regret in courteous terms, but they saw no reason for any action by the government. It was not their fault that the bank had landed itself in this mess. It would have to extricate itself as best it could. Mr. Kennard (now Sir Howard Kennard), the British Minister and a staunch and hard-working champion of British commercial interests took privately very much the same view.

In the circumstances our only hope was to obtain from Vojnovič a mortgage on his Montenegrin concession. This, too, entailed long negotiations. Vojnovič's tactics varied from blustering aggression to smiling submissiveness. But he was always evasive and fought every inch of the way. The delays were tedious, but Belgrade was not without its compensations. The weather in that November was like the ideal English summer. The sun shone all day from a clear blue sky. The nights were cool and pleasant. In my interview with Voya Marinkovitch, the Yugoslav Foreign Minister, he had spoken in glowing terms of the Yugoslav army. On November 7th I had an eye-witness's view of its efficiency at the funeral of Marshal Poutnik, the hero of the Serbian retreat in the Great War. Not even in pre-war Germany have I seen finer marching or a more impressive body of troops. And, strangely enough, although the Serbians are a race of peasants, the officers were as smart as any British guards officer. In the early morning I worked hard at my Serbian, which with my knowledge of Russian and Czech I picked up easily. In the daytime I found amusement in studying the contrasts of human nature during the dialectical duels between Dickson and Vojnovič. In the evenings I went to the opera or the ballet or talked with Dickson. Thirty years before he had been Lord D'Abernon's private secretary in the days when this future ambassador was Governor of the Imperial Ottoman Bank. As a young man Lord D'Abernon (then Edgar Vincent) had gone to Greece. Six months later he was master enough of the language to write a Greek grammar which is still in use. At twenty-nine he was Governor of the Imperial Ottoman Bank and the most picturesque figure in the Near East.

Dickson, a good raconteur, had many stories of his former chief. Most of them referred to his capacity for quick decision and to his terseness of speech. On one occasion the manager of the Adrianople branch of the Ottoman Bank had been transferred to some more outlandish post. In despair he sought and obtained an interview with Lord D'Abernon in order to have the decision reversed. First, he stated that he had private business interests of his own in Adrianople which he could not neglect.

"Ça c'est *votre* affaire," replied Lord D'Abernon. Then, with much feeling, the unfortunate manager pleaded that his wife's health would not stand the change. "Ça c'est *son* affaire," was the laconic reply. Finally, the manager played his last card. He knew the business life of Adrianople better than any man living. His transfer would do serious harm to the bank's interests.

"Ça c'est *mon* affaire," said the young Governor, and the interview was ended.

I enjoyed my talks with Dickson. I enjoyed my work. I was very ascetic. There were, I thought then, worse places in the world than Belgrade.

At last, after three weeks of haggling, we succeeded in obtaining from Vojnovič a first mortgage on his Montenegrin forest. The next step was to ascertain (1) whether the forest existed, (2) whether Vojnovič's claim to it was valid, and (3) whether the timber could be worked at a profit. This meant a visit to Montenegro, and to Montenegro we set out. On the day on which the mortgage deed was signed, I was in Zagreb, having gone there to consult our Croat lawyers. I therefore arranged to make my own way to Ragusa, which was to be the starting-point of our expedition, and to meet Dickson there.

I left Zagreb on the evening of November 10th and, changing trains at Brod in the middle of the night, arrived by a quaint narrow gauge single track railway at Sarajevo at 1 P.M. on Armistice Day. Here I broke my journey for four hours. Sarajevo on Armistice Day was an emotional experience that could not be missed. With the enthusiasm of an American tourist I set out to "do" the sights. The sun was so hot that I took off my flannel jacket and carried it on my arm. There was a stillness in the air which produced in me that same uncanny feeling inseparable from all volcanic centres. The town itself, a symphony in blue and white with minarets towering needle-like against a background of green hills, seemed asleep. In the market-place cross-legged Slavs with "fezes" sat and smoked in silence. Others, immobile as Buddhas, watched their coffee simmering in little brass pots. Sarajevo, most Western of Mohammedan outposts, retains to-day the atmosphere of the East in a far higher degree than the remotest corner of the new Turkey. Here the men were philosophers. Only the women worked, and in the public washing place, through which ran a little stream, veiled harridans rubbed the coloured print pants of their husbands with pumice stone. They were fat and unattractive.

One lovely vision I did see—a young girl with Eton crop, print dress, long white gloves, modern shoes, and an intriguing black yashmak. She could not have been more than fifteen or sixteen. As she passed, the cross-legged philosophers looked up. Their eyes followed her slowly, but they registered neither approval nor disapproval. She was a symbol of that compromise between East and West which is overtaking even this last stronghold of Mohammedan conservatism. I felt, however, that the transition would be slow of accomplishment. At three I took an old-fashioned cab, roomier and more box-like than a London "growler," and drove out to the corner of King Peter's Street where the Archduke Franz Ferdinand was murdered. The spot is close to the bridge over the river, and a plaque, severely correct in language, indicates as much as decency permits Serbian approval of the deed, which provoked the World War and which may one day be the chief landmark in the collapse of Europe's world domination. The street was deserted. But for the presence of a solitary Serbian policeman I could have knelt down and prayed undisturbed. That evening, as my train drew out of the town, there was a glorious sunset, changing the blue and gold cupolas of the mosques to a soft saffron and flooding the green valley with a delicate pink light. If peace reigned anywhere in the world, it reigned that afternoon in Sarajevo.

Most people have made their first approach to Ragusa from the sea. I entered it from the east after a steep descent from the mountains. It was six-thirty in the morning, and the sudden vision of so much loveliness took my breath away. The blue stillness of the sea, the grey-white walls of this miniature and as yet unspoilt Venice, and the rows of solemn cypresses endeared the place to my heart at first sight. Sverljuga had said that the Dalmatian Coast would satisfy my sense of beauty more fully than any place I had ever visited. To-day, after many visits, I am prepared to agree with him. Nature has nothing more beautiful to offer than this mountain-walled strip of coast line, and the pearl of its loveliness is Ragusa.

Leaving my luggage at the hotel, I went out into the Stradon, the main street of the city. As I passed through the Porta Pile, a group of Dalmatian peasant women in their bright-coloured national costumes were swinging sturdily down the street. As I stood watching them, a priest passed me and, turning to the left, disappeared through an archway. I followed him and found myself in a cloistered garden with palms and orange and lemon trees heavy with fruit. In the centre of the garden path was a little fountain with a statue of St. Francis. Full of gratitude for so much loveliness, I went to Mass and then hurried out into the street in order to see as much of the town as I could in the limited time at my disposal. Until Napoleon captured it in 1812 and incorporated it in the kingdom of Illyria, the city had been an independent Republic. In 1814 it was given to Austria, who kept it until the end of the Great War. Now it had been restored to its original Croat owners. The inhabitants, mostly sturdy, handsome Slavs, retained the proud traditions of their ancient independence, but the glory of the architecture was Venetian. Almost every house was perfect. Almost nothing had changed since the sixteenth century. Another gate closed the south end of the street, and, passing through it, I came upon the fish market where a score of sun-browned fishermen were hauling in their nets. Before me, shimmering in the morning sun, lay Lacroma, once the island home of the ill-fated Emperor Maximilian of Mexico. Since then I have explored every corner of Ragusa. I have crossed over to Lacroma a score of times to watch the sunrise and the sunsets. But when I try to visualise the place, it is my impressions of that first November morning which return to me. Never have I passed two such perfect hours. When I first thought of time and looked at my watch, it was nine-thirty. At ten we were due to start by car for our Montenegrin forest.

We set out in a powerful Fiat along the old military road built by Marmont. On our right were the blue waters of the Adriatic, on the left the mountains, sinister and menacing in their volcanic barrenness. Between sea and mountain lay a narrow strip of fertile land planted with vines and olives. I lay back in the car and watched the scenery with thoughts far removed from the business which lay before me. The sun brought a new warmth to my heart, and I was at peace with the world. I liked these smiling Dalmatians, all devout Catholics, who smiled with rows of gleaming white teeth as we passed. They rode on donkeys. Seated between two packs, with their feet almost touching the ground, they looked gravely ridiculous.

After passing Castelnuovo, we came suddenly upon the Gulf of Cattaro. Under a Northern sky the Boka, with its grim, overhanging mountains and its dark, unfathomable waters, would look like the entrance to the valley of the shadow of death, but in the sunshine of the South the beauty of the panorama subdues the sense of awe and respect which an all-powerful Nature inspires in these volcanic regions. As we drove round the first bend of the gulf, we crossed a roaring torrent which hurled itself into the sea from a hole in the mountain. It was the mouth of one of those subterranean rivers which characterise this coast. The mountains seemed to close in on us. Here was a land where man seemed no larger than an ant. Somewhere above these 4,000 feet of precipice stood our forest.

As we approached the next village, I saw a group of men, supported by some twenty mounted gendarmes, standing by a small wooden bridge. They waved their arms, and we pulled up, not quite certain whether our reception was to be hostile or friendly. Then I caught sight of Vojnovič smiling rather sheepishly. The gentlemen with him were the Mayor of Risan and the Prefect of Cattaro, who had come to welcome us. The gendarmes had been sent by orders from Belgrade to ensure our protection from bandits if and when we made the ascent to the forest. We had arrived at our destination.

Risan, once a haunt and hiding-place of the Illyrian pirates, was the port and office headquarters of Vojnovič's timber concession. That gentleman showed us the sights with the assurance of a Roman Emperor. Here—he pointed to a wooden shed—was the sawmill where the timber was to be sawn. There was the rope railway which was to bring the logs down to the mill. He waved an arm towards the mountain-side. A succession of small scaffolds, rather like two telegraph poles with a plank across them stood out perilously on the rocky side of the precipice. I shuddered. It was a ramshackle affair which did not look strong enough to support a dead cat. These preliminaries ended, we formed into a procession and proceeded to Vojnovič's villa, where a magnificent luncheon had been prepared for us. A cynical thought that the food and wines set before us were part and parcel of the bank's £100,000 guarantee flashed through my mind and departed as quickly.

From the window my eye had already found a new attraction—a ruined Venetian township with a score of palazzi and deserted villas and campanile. It was Perasto. Here, in days gone by, the great Venetian and Croatian captains made their homes and built their palaces and churches. For, in the fifteenth and sixteenth centuries, the Croats under Venice were sailors worthy to be ranked with England's best. And, as the Boka furnished the best sailors in the Adriatic, so Perasto produced the best sailors in the Boka. They were a race not only of mariners but of fighters whose whole life was a battle against the sea and the Turks. To-day, the glory of Perasto has vanished with the glory of Venice. But the little village, nestling in the sun beneath the precipices of St. Elias, with its two little islands of St. George and the Madonna of the Rock standing out like two pearls on the black velvet of the water, is the gem of the whole Boka. The mighty mariners have gone to their last rest, but the Madonna herself is still worshipped by every true sailor, no matter what his origin.

The Madonna has a curious history. When the sirocco blows, the Boka can be very rough, and terrible is the toll it has taken in ships and in human lives. The entrance to Perasto is guarded by a narrow entrance called The Chains, so named because the inhabitants used to throw a barrier of chains across the channel in order to keep out the constant stream of pirates. Until the middle of the fifteenth century the island which the Madonna now graces was unknown. Indeed, it was only a submerged rock. One night, however, after a violent storm, a ship-wrecked mariner was found clinging to the reef with the miraculous Madonna in his hands. No one knew how the picture came to be there. From that day the Madonna has been the special guardian of all Catholic sailors. Her island has been built up piously with stones brought from far and wide by grateful sailors, and the Madonna herself, a beautiful painting of the early Renaissance period, is enshrined in a church surrounded by cypresses. Even to-day, every 15th of August, sailor pilgrims of every race and nationality come to pay her homage and to add a stone to her island home. The visit of Lord Beatty and the British Fleet in 1926 is still the chief event in the life of the modern Perastino.

All these facts (I have since verified them by numerous visits to the island itself) I obtained from the Prefect, a tiny little man in a threadbare frock-coat, while Dickson and Vojnović discussed the prospects of the timber concession. The ascent to the forest demanding a full day's time, we slept that night in Cattaro under the shadow of the mighty Lovchen, the black mountain which guards the fastness of Cettinje, the capital of Montenegro. Our hotel had no bathroom, but my bedroom had a loggia and from its balustrade I could pick oranges and pomegranates from the trees in the garden below.

The next morning we rose at six and drove by car by a wonderful and terrifying serpentine up the mountain behind Risan. Leaving the road at its highest point, we walked for about an hour until we were met by the foresters with midget ponies. My heart sank to my boots. Before us was a rough ascent which was more like a precipice than a slope. It looked uninviting enough for a man or for a pony alone, but for a man on a pony it seemed an uncomfortable approach to suicide. When I saw Jones, our timber expert and a giant of a man, mount and the pony go ahead as if he were carrying a feather, I plucked up my courage. I soon learnt the trick. All one had to do was to hold on to the saddle, to ease one's seat as much as possible, and to leave the rest to the pony. My own, a little lady called Brownie, was marvellous, picking her way with the agility of a mountain goat and never stumbling once. The sun was hot and the air as still as death, and by the time we reached the forest I was in a muck sweat. There *was* a forest—a large forest. Certification of this fact was the sole concrete result of our Odyssey as far as Dickson and I were concerned. For the rest we were dependent on the advice of our timber experts. We had no knowledge of the value or number of the trees. The beeches looked magnificent. The pines, we were assured, were as fine as any in Europe. As bankers, however, we had done our duty.

On our way home we stopped at the plateau where we had left our car and had a meal and quenched our thirst with excellent Dalmatian wine. Then we lay down on the grass and rested. Here we were on the old frontier of Montenegro and Austria. All around were rings of dismantled Austrian forts, one still mounted with armour platings weighing twenty tons and with large howitzers. The view over the Boka was superb, and, taking my copy of *Fleurs d'Ennui* from my pocket, I began to read again Loti's romance of Pasquala Ivanovitch. Fifty yards away was a tiny Montenegrin village, and on a flat stretch of grass before the village huts a band of boys and girls were dancing the "kolo," a dance which bears a faint resemblance to a Scottish reel. They were raggedly dressed and obviously very poor. There was a girl, with dark eyes and attractive colouring but with the thick ankles and sturdy legs of all Montenegrin women, who might have been another Pasquala. Loti had sat out on the mountain-side with his Pasquala, a little shepherdess, and to the chirrup of the cicadas had felt her heart beat against his hand. Loti must have been younger or less fastidious than I. My Pasquala scratched her head and looked as if she wanted a bath or a tin of Keating's.

My thoughts became more serious when Vojnovič came over to me and, pointing to an overgrown fissure in the ground in the opposite direction, said: "The village used to be over there." "What do you mean?" I asked. "Well, you see, there was an earthquake." We were in a district where earthquakes were an almost annual occurrence, and I marvelled at the courage of these mountaineers who danced gaily on the brink of a volcano. They reminded me sadly of Europe; only here the enemy was not self-seeking politicians and ruthless capitalists but Nature herself. When Nature was so chaotic, what else could one expect from man?

Our business was now finished. The next day was a Sunday, and, fearful lest the conscientious Dickson should wish to set out immediately on the long journey home, I rose at 6.30 and went to

Mass in a tiny chapel close to the Cattaro Cathedral. I did not wish to leave the Boka without making the trip over Lovchen to Cettinje. In an excess of business zeal I was equally determined not to be the first to make the suggestion. My prayers were answered. Over our morning coffee Dickson, who had worked like a hero, sat back in his chair and lit a cigarette. "It is a glorious day," he said. "Let us put off our return until to-morrow and go to Cettinje."

We made the trip by car on a wonderful and fearsome road built in an endless series of serpentines on the rocky side of Lovchen. On the way we passed a band of Montenegrins setting out on foot on their long trudge home. They were an extraordinary sight. As Champlain said of the Indians in Canada, their women were their mules. One old harridan carried a whole household compendium: a great sack of potatoes on her back, a couple of heavy kerosene tins slung across her shoulders on a pole, and a mass of carrots and onions hanging like a Samoan skirt from her girdle. With head bent forward until her back made a complete arch, she still had her hands free for her knitting. The men, picturesque, fierce-looking and splendidly proportioned, followed leisurely behind, idle but magnificent. They carried nothing. It was their established right. Montenegro, I decided, was a man's country.

All the way up the mountain-side we had a glorious view of the Boka and of the Adriatic. Near the head of the pass we stopped at Njegus, the ancestral village of the Montenegrin dynasty, and saw the house where Nikita, the last King of Montenegro, was born. It was little better than a peasant's cottage. But it was a mountaineer's home four thousand feet above sea-level. Farther on, an eagle soared above our heads, seeking God knows what prey among these barren burnt-out rocks. Our chauffeur waved an arm towards the summit of Lovchen. A stream issues from its side. Here Ivan Černojevič, the fifteenth century Barbarossa of Montenegro, watered his horses. According to Montenegrin legend he now sleeps in a cavern in Ivanograd, refusing to wake until the Turks are chased from Europe. The Turks are all but gone, but Ivan still sleeps. Here, too, is the grave of Vladika

Rada, the great Montenegrin poet and spiritual chief. During the war the Austrians, in the insane belief that the demolition of a grave can kill patriotism, destroyed the monument which marked the spot. In 1925 it was rebuilt and opened again with imposing ceremony by King Alexander of Yugoslavia, who himself is a grandson of King Nikita.

At the end of our ascent we came to a broad plateau with a view extending far into Macedonia and Albania and revealing the wide expanse of Lake Scutari. Cettinje itself was disappointing. Its glory has vanished with its independence. The administration is now entirely Serbian. The Legations of the foreign powers have been turned into government offices or hospitals. The British Legation is now a school. The poverty of the population is pitiful. Even in the days of Nikita the bulk of the young men emigrated to America and the parents eked out their scanty incomes with the remittances from these exiles. To-day, the war and the American immigration quota have put an end to this outlet, and the present generation lacks the initiative to break new ground. The Serbians have increased educational facilities, and to-day the young Montenegrin has only one ambition: to matriculate and to go to the University in Belgrade. Like the clans in Scotland after the Forty-Five he is being rapidly turned into a bourgeois. And like the kilt the Montenegrin national costume is disappearing.

Returning the same evening to Cattaro, we slept the night at our hotel, and the next day we motored to Spalato, covering the two hundred and fifty miles in ten hours and finishing up with a ghostly moonlight drive through the desolate Karstgebiet. We spent a whole day in this beautiful port. In the morning I explored the palace of Diocletian, the first wise man to discover the peaceful solitude of this enchanting coast. I climbed up the campanile and spent a happy hour watching the ships, their sails a gay medley of brown and orange and salmon-pink, unloading their cargo of lemons and apples and olives. In the afternoon we went out to Trogir or Trau, another unspoilt relic of old Venice with the most glorious Venetian square hedged in by a loggia, a magnificent cathedral, a palazzo, and an old town-hall. The dirt and smell, it is true, were overpowering, but the sunset over the bay was of the kind which makes one wait until the last ray of light has passed into blackness, and I would still change all the baths and central-heating of America for a country where an overcoat is unknown and where a litre of wine costs no more than twopence.

That night we left for Zagreb and home. We had no sleepers. The train bumped and jolted unceasingly. But I never noticed the discomfort. I was still living in the memory of the past week. For seven days the sun had shone in a blue sky. Not a cloud had darkened the serenity of my own thoughts. Never since the war had I felt so completely at peace with the world. I was going back to a sea of trouble, but I did not care. Deep down in my soul, I was grateful to the bank, to Vojnovič, and even to the unfortunate Serbian manager, whose error had set me on the road to this land of dreams.

CHAPTER FIVE

I RETURNED to England at the end of November, 1926, but my stay was short. Early in the new year I was back again in Yugoslavia. Dickson and I had obtained the mortgage on the Vojnovič concession, but unless the concession could be worked the bank was not likely to recover its money. Vojnovič had no capital, and we had no intention of supplying it. My directors had now a new policy: to find a reliable purchaser who would take over the concession from Vojnovič. General Lawrence, our chairman, found the man, a certain Victor E. Freeman, and I was ordered to accompany him to Yugoslavia in order to see what could be done.

Freeman was a dapper little man with broad shoulders and a bald head. Although a British subject, he spoke English with a strong Jewish accent. I imagine that his mother tongue was Yiddish. He was one of those men who had made money during the immediate post-war boom and, unlike others of his type, had kept it. He had large timber and transport interests in Central Europe. Shy and nervous in society, he had a Napoleonic ambition in business. His chief desire was to establish himself with the best people in the City. His private life was exemplary. He had a large house near Dorking where he lived with his son and daughter. The house was rather grotesquely furnished. There was a sham Arthurian hall, a collection of doubtful old masters, and a library with rows of books with rather glaring bindings. A fountain played from the centre-piece, filled with goldfish, on his dining-room table. He had a model farm with new and spotlessly clean buildings and a really beautiful garden. In its incongruousness Leladene reminded me of Pierre Loti's house in

Rochefort. Otherwise, Freeman had no extravagances and no excesses. He had won the confidence of General Lawrence. An independent inquiry which I made at a well-known Scottish bank elicited the satisfactory information that he was good for a credit of £250,000. My first impression of him was unfavourable. When I learnt to know him better, I liked him. If there was more "bluff" than solidarity in his make-up, he was an honest and courageous "bluffer" who, when he had given his word, did his best to live up to it.

I made two long trips with Freeman to Yugoslavia. They covered much the same ground as my previous trip with Dickson, but were richer in adventures. For weeks we negotiated with Vojnovič, who repeated all his old tactics. We visited the forest again. We made the same journey to Cettinje. We wrangled with lawyers and timber experts in Zagreb. We wrestled with ministers and government officials in Belgrade. Freeman tackled the Zagreb end. In the Croatian capital he was a little king. The interviews with the ministers in Belgrade, where he was not so popular, were left to me. The difficulties were enormous. Acting on instructions from my directors, I had only one object: to relieve the bank of its responsibilities. I wanted Freeman to take over and finance the concession. Freeman, at first, was willing to act only in the capacity of the bank's agent. When finally Freeman came round to our way of thinking, Vojnovič refused to part with the concession except against a large cash payment. For a long time there seemed no issue out of the deadlock.

During my comings and goings between Montenegro and Belgrade and Zagreb I got into trouble twice over matters not strictly connected with the bank's business. The first occasion was in Belgrade. At that moment there was high tension between Italy and Yugoslavia over Albania, where Italy, who by a ridiculous decision of the Ambassadors' Conference in 1921 had been given the mandate to protect the integrity of Albanian independence, seemed intent on establishing a permanent protectorate over the country. Feeling between the two countries was not improved by the publication of a cartoon in a Belgrade paper which showed 10,000 Italians giving the Fascist salute to a Napoleon-like Mussolini in the arena of the Coliseum in Rome. Mussolini's tricorne was a bowler-hat stuck on sideways. At one of the entrances stood a party of English tourists with an Italian guide. The first Englishman is addressing the guide. "Who are these people," he asks, "and why do they stand like that?" "Ah, milord," replies the guide, "these are the Italian Fascisti. They grew tired of holding both hands up in the war."

Three years later, when I became a journalist, I quoted this story in my newspaper. It produced an immediate repercussion in Rome—an order to the Italian Embassy in London to make an immediate protest. I was with the editor when the card of the Italian Counsellor of Embassy was brought in. He was standing in the passage outside. His business was urgent. The editor handed me the card. The Counsellor was an old colleague, who had been with me in Prague. Our farewell dinner to him, when we let him down on a rope-ladder of table-cloths from the balcony of a Nachtlokal on to the stage below, I have already described. In spite of this intimacy I did not feel that I could face him at that moment. I could not leave by the door. Fortunately, however, there was a private lavatory in the editor's room. I beat a hasty retreat, pulled the bolt, and waited there until the interview was ended.

My second adventure was in Cattaro and was provoked by no fault of mine. I had gone there with Alcalay, our Belgrade lawyer, to check the legal validity of the concession and was lunching with him quietly in a restaurant. At the table next to me were three huge Montenegrins who were engaged in a noisy altercation with another Montenegrin sitting alone at a table on the other side of the room. All four had come down from Cettinje to attend a shareholders' meeting of a shipping company, which had been started in the boom period just after the war, and which, like nearly every other concern of its kind, had gone into liquidation. At first the conversation was merely aggressive. There was much talk of shares and swindles. From swindles they switched back to the war. Then the atmosphere became electric. The group next to me had been partisans of King Nikita and had approved his surrender to the Austrians. The gentleman opposite had fought with the Serbians to the bitter end. In a rash moment he used the word "coward." With a yell the giant next to me seized a knife and sprang to his feet, knocking my table sideways and upsetting a plate of hot soup over my lap. Frantic with pain and rage, I, too, gave a roar and was dashing off in pursuit, when Alcalay seized me and, grasping me round the waist, dragged me back to my seat. "Sit down," he whispered hoarsely. "Do you want to be murdered?" At that moment I did not care if I were. My legs were scalded. My trousers were ruined. I wanted vengeance.

By this time the room was in an uproar, which was ended only by the appearance of the Prefect with four gendarmes. His first concern was for me. I learnt afterwards from Alcalay that at the first commotion the hotel proprietor had dashed round to the Prefect's office and had told him that I was being murdered! The Prefect looked pale and frightened, but was full of apologies. My assailant would be punished. He would be arrested at once. In vain I explained that the whole affair was an accident as far as I was concerned and that I had no complaint. Already the Prefect was working out in his mind a report to Belgrade in which, thanks to his energetic action and devotion to duty, he had saved the life of a distinguished British visitor. Already he saw himself promoted. My embarrassment was relieved by the appearance of the gentleman with the knife. His would-be victim had escaped. The murderous glint had disappeared from his eyes. He looked at my potato-soup-stained trousers and realised his enormity. He apologised handsomely. We shook hands. It was a case of "hot blood cools quickest." We warmed it once again with the best wine which the hotel could supply. The Prefect, his dream of promotion destroyed, drank with us.

At last, after weeks of financial fencing, I succeeded in bringing Vojnovič and Freeman to terms. The basis of the deal was as follows: Freeman would take over the whole concession and would be responsible for the felling of the forest within six years. He would provide the capital for the running expenses. The bank would pay for the completion of the plant; that is, the bank would put the aerial railway into working order. In return for the transfer of the concession Freeman would pay to the bank a royalty on every cubic foot of sawn timber. Vojnovič was also to receive a small royalty and a yearly cash payment. Provided that the aerial railway worked and that the forest was as large as the experts stated, the bank would not only recover the original £100,000 paid out irregularly to Vojnovič by the Serbian manager, but would make a handsome profit. It seemed a miraculous escape from an impossible position.

Afraid lest Vojnovič might change his mind, I spent a feverish afternoon preparing a draft agreement, and that same evening in Zagreb Freeman and Vojnovič initialled it. The actual transfer of the concession required several formalities before it could be completed. I had to go to Belgrade in order to secure the approval of the Yugoslav Government. The legality of the signatures had to be attested on the spot. Once again I made the beautiful trip to Boka, this time accompanied by a whole circus of lawyers and by Freeman and Vojnovič. The final signing of the transfer had a romantic setting. It was signed in the ruined villa of a fourteenth-century sea-captain in Perasto. The roof was gone, but the first floor was occupied by the local notary. He smelt of garlic, but through the open window I could see my two little islands with the church of the Madonna of the Rock. It seemed a happy augury. I returned to England with my agreement. It was approved by my bank, and I received the formal thanks of my directors. As things turned out, the thanks were premature. There were vexatious delays in connection with the new aerial railway which proved unsatisfactory. Within three years Freeman himself had crashed, a victim, partly of his own megalomania and partly of the collapse of the Austrian Credit-Anstalt. He died suddenly in January, 1931, leaving his affairs hopelessly involved.

For the moment, however, my prospects seemed to have taken a turn for the better, and my hopes of a successful business career revived. True, I was still in debt and in the toils of the money-lenders again. The policy of the bank, too, was one of continuous retrenchment. While I was away in Yugoslavia, we had sold a large block of our shares in the Anglo-Czechoslovak Bank to a Czech concern. At that very moment we were trying to reduce our Yugoslav commitments by an amalgamation of the Croatian

Discount Bank with another Yugoslav bank. The writing on the wall was plain enough, but I refused to read it. Freeman had taken an interest in my career. His influence in the bank was growing rapidly, and later, when our Croatian amalgamation was on the point of completion and threatened to fail over a sum of £75,000, Freeman put up the money himself and was made a director of the new bank as a reward. His star was in the ascendant. Mine rose with it, for, having apparently succeeded in the Vojnovič affair, I was sent out again on another liquidation; this time of our interests in a Hungarian shipping concern.

The business was a complicated affair of no particular interest to the reader. Briefly, my task was to obtain compensation from the Hungarian Government for the company's ships which they had commandeered during the war, and, failing this, to attempt to sell the ships to the Italian Government or to an Italian shipping company. I failed ignominiously, but the affair gave me two exciting and not unpleasant months in Budapest, Venice, and Rome.

I arrived in Budapest early in May, armed with letters of introduction, including one to a young Hungarian count, who belonged to a famous family and to whose relations I had been able to render a small service when I was at our Legation in Prague. My days were spent in endless business discussions. I enlisted the help of the British Minister and of Sir William Goode. I had several interviews with the Hungarian Minister of Finance. I used all the private influence that I could command. But I made little headway. The truth was that every one knew that our bank was retrenching, and like every other Central European nation the Hungarians were not interested in banks bent on retrenchment.

Out of business hours I was in the hands of my Hungarian Count, and during a whole fortnight I had a marvellous experience of Hungarian hospitality and a revealing insight into Hungarian mentality. My count was an ardent patriot, who, according to his own account, was mixed up in every kind of irredentist intrigue. Like many Hungarians he had a considerable respect for the Serbs. Like most Hungarians he hated the Czechs. How could gentlemen who had lived for a thousand years in castles be expected to shake hands with a race of domestic servants? His views on treaty revision would have been comic if they had not been put forward with such obvious conviction. The Croatians would return to Hungary of their own accord. Hungary would then make an alliance with the Serbs. Then she could take back Transylvania and Slovakia when she wanted. The Czech army! The Rumanian army! Bah! They were not soldiers. They would run at the first shot. I shuddered. Was it possible that this cultured, young man who spoke half-a-dozen languages without a trace of accent, believed these things? Did he really think that the doctrine of feudalism could be maintained in a world which had long since discarded it? On every side of her frontiers Hungary was surrounded by peasant peoples who had thrown out the feudal landowners and who now owned their land. Would the Hungarian peasant continue indefinitely to support a system which denied to him the same rights as his neighbours? In Budapest life was luxurious enough. But when I went out into the country, I was amazed at the servility and the poverty of the Hungarian peasant. I made no attempt to argue with my count. It would have been useless. His views, I discovered, were the secret or open views of ninety per cent of the Hungarian squirarchy.

In every other respect he was a charming companion and one of the best-looking men I have ever seen. His prodigality was Napoleonic in its extravagance. At the time he was in love with a beautiful young Hungarian actress, and every night I accompanied him to the theatre, where we had the largest box. She was the mistress of another and richer man, and his suit did not prosper. He sat through the performance with his eyes glued to the stage and his head leaning on his hand in a Byronic attitude of despair. By day he flew his aeroplane over her villa and dropped flowers on it. The intensity of his passion moved me to a genuine sympathy.

After the theatre he always took me to hear the gipsies. He was insistent that I should hear the best that Budapest could offer. Everywhere we went the same ritual was observed. When he entered the room, the other guests ceased to count. The maître d'hôtel, the waiters, the orchestra, and the Animierdamen preened themselves in eager anticipation. The gipsies played only for him. He distributed champagne and largesse with a recklessness of noblesse oblige which I had never seen equalled even in Russia. But we sat alone, listening to the music or talking of love. He could not live without gipsy music. Every time he heard it it seared his soul.

He did not care for English and American women. They were pretty in a doll-like kind of way, but artificial and vitiated. Once there had been an American girl very rich and very beautiful. He had fallen madly in love with her. He had taken her everywhere in Budapest. But she had been cold to all his advances. Before she left, he had begged her to see something of the Hungarian countryside. She had laughed and had imposed conditions. She would come (1) if there was a proper chaperon and (2) if he would provide the best gipsies in Hungary. He had gone away to Lake Balaton and had hired a villa. Two days later he had wired her, saying that everything was prepared. The night she arrived they had dined on the verandah with the moonlight shining on the lake. The verandah had been divided into two by a wall of roses brought all the way from Nice. They had dined almost in silence. When the coffee was brought in, gipsies, hidden behind the wall, began to play, first, softly and plaintively, and then wildly and more wildly. As he told me the story he sighed. "It must have cost you a fortune," I said. "Was the money well spent?" "Of course," he answered gravely. "No woman can resist flowers and gipsy music." Then, flicking his ash on the floor, he added: "She had no soul; she bored me."

After two weeks of fruitless negotiations in Budapest, I left for Rome on a rather hopeless mission to persuade the Italians to buy some of our ships. I was accompanied by one of the managers of our Budapest branch, and on our way we stopped at Fiume, Abbazzia, and Venice, where we interviewed various shipping agents. I did not know Italy well, although I had passed through it often enough. Nevertheless, even to a superficial observer the contrast with 1920 and 1921 was startling. Then I had not dared to leave my compartment in the train for a minute, let alone go to the wagon-restaurant, for fear of having my luggage stolen. Now a Fascist guard watched my effects while I ate and, when I put my feet up on the seat, ordered me to place a newspaper under them or to remove them from state property. Rome, then in process of being rebuilt, was a tornado of dust. But the order and the enthusiasm were remarkable. Perhaps the enthusiasm itself was ordered. At any rate there was a noticeable restraint in the general atmosphere, and I found it well-nigh impossible to elicit any information about the state of the country from the businessmen with whom I came into contact. Criticism of the régime could be gauged only by what was left unsaid.

Both from the Italians and from Sir Ronald Graham, the British Ambassador, I ascertained that there was no hope of success for our mission. The Italians, however, kept us waiting for four days before giving a final answer, and I put them to good use. I saw as much of the city as a man can see in such limited time. With Baedeker in hand I "did" the Vatican and the Forum. I motored out to Ostia and bathed in the sea. I dined al fresco in the garden of the Hotel de Russie. As a good Scot, whose maternal ancestors gave their lives for the Stuarts at the Battle of Cromdale Haughs, I made my pilgrimage to St. Peter's and stood bareheaded and emotional before the Canova monument to the last of my country's rightful kings. Then I packed my suitcase and took the train for London.

But for one incident it was an uneventful journey. I shared my compartment with an American painter who was returning home after four years in Rome. He was a first-rate raconteur, and he told me many strange stories of life in Rome and of the inquisition methods of the Fascists. When the wagon-restaurant attendant came round with the dinner-places, my American friend took a ticket for the first service. Making the excuse that I could not dine so early, I took mine for the second. On entering the train, I had already noticed a beautiful young woman with a sad, madonna-like face in the next compartment. She was dressed in black and was obviously an Italian. She was travelling alone. My instinct told me that there was a mystery behind her sadness. I made friends with her by offering her a match to light her cigarette, as we stood in the corridor watching the sunset. She came to sit in my compartment. We dined together, and over coffee she told me her story. Her husband was a Liberal and a bitter anti-Fascist and was in prison. She herself had been under domiciliary arrest. Now, after months of waiting, she had at last obtained permission to leave the country and was going to Paris to join her brother.

Chance acquaintances in Continental expresses are dangerous, but I found her fascinating. She seemed so obviously sincere. At one moment her whole face would light up with the anticipation of freedom. A minute later a troubled look would come into her eyes. Before she left me, she gave me her name and her Paris address. It was a Friday night, and, as I went to bed, my thoughts were already playing with the idea of breaking my journey in Paris and going on to London by the Sunday night boat. I slept soundly, being wakened only for a second or two by the sound of angry voices in the corridor in the early hours of the morning. When I went along to the wagon-restaurant for breakfast, we were already in France. My beautiful neighbour had disappeared. She had been taken off the train at Ventimiglia. When I asked the chef du train what had happened, he shrugged his shoulders. "Probably a spy or a smuggler. It happens every week," he said.

His cynicism shocked me. I did not believe that my madonna was either a spy or a smuggler. Every woman can fool almost any man, but this time I was convinced that my judgment was right. To prove it I broke my journey in Paris for two hours and drove out to the hotel address in the Champs Elysées, which she had given me. I went straight to the manager. "Has Signora ——— arrived?" I said. "I have an important message for her." Without even referring to his books, he replied at once: "No, but she is expected to-day. Her rooms were booked some time ago." I told him that she was not likely to arrive, having been taken off the train by the Italian police. He whistled softly. "It is very sad," he said. "They are old clients of ours. The husband, you know, is the famous Professor ———." Italy, too, has her Ogpu. It is not so spectacular and not so blood-thirsty, but its methods are not dissimilar and certainly not less efficient.

CHAPTER SIX

THERE are moments in the life of every man when the presentiment of failure chills even the most cheerful optimism. The lack of success which had attended my Budapest and Rome mission made me anxious again about my future. On my return to England I was once more face to face with all my financial troubles. There were my money-lenders' bills to be met. They had arisen in this way. My bank was generous about expenses. I had, too, a good friend in Malcolm Turnbull, the able secretary of the bank and my immediate chief. He was a Scot who had travelled widely and who, although rigidly ascetic in his own scale of expenditure, understood the importance of entertaining as an adjunct to business in foreign countries. He was, however, such a faithful watchdog of the bank's interests and so gentle in his insistence on economies that when I came to make up my accounts I reduced my entertainment expenditure to about a quarter of its actual amount. In this manner any trip I made abroad left me a hundred pounds or more out of my pocket. My remedy was always the same. Knowing my own weakness, I repaired in advance to my Russian-Jewish friend with the Scottish name, hoping always that I should bring off some coup like the sale of the De Forest estate which would enable me to meet his interest charges.

To relieve my most pressing needs I raised a loan from my uncle, pledging to him in return the problematical royalties from my book of Russian memoirs which I had always intended to write but which I had never started.

Freed from my immediate embarrassments, I settled down to a humdrum existence in London and found it irksome. The plain truth was that, after more than twenty years spent abroad, I could not adapt myself to English life. Its apparent levity shocked me. In my notebooks I found a description of the Athenians in the period of their decline: "In the fifth century before Christ Athens was at the height of her glory. Five hundred years later all the Athenians and foreign visitors to Athens occupied themselves with nothing else than repeating or listening to the latest novelty." It seemed to me a true picture of English society in 1927, and, when in September I took my leave, I spent it on the Continent, revisiting in turn Bavaria, Slovenia, and my beloved Dalmatian Coast.

I was in Munich on October 2nd for President Hindenburg's eightieth birthday. The city afforded several painful contrasts with my previous visits. In an orgy of flag-flying practically no Republican flags were flown. The official buildings hoisted the blue and white Bavarian flag. Private people flaunted the old Imperial black-white-red without protest or interference. In the streets, too, I saw bands of young men with tell-tale slashes on their faces. Duelling was forbidden, but the Mensur had been restarted. Germany was going back to her old gods. In the evening I attended the gala performance of the Meistersinger at the opera. Every seat was occupied, and the atmosphere was electric. When Wilhelm Rode finished the famous Hans Sachs' song: "Despise not the old German masters; too long have foreigners triumphed in our land," the whole audience rose and cheered itself hoarse in a tornado of patriotic emotion. It was a little terrifying, a little too like the spirit of 1914, to be pleasant. This time, too, having more leisure, I made a tour of the Dalmatian Islands: Hvar, the Madeira of the Adriatic, Korcula, first colonised according to tradition by Æneas, Lissa, where in 1811 the British admiral, Sir William Horte, met and destroyed a vastly larger French fleet, and, above all, Lacroma.

In comparison with the stony "Karst" of the other islands, Lacroma is like a green oasis. Its hilly slopes are covered with a profusion of cypresses, laurels, aloes, pistachios, and the fascinating strawberry tree, while the undergrowth is a wilderness of wild flowers and erica. After a short walk through this enchanting forest one comes, like the Prince in the Belle au Bois-Dormant, to the old Benedictine monastery with its palm-crested park and its rosemary-bordered gardens. And the rosemary is indeed for remembrance, for Lacroma is as old as history itself. Here Richard Cœur-de-Lion, fleeing from the storm, was miraculously brought to shore and in gratitude for his deliverance left money to the monks for the erection of a church. In these friendly cloisters King Radoslav of Serbia sought refuge from the murderous intents of his treacherous nephew. Here, too, King Sigismund of Hungary was glad to find a resting-place after his flight from the victorious Turks.

If there is one spirit of the past, however, which walks alive in Lacroma to-day, it is the ghost of the ill-fated Emperor Maximilian, who converted the monastery into a residence for himself and laid out the park and gardens which, with the sunsets, are the real glory of Lacroma. Here, on a stone terrace commanding perhaps the finest view in Europe, surrounded by pomegranate and orange trees and great clusters of roses and bougainvillæa, he would sit every evening, building his daydream of Mexico and watching this wonderful panorama of ever-changing sunsets, the sky now flame-coloured, now pink topaz, and the sea a riot of blue from the palest aquamarine to the deepest of indigo. Did he dream of that other island and of the fate of a still more ambitious Emperor?

Every time I visit Lacroma my mind goes back to Manet's picture of the shooting of Maximilian in the National Gallery in London. I see again the dark-grey uniforms, the white belts and white spats, the aimed rifles of the Mexican revolutionaries. I remember that it was in honour of their leader, Benito Juarez, that Mussolini was given his own Christian name of Benito. And in the picture that I conjure up in my mind I see the symbol of the struggle between the old and the new which is being fought out in Europe to-day and of the ancient, deep-rooted hatred of Austrian for Italian and Italian for Austrian.

Some day perhaps an unknown writer will find in Lacroma, and in the unfortunate Habsburg, the materials for a great tragedy. For the spirit of tragedy lies heavily on Lacroma, and, although the island is of the softest beauty, the cliffs are sheer and forbidding, with sinister grottos down which the Ragusan senators used to drop their political prisoners. Who knows, too, what further tragedies await Lacroma? As I watched for the last time the sun go down behind Lopud, I asked my chauffeur, a Slav Sandow, who had aspirations of swimming the Channel the next year, what would happen if the Italian fleet were to occupy Lacroma. His eyes flashed. "We have a society here," he said, "in which every member has to take an oath to leave wife and child and all that he has and, armed or unarmed, never to rest so long as a single Italian soldier remains on Dalmatian soil." "I am a member," he added quietly.

As I entered my boat to return to Ragusa, the moon came out from behind the Montenegrin mountains, and in its pale light we saw a flotilla of English destroyers slip silently like wraiths round the corner from Gravosa. Some day perhaps the British Navy, through constant absorption of so much beauty, will give us a Claude Farrère or perhaps even a Pierre Loti.

At the end of October I was back again in Yugoslavia on business. There was some talk of an English loan to the Yugoslav Government. It was to be arranged through the medium of our bank, and I had to go to Belgrade to make the preliminary arrangements for the visit of M. Bark, who was our heavy gun in these matters. Unfortunately, it came to nothing.

At the end of November I appeared as a Crown witness in the curious case of Aronowitz against the King. When I was head of the unofficial British Mission to the Bolshevik Government in 1918, I had had to raise a considerable sum of roubles in irregular ways owing to the closing of the banks and to the fact that Russia was then completely shut off from the rest of the world. The procedure, which was also adopted by other foreign missions, was a simple one. There were many Russians who had secret stores of roubles which they were anxious to dispose of against foreign currency. The Allied Missions wanted roubles. In my own case I employed an outside agent, an English businessman, whom I had known for several years. The agent collected the roubles from these well-to-do Russians and brought them to me.

In order to induce the Russians to part with their roubles, I either backed our agents' sterling cheque or gave him an official certificate stating that he was good for the money in London. At the end of the war the agent presented his accounts and was paid in full in order that he, in turn, might meet his liabilities to his Russian clients.

Several years later, however, one or two of my certificates began to turn up in London. They were presented, first, to the agent and, when he was unable to pay, they were brought as a claim against the British Government. In each case the holder of the certificate declared that he would never have parted with his roubles without the certificate of the Head of the British Mission. In at least one case the British Government had paid up without protest. Mr. Aronowitz's claim was the third or fourth of its kind, and, when it was presented, the Government began to be suspicious—not without reason. The certificate had passed through several hands. There was nothing to prove that the original lender of the roubles had not been paid already. To pay twice would be to establish a dangerous precedent, and in the case of Mr. Aronowitz's cheque the Government determined to test the case in the Courts. I was the chief witness. I was cross-examined by Sir Leslie Scott for Aronowitz, and by Lord Hailsham for the Crown. The whole case turned on the question of my authority to issue these certificates which were accepted by the Russians as Government guarantees. I had to admit that I had acted without the authority of the Foreign Office. It was strictly true. There was at the time no means of consulting London. In his final speech for the Crown, Lord Hailsham praised me for assuming responsibility in times of exceptional difficulty but maintained that I had acted ultra vires and could not therefore be said to have pledged the King's credit. The judge, the late Mr. Justice McCardie, upheld this point of view and gave judgment in favour of the Crown. The Crown, having achieved its object which was to establish a precedent which would put a stop to similar demands, then paid full compensation to Mr. Aronowitz. My ordeal as a witness was less terrifying than I had expected. It was my last excitement of 1927.

The year 1928 opened catastrophically. In January, Spencer-Smith was killed in a motor accident. His death at the age of forty-six affected me profoundly. His original conception of an English bank which would help to bring the factious nations of Central Europe together had been sound enough. Although he lacked experience of foreigners, he might have succeeded, for he had great qualities of leadership, courage, charm, an infectious optimism, and an admirable sense of fair-play. But the Peace Treaties and, above all, their rigid application during the immediate post-war years were against him, and the task was beyond his powers as it would have been beyond those of any other Englishman. The French had the bayonets and we had not, and since 1919 bayonets have dictated policy in Central Europe both in the case of the victors and of the vanquished. A man of high character and real generosity, he had been a very good friend to me, and I felt his death as a great personal loss.

This tragedy advanced the prospects of M. Peter Bark, the former Tsarist Minister of Finance, who now became our Managing Director. He had always taken a friendly interest in my career, sympathised with the difficulties of my position, and did all he could to advance my interests. Soon after Spencer-Smith's death we had a long talk, and he promised to do his best to have me elected a director of our reconstructed Czechoslovak and Yugoslav banks. He also held out some hope of a job with Rothschild's, who were then considering the possibilities of a loan to the Yugoslav Government. The jobs never materialised. As far as the Czech and Yugoslav banks were concerned, our policy of retrenchment had affected our influence. We were now minority shareholders, and when the new boards were elected my name did not figure in the lists.

I accepted this failure as the final blow to my hopes of a banking career, and, having meditated over this step for nearly three years, I suddenly made up my mind to seek some other vocation. Recently, as a free lance, I had begun to contribute to the *Evening Standard*. Even during my long residence abroad I had never entirely lost touch with Lord Beaverbrook. Owing to my debts it was essential that I should earn a larger salary than I was receiving from the bank. If I were to become a professional journalist, there was no newspaper concern in England which could pay me so well as the Beaverbrook Press.

On February 21st I dined with Lord Beaverbrook at his little house, The Vineyard, in Hurlingham. There were half-a-dozen other guests including Duff Cooper and Lady Diana Cooper. During dinner the conversation was brilliant but flippant. After dinner the others went on to some party, and I remained alone with Lord Beaverbrook. I told him of my difficulties in the bank and of my dislike of a City life. He talked to me very seriously and warned me of the dangers of frittering away my time and my substance in social levities. It was sound advice. Indeed, I know no one who is more capable of giving good advice on a difficult situation than this strange little man whose make-up is two-thirds genius and one-third puckishness. Finally, he offered me a job as a diary-writer on the *Evening Standard*. It was a good offer. I made no attempt to bargain over my salary. Nevertheless, I hesitated and asked for a few days' grace for reflection. I told him that I should like to accept, but that I wished to write my Russian memoirs before joining him and that in any case my acceptance was dependent on the terms of my final settlement with my bank. Then, armed with my new offer, I went to see M. Bark. I told him that I had an offer of a well-paid job with Lord Beaverbrook, but that before I joined him I wished to write my book. I explained that what I really wanted was the eight months' necessary leisure for the writing of my book. I pointed out that leisure required money. I knew that other employees of the bank, who had been dispensed with, had received some compensation. I touched diplomatically on my services to the bank in the early stages of its existence. The directors treated me with noble generosity. They gave me a year's salary with no further obligations on my part than the writing of the leading article for the bank's monthly report. The Czech bank voted me a small bonus in recognition of the help I had rendered it at the time of its creation.

Then, having successfully rid myself of the old love before I was quite on with the new, I carefully sounded the views of my relations and friends. My relations, who knew little of journalism and who were tired of paying my debts, were pleased enough. My friends were horrified and warned me in plain language that I was selling myself into slavery and that in Fleet Street I must lose either my self-respect or my pants. These truisms did not affect my decision. I had no illusions about what I was doing. After more than twenty years of almost complete independence during which I had always been able to give full expression to my own views, it meant self-negation and, above all, a necessary and tactful self-repression. But there was no alternative. I was in debt. There was no future for me in a bank which had failed to realise its early hopes. Sorrowfully and reluctantly, I came to the conclusion that Continental Europe offered too many temptations to my tempestuous temperament and that English discipline would have a salutary effect on a rather volatile character. I went back to Lord Beaverbrook and told him that, if his offer were still open, I should be glad to join him in the autumn. I made only one stipulation, that I should be given frequent opportunities of going abroad. "Good boy!" said Lord Beaverbrook. The good boy smiled a little nervously. He had made up his mind that the servant at least should be worthy of his hire. He found a momentary consolation in the reflection that between Lord Beaverbrook and the bank he had bought himself eight months of leisure and freedom.

Did I write my book? I did not. Having decided to turn my back on Central Europe, I repented immediately. A sound instinct told me that rarely, if ever, again would I revisit the Continental scene, and certainly never with the same leisure. Conceiving Europe in the terms of a last farewell, I undertook a European tour in the grand manner and spent five of my eight months abroad. It was a holiday which I have never regretted and to which I look back to-day with a nostalgia that is sometimes acutely painful. I led a life of complete decorum and sobriety. Untrammelled by my business ties, I enriched my detailed experiences of the past ten years by a detached and impartial observation. It was a period of almost complete happiness clouded only by one missed opportunity and by one great sorrow.

In March, I dined at the Embassy Club in London with Mr.

Sam Goldwyn, the Hollywood film-magnate. Aided by the vivid imagination of Lord Castlerosse, I discoursed eloquently on my experiences in Bolshevik Russia. For once Hollywood listened instead of talking, and at the end of the evening Mr. Goldwyn invited me to tea with him the next day at the Carlton Hotel. I went, and to my surprise he made me an attractive offer to come to Hollywood and to write a scenario of my Russian adventures. Pleading for time on the grounds that I had a book to finish, I promised vaguely to consider the matter later. Then I dismissed it from my mind. Instead of writing my book, I supplemented my bonuses by writing articles on the Central European situation for the English reviews.

In May, my mother, who had been ill for two years, underwent a serious operation in a London nursing home. Although she was sixty-four, she stood it marvellously and at the end of ten days was pronounced out of danger. I stayed in London throughout her convalescence, seeing her every day. Her cheerfulness was remarkable. She felt better than she had been for years. She talked happily of going to Scotland in a fortnight's time. The doctor had said that within a month she would fish again. Then one Saturday morning I went to see her. She was in high spirits. She insisted on my going away for the week-end. My father would be with her on the Sunday. She was to leave the home on the Tuesday. Her doctor himself had gone to Devon for the week-end. I went. On the Monday morning I was walking in the woods at the Rosslyns' place near the Sussex Downs. It was nine o'clock on a perfect May morning. Suddenly I saw Lady Rosslyn walking down the path. Her face was set. She took me by the arm. "Bruce," she said very quietly, "you're wanted on the telephone. I'm afraid there's bad news." Knowing the worst, I went to the telephone as in a dream. My aunt was speaking. Her voice sounded a whole world away. Dumbly I listened while she told me. My mother had been doing a cross-word with my father. Suddenly she had put her hands to her head and had fallen forward. When my father lifted her back, she was dead. I, who weep with ridiculous ease at cinemas and theatres and over books, would have liked to cry. But the tears refused to come. Starkly my association with her filmed itself in my mind in a series of kinematic flashes. I saw again ridiculous little incidents: how she had spanked me when I was six for going to a football match without permission and getting my feet wet and how my father, always sympathetic where rugby football is concerned, had patted me on the back and had stemmed my tears with a bluff: "Never mind, old boy, you'll be a man before your mother." Clearest of all, however, I saw her virtues, her patience, her pride in her five sons, all of whom except me, her eldest, had never caused her a moment's anxiety, her self-denial, her unfailing kindness to me, and her ever-willing readiness to sacrifice everything to pay for my selfish self-indulgence. Now there could be no reparation in this world. In a dream I hired a car and drove to London. My father had aged ten years in a night, and I made arrangements for the funeral. Against my will I went with him to see her for the last time at the undertaker's. Her face was very peaceful. Her wedding ring had been stolen from the unclosed coffin.

On the night before the funeral Gerald Barry, then editor of the *Saturday Review,* rang me up. He wanted urgently a leading article on the Bank of England and the new Currency Bill. He must have it the first thing in the morning. Would I do it? I knew nothing about the new Currency Bill. I know nothing about it to-day. But I had just discovered the secret of Mr. Montagu Norman's marvellous memory and wished to impart my knowledge to others. That great man, when he received a visitor, sat at a desk entirely free from papers of any kind. He never made a note. Yet he never forgot a conversation. The truth was that in the right-hand drawer of his desk the Governor kept a diary, and, when his visitor had left, the date, the time and the salient features of the talk were carefully entered into it. Moreover, I remembered that at the time of his father's death Arnold Bennett had sat up all night writing his first article for a Five Towns newspaper and registering his mental reactions during the process. I worked at my article most of the night and finished it at four in the morning. I, too, decided that I had something of the journalist in my make-up.

After the funeral I went abroad again and spent a peaceful

fortnight in Bavaria, motoring all over the country, going to the opera in Munich, attending Mass in the Hofkirche, and fishing again on the Semt, where one afternoon I caught six trout weighing eighteen pounds. Munich was a little shabbier than on the occasion of my last visit. The lot of "the little man" was harder. The cleavage of opinion was wider. There were more students with duelling slashes on their faces. A new feature was the open appearance on the streets of men in brown shirts with swastikas on their arms. Even the Germans laughed at them. But in the Reichstag elections that year the National-Socialists had returned twelve deputies. It was their first tangible proof of success. Every Muenchener was pro-English, but the feeling against France was more bitter, more resentful, than ever before. Hope deferred was making the German Republic sick.

From Bavaria I went on to Slovenia and to Dalmatia. On this occasion the customary peace of my Yugoslav holiday was disturbed by an event of European importance and significance. I was in Zagreb, the Croatian capital, on the day on which Puniča Račič, the Montenegrin deputy, murdered the leading Croatian deputies in the Skupština in Belgrade. Goaded by the jeers of the Croat deputies, he took out his revolver and picked off the leaders, one by one, as they sat on the front opposition bench during the debate. Among his victims were Stepan Radič and his brother Pavle. The excitement which this brutal act provoked in the Croatian capital was immense. The inhabitants poured out into the streets. A black flag hung from every window. There were sullen looks on every face. But the restraint of the people was admirable. Had I been a Serbian, I should have felt uneasy. This spectacle of a whole people in mourning had a deeper significance than any violent outburst. A year before I had met Puniča Račič in Belgrade. He was a violent adventurer with an uncontrollable temper and a bad political record, the kind of tool which is at the service of every Balkan Government. I was not surprised when a Belgrade chauvinist newspaper hailed him as a patriot. It was obvious that he enjoyed protection in high places, and at one moment it seemed probable that he would never be brought to trial. In any case his sentence was light, and long before the case was ended a Europe, already inured to political assassinations, had forgotten it. Radič, too, I had known. He had many faults. Much of the futility of the Skupština during the early post-war years was due to his verbosity and dialectical vacillations. But he had rendered one service to his people and also to the Serbians. In December, 1918, the Croat peasantry might easily have been led along the path of Bolshevism. To Radič, a brilliant orator, the temptation must have been great. Yet he resisted it. Now by an incredible act of folly, the Serbians had made a martyr and a national hero of this unpractical and rather grotesque demagogue. It was a stupendous blunder, but, like the march on Rome, it was a landmark in the shifting sands of post-war politics and in the protracted crisis of the great post-war transition. Its significance was not to be mistaken. It meant the end even of the pretence of democratic government in Yugoslavia. It gave a free rein to the policy of Serbian domination. It was a blow to common sense and decency. It was a stimulus to that madness of exaggerated nationalism, backed by armaments and yet more armaments, which has overcome an impoverished Europe apparently bent on self-destruction. It would be remembered long after Locarno and the long series of Geneva pacts and conferences had been blurred in the memory of men.

In July I returned to England or rather to Scotland and spent three pleasant weeks on the western coast of the Outer Hebrides. I was supposed to be fishing, but my suitcases were full of Jacobite literature, and, alone upon the moors with never a living soul to cross my path all day, I read again with a new delight the story of the Forty-Five. At Callernish I saw a Druid circle, grander and more complete than that of Stonehenge, and felt as pagan as my early Celtic forbears. At Callernish, too, I saw men living in a poverty and squalor worse than any I had seen even in Ruthenia. It was their woeful Scottish pride which kept them in this wretched state. Twenty years before a great English capitalist, the late Lord Leverhulme, had taken an interest in the island and was prepared to develop its resources and to raise the standard of living of the tribesmen. But he had called himself the Lord of the Isles, a title which belonged by right to the Kings of

Scotland. This usurpation was more than Scottish blood could stand from an Englishman, and so the great reconditioning schemes of the would-be benefactor came to nothing.

Sinful pride certainly; yet it was this same pride which in the campaign of the Forty-Five kept the ancestors of these men loyal to the Stuart. For the real romance of what the English call the Jacobite rebellion lies not in the charm of Bonnie Prince Charlie or in the nobles who gave their lives for the cause, but in the loyalty of and devotion of the poor clansmen who rallied to the Stuart standard. The Forty-Five was made possible only by "the little man," and as in all wars and as in Europe to-day, which is warring and yet not at war, it was "the little man" who paid the heaviest price. Yet in spite of the temptations of English gold there was no Scottish traitor throughout the campaign. When, after Culloden, Charles Edward, fleeing for his life and with a price of £30,000 on his head, stumbled into the remote hut in Glenmoriston, where seven Highland outlaws were seeking refuge from justice, he was safer than in the castle of any Scottish noble. For weeks they guarded him and fed him until they could bring him into safety. The seven men have found a permanent place in history. To-day, the Highland blood in me still quickens with pride at the thought that one of these was a Macgregor and an ancestor of my mother.

I am a little ashamed of my enthusiasm. By the conviction of reason I am an internationalist. My nationalism is the purest romanticism. It has its roots only in the past and has no relation to the modern world. Yet it has taught me how easily what is a genuine sentiment among the ignorant masses can be exploited by the unscrupulous and how far distant we are from the ideal of a perfect humanity.

Early in August I went to Switzerland in order to spend a month with my wife and son at Villars. It was my first prolonged stay in the Swiss mountains. It was also the occasion of my first visit to Geneva. I have an abiding and inalienable affection for Lake Geneva. I love the quiet peacefulness of its shores, the warmth of its sunshine, the rich kaleidoscope of its sunsets. I enjoy seeking out the ghosts of its romantic past. Baedeker in hand I have made the tour du Lac on countless occasions and have followed the traces of Byron and Shelley, of Gibbon, of Rousseau, of Tolstoy, of Gambetta, and of the great army of writers and political exiles who have found solace and inspiration by its shores. Posing as a Boer, I have even sought admittance to the Dubochet villa at Clarens where Paul Kruger, the Boer President, breathed his last. It is by the placid waters of Lake Geneva that I should like to write the book which I shall never even begin.

But it is the south-western end of the Lake which has captured a place in my heart. From the first moment Geneva itself filled me with a repugnance which I cannot explain and which subsequent visits have been unable to allay. Had the choice lain in my power it is the last place I should have selected for the League of Nations. It is too cold and uncompromising like the spirit of that Calvinism to which it gave birth. I do not deny its beauty. There is no finer monument in Europe than the magnificent bas-relief of Calvin, Knox, Farel, Bèze, Cromwell, and the other Calvinists on the famous ramparts. Yet in that moment I saw the symbol of the failure of the League. The Calvinists stand facing Rome, itself potentially the greatest League of Nations. Their attitude, unbending and uncompromising, was like the attitude of the victorious Allies, who had turned the League into an instrument for the perpetuation of their victory and a criminal dock for their enemies. I admired the coloured orderliness of the gardens of Geneva. The League, too, had started as a garden of new ideas, but it had been choked from the start by the weeds of the Peace Treaties. At the League and at the International Labour Office I found many old friends: Phelan, a brilliant young Irishman, who was with me in Russia in 1918 and who, if he had cared to go back to Irish politics, might have been Mr. De Valera's foreign minister; the late Albert Thomas, also an old friend of Russian days and the most loyal and hard-working servant the League has ever had; and a whole host of foreign diplomatists whom I had met in different parts of Europe. In the permanent staff of the League I found inspiring signs of a genuine League loyalty. Then the Council and the Assembly met, and at once the whole place was enveloped in an atmosphere of intrigue. First principles were abandoned in an unedifying struggle for personal advantage. Journalists raked in a rich mud for scandals and found them without difficulty. The delegates of the different nations voted as their governments wished them to vote. It was a depressing spectacle.

On the whole I preferred Geneva when the Council delegates were absent. Then I could roam about the book-shops undisturbed. Most of my time I spent in retracing Lenin's life as an exile in Geneva. I tried to find the spot where, when riding his bicycle from the Carouge to attend a Social-Democratic meeting, he had collided with a tramcar and nearly lost his life. Idly I speculated on what would have been the course of world history if, instead of a push-bike, he had had a motorcycle. I had my table at the Café Landolt, where he used to sit, and, with my eyes fixed on the Salle de la Reformation just across the road, wondered what kind of figure the Bolshevik leader would have cut among the delegates of the Assembly.

I remembered my conversation with him in the Smolny Institute in Petrograd early in 1918. "Against a united capitalism," he said to me with his cold, logical self-confidence, "we should have no chance. Fortunately for us," he added, "it is in the nature of capital to fight against itself." I thought of the Lenin mausoleum on the Red Square in Moscow. Was the suggestion of a smile on that mummified face purely imaginary or was it inspired by the spectacle of a capitalist Europe determined on suicide and rushing like the Gadarene swine to its own destruction? If he were alive to-day, Lenin would have laughed.

Many portraits of Geneva personalities are photographed in my mind. I see again Mr. Bernard Shaw stalking out of the dining-room of the Residence, an object of greater hero-worship and reverence to the throng of League visitors than any political delegate, with his wife following humbly behind. I see again the venerable figure of the octogenarian Count Apponyi replying in dulcet periods to the fierce challenge of M. Titulescu on the question of the Hungarian optants and the Maharajah of Kapurthala leaning across to my wife and whispering: "There is a great gentleman. That's what comes from 700 years of breeding." But if I would symbolise the League in one concrete vision, I would go back to the other end of the Lake and I would present to you the tall, gaunt figure of M. Romain Rolland walking vigorously on his daily seven-mile walk to Montreux and back. To-day, he lives in voluntary exile in Villeneuve, an honest and fearless prophet execrated in France because he has dared to fix the responsibility for the hate, which to-day divides Europe, on his own countrymen.

CHAPTER SEVEN

CHANCE, which more than once has thrown me across the path of great events, favoured me throughout that year of 1928. In the autumn, conscious that it might be my last visit, I went to Berlin for a fortnight, partly to see Jenia and partly to acquire "copy" for the journalistic career on which I was now entering. I had a personal letter of introduction to the Crown Prince from Millicent, Duchess of Sutherland. The Crown Prince was not in Berlin. Instead, I fell metaphorically into the arms of the ex-Kaiser.

The manner of it was in this wise. Very conscientiously I had looked up all my old friends. I had called on Sir Horace Rumbold, our Ambassador, and had explained to him that I was embarking on a new profession. I had renewed my contacts with General Seeckt, Baron von Reinbaben, Meissner, the right-hand man of President Hindenburg, and Roland Koester, an old Prague colleague and now German Ambassador in Paris. I had seen Gustav Stresemann, still full of vigour but already a sick man with one kidney affected by the disease which was so soon to take him to the grave. I had spent Armistice Day in the Imperial Palace. The place was almost deserted, and, as I inspected the ex-Kaiser's desk made out of an oak beam from Nelson's "Victory," my mind went back to the lonely Armistice Day I had spent in Sarajevo the year before. Then it had been hot as summer. Now an icy wind raked the sidewalks of Unter den Linden. Here in Berlin there was no two minutes' silence, no outward sign of thanksgiving for the end of a war which had brought defeat and shame to a proud nation. I had been royally entertained by my German banking friends. I had filled my diary with useful notes without acquiring any information of a sensational or even "newsworthy" nature and was preparing to depart when I received an invitation to luncheon from Richard von Kuehlmann, who had been German Foreign Minister at the time of the Brest-Litovsk Treaty. At that luncheon, served in his Wilhelmstrasse apartment with a charming background of old china and seventeenth-century prints, I met Karl Friedrich Nowak, the historian and man of confidence of the ex-Kaiser.

Nowak was an extraordinary little man with a head almost as large as his body, a prodigious memory, a dyspeptic complexion, and a nervous energy which was both restless and apparently tireless. At the time he was trying to combine publishing with writing books. Fortunately, I had read and admired his "Downfall of the Central Powers" and his "Versailles" and was able both to compliment him and to discuss both books with sufficient knowledge to flatter his literary pride. We took to each other from the first moment. He asked me to dine with him. We sat up for most of the night. We lunched again the next day, and then, after having tested me thoroughly and, doubtless, after consulting Kuehlmann about my reliability, he sprang his mine. Could I help him in a very confidential manner? The ex-Kaiser was furious at the publication in England of "The Letters of the Empress Frederick" which had appeared that autumn with a preface by Sir Frederick Ponsonby, the Keeper of the Privy Purse. The letters had been smuggled out of Germany. As his mother's heir, the ex-Kaiser was the holder of the copyright of her letters. He wished to take out an injunction against the book in England and to have it withdrawn. The handling of the affair had been put in Nowak's hands. Could I recommend him a good English barrister?

I recommended Mr. Theo Matthews. At the same time I advised Nowak very strongly not to have the book withdrawn in England. I pointed out that an injunction would attract still wider publicity to the book and that a case in the British Courts would give great and perhaps unpleasant notoriety to the ex-Kaiser's name. "What then would you do, for something must be done?" said Nowak.

"Why not suggest to the ex-Kaiser that he should write a

dignified explanation of his relations with his mother and have it published in England and Germany?" I replied.

Nowak took up a fork and began to trace patterns on the tablecloth. At last he spoke. "It is an idea," he said. "We might publish a German edition of the Letters and His Majesty could write the preface."

"In that case," I said, "you will give me the English translation of the preface to publish in my newspaper. It will be a good kick-off to my journalistic career."

I returned to England. The ex-Kaiser took Counsel's opinion in London. He was informed that not only did the copyright of the letters belong to him but that under a statute going back to Queen Anne he could sue as a British subject in the British Courts. Fortified by this opinion, the ex-Kaiser showed his magnanimity and, I think, sound sense by accepting Nowak's and my advice. With Nowak I called on Sir Frederick Macmillan, the publisher of the book, and arranged with him for the publication of a German edition with the ex-Kaiser's preface. With Nowak I went to Doorn on November 24th and 25th. I was not received in audience, because the ex-Kaiser had made a vow that so long as British troops were on German soil he would receive no British subject at Doorn. But we met in the garden without speaking, both saluting gravely as we passed. Moreover, I obtained the exclusive right to publish the English translation of the ex-Kaiser's preface in my newspaper and a promise that, as soon as the British troops left the Rhineland, I should be granted the first authentic interview given by the ex-Kaiser since his abdication.

I received the preface in due course. I translated it myself. It was published in the *Evening Standard* on February 12th, 1929. It was a frank and impressive statement of the ex-Kaiser's case. I was well satisfied with a delicate job well ended. I dismissed the promised interview from my mind, regarding its fulfilment as improbable. During the whole period of his exile the ex-Kaiser had maintained a dignified silence which had won him considerable sympathy. Why should he break it for me? I had, however, mistaken my man. The evacuation of the Rhineland by the British troops began on September 14th, 1929. On the 25th of the same month I received the following letter from Doorn:

Haus Doorn, 25. IX. 1929.

To:
Mr. Lockhart Esqu.

Sir,

I have the honour to inform you, that His Imperial Majesty the German Emperor has graciously decided to accord you an audience in the second half of November. His Imperial Majesty is moved by the wish to be able personally to express to you his gratitude for the pains you took on His Imperial Majesty's behalf respecting the publishing of the Emperor's Preface to the Letters of Empress Frederick his august Mother and your kind help towards facilitating other publications concerning the Emperor personally.

I remain Yours,
(Signature)
Acting Chief of the Imperial Household.

The last British troops were evacuated on December 12th, 1929. My visit to Doorn took place during the week-end of December 14th and 15th.

To save a night's sea-crossing I had made up my mind to fly, but when I arrived at Croydon on the Saturday morning there was a thick fog, and both the British and the German aeroplanes cancelled their flight. I could have cried with vexation. I had to be in Utrecht that afternoon to meet Nowak. There was now no time to make the sea journey. Already I saw myself disgraced for having missed my interview at the last moment, when the pilot of the Dutch plane took pity on me. If I could wait till twelve, he might be able to get across. He had the mails to carry and was determined to go if the visibility was only half-way possible. At two o'clock the mist lifted a little, and my Dutchman decided to take the risk. I was the only passenger on a flight which was thoroughly unpleasant. After skirting Dunkirk, we did most of the rest of the journey over the sea, flying so low that we seemed to be skimming the water. Fortunately, at Rotterdam the fog cleared, and we made a good landing. It was an experience which I should not like to repeat, and I took a large schnapps before leaving by car for Utrecht, where four hours late I joined up with Nowak and his Secretary, Princess Kropotkin. That night I prepared with Nowak the list of written questions which I had undertaken to submit to the ex-Kaiser.

The next morning the ex-Kaiser's car called for me at our hotel, and in drizzling rain I set out on the twenty-mile drive to Doorn. As we were borne along the narrow, muddy road lined with weeping poplars, my mind went back to my Scottish forefathers who had accompanied the Stuart into exile in this flat, water-logged country where the rain never ceases. I could imagine no more depressing place for an exile. As we passed through the red-and-white shuttered Tower House which guards the entrance to Doorn, the rain stopped. The ex-Kaiser was standing in the drive. He was wearing a soft Homburg hat, knickerbockers, and a long, loose Byronesque cape. He carried a stick. His magnificent Alsatian, Arno, was by his side. We pulled up and got out, and at once he took me by the arm, welcomed me to Doorn, and in quick, animated sentences began to thank me profusely for the service I had rendered him in the matter of his mother's letters. These remarks were followed by questions about his English relations. How was the Prince of Wales? Was he still hunting and still falling off his horses? He had last seen him in 1912 and remembered him with affection for his boyish good looks and charming modesty. He was a little hurt that of the British royal family only Princess Beatrice had written to condole with him on the Kaiserin's death. He had received only three other letters from England, and he treasured them still. One was from General Hely-Hutchinson Waters, who was British Military Attaché in Berlin at the beginning of the century. He is to-day the most intimate of the ex-Kaiser's English friends.

On entering the house, the ex-Kaiser went upstairs to change and wash, and then in a few minutes I was summoned to a private audience in his study upstairs. It is quite a small room in the upper storey of the Tower with a view looking out on the garden. Here among rows of books and surrounded by his collection of family miniatures and photographs, the Imperial exile spends his afternoons in reading and writing. We sit down opposite each other at a small writing table, and I hand to him my list of written questions. Some of them are of a delicate nature. Will he answer all, or some, or none at all? As he reads them through, I calculate the chances. The last question, which is about religion, interests him. "Here is a question on which I could write much," he says gravely. He switches back to a previous question about whom he considers the best democratic brain in England. His face lights up, and he replies at once. "Here is a question which I can answer straight off. Bernard Shaw, of course! Have you read his 'Apple Cart'? A great play by the greatest of living satirists. What genius and what humour! But then Shaw is an Irishman. I wonder if anybody understands the moral of the play. This is how I interpret his meaning. With a stupid king and clever ministers, the ministers do what they want. With a clever king and stupid ministers the situation is only partly reversed. With a stupid king and stupid ministers everything goes wrong. And the ideal government is a clever king *and* clever ministers."

He is off on Shaw now, and there is no stopping him. As he talks, his whole face lights up. His eyes sparkle. His voice is the voice of a young man. There is a glow of health in his pink cheeks. He is vigorous and robust and looks remarkably well. As I listen, my confidence returns. I feel that my questions will be answered fully. He admires Shaw. "An American journalist," he says, "once compared my personal appearance with that of Shaw. He wanted to know whether I tried to make myself look like Shaw or whether Shaw strove to cultivate my appearance." The conversation is switched off to Russia and Japan. As an intensely religious man he hates Bolshevism. As the prophet who before the war predicted the danger to Europe of the yellow peril, he still visualises the necessity of Europe uniting against the East. I was amazed at the extent of his reading. Here surely is one of the world's greatest dilettante, a man who can talk with some authority on nearly every subject. He is and has always been a voracious reader. The books he prefers are travel descriptions, memoirs, and historical novels. In English literature he passes the

Baldwin test, for his favourite English authors are Dickens, Scott, and Marryat, all of whom he has read and loved from his childhood days. More recent favourites are Mr. Warwick Deeping and Mr. P. G. Wodehouse. He is not to be drawn regarding his hopes of a Hohenzollern restoration. "My attitude is straightforward," he says. "I shall return to Germany only if my people invite me." He is more forthcoming in reply to a compliment about his remarkable health. "All due to the simple life," he says with a smile. His every day, in fact, is regulated like clockwork. He is up at seven and dressed by eight, when he goes for a vigorous walk. At quarter to nine there are family prayers, at which he always reads a chapter from the Bible. Breakfast is at nine and is his principal meal of the day. From 9.30 to 11.30 he works in his garden, felling trees or planting roses. Every flower, every rose-bush, has a little tin ticket with the date of planting and an inscription "planted by Seine Majestaet." The rosarium reminds me of Frances, Lady Warwick's Garden of Friendship at Easton. From twelve to one he receives the reports of his secretaries, discusses the newspapers, and attends to his correspondence. Luncheon is at one and is a simple meal of two courses. After a short rest he retires to his study where he works until tea-time. After tea he goes back again to his study and reads or writes till eight. Dinner is at eight and is an even more frugal meal than luncheon. He is very temperate in all his habits. He eats sparingly, and the only alcohol he drinks is a glass of sparkling claret mixed with water. He smokes a long Turkish cigarette and an occasional light cigar. After dinner the household assembles in the smoking-room and listens while the ex-Kaiser reads aloud. At 10.15 the day is ended, and he retires to bed.

As I listen to the account of this exemplary existence, a gentleman of the household enters the room. "Quarter to one, Your Majesty!" he says with a profound bow. "All right, all right," says the ex-Kaiser cheerily. "You can go away. I haven't committed any indiscretions yet." He shows me his miniatures and his photographs. The miniatures are mostly presents from former crowned heads of Europe. There is a box from King Edward with his miniature set in brilliants and an almost identical box with a miniature of the late Tsar of Russia. As I look at the wistful face of Nicholas II, I feel that I would rather live in a hut on the moors and be free than live as the ex-Kaiser lives in Doorn, but that Doorn at any rate is preferable to the dark horrors of Ekaterinburg. The photographs include numerous pictures of himself in every stage of his career. There are photographs of him as a boy in kilts at Balmoral, in a sailor suit at Cowes. His own favourite is one of himself as a child of two in skirts. It is painted by Queen Victoria, who lives in his memory as the kindest and most understanding of his English relations.

The legend of the favourite grandmother and the favourite grandchild is maintained in a more concrete manner. Just before luncheon I am handed over to one of the gentlemen in waiting. We assemble in an anteroom. Here I meet the gentlemen of the household: Count Finckelstein and Count Hamilton, a Swede of Scottish descent, and am introduced to the Princess Hermine, his second wife, and his little stepdaughter. We wait for the ex-Kaiser. When he comes down again, he has changed again. He now wears a short black coat with winged collar and striped tie. In the tie is embedded a pin with a cameo of Queen Victoria.

Fortunately, Nowak has put me wise to this idiosyncrasy. Had I been a Turk, the ex-Kaiser would have worn some Turkish order or emblem. The cameo of Queen Victoria is in my honour, and I tactfully praise the beauty of the workmanship. At luncheon there is little formality. The Princess Hermine goes in first, followed by the ex-Kaiser, who holds the hand of his step-daughter and romps in with her. The Princess or Kaiserin, as she is always called at Doorn, is a dignified, self-possessed woman. I can guess that she has considerable influence over the ex-Kaiser. The conversation is in German and is mainly a duologue between the ex-Kaiser and myself. He plies me with questions. The range of his subjects is wide. He talks of his visits to the New Forest, of Lord Malmesbury and of the latter's grandfather, Admiral Sir E. A. J. Harris, who taught him tennis and who gave him James's Naval History—a monumental work in sixteen volumes. "I'm the only sailor in the world," he says with pride, "who has read the work through from beginning to end." After luncheon there is more conversation in the smoking room. He draws me into an alcove. He has more questions to ask. Why are our great English families selling their places and their art treasures?" I reply that they are being taxed out of existence. "It is the same in Germany," he answers and shakes his head. There are more questions about the Anglo-Catholic movement and the Prayer Book controversy in England. Here I am out of my depth, and, amazingly well informed about this, as indeed, about all religious developments, he himself supplies the answers. "The materialism of the present age will pass," he says. "Man's spiritual development has not kept pace with his material progress. The great races, especially England and Germany, will experience a religious revival."

After some twenty minutes his step-daughter comes up to him. "Mamma wishes to know if you will go upstairs," she says. The ex-Kaiser summons one of his gentlemen, who goes away and returns with a large scroll. The Kaiser unrolls it and hands it to me. It is a coloured portrait of himself. It is already signed with the date of my visit and the signature Wilhelm I.R. Written across the bottom in the ex-Kaiser's handwriting is a saying of Abraham Lincoln: "Nothing is settled finally until it is settled right." "Put it away in some corner," he says jocularly. "It may compromise you." Then with a warm goodbye and an energetic "you will have the answers to your questions in an hour," he gives his hand to his step-daughter and lets himself be led from the room.

With Nowak I go for a walk in the park. Doorn is not St. Helena. There are no Hudson Lowes. But it is depressing and flat enough for any one but a Dutchman. It is a kingdom of damp. Every one, including the Princess Hermine, suffers from rheumatism. Even the pigeons which swarm the park look bedraggled and jaded. There is only one exception to the prevailing gloom—the ex-Kaiser himself.

Exactly to the hour I am handed the replies to my written questions. They are in the ex-Kaiser's own neat and vigorous handwriting. I reproduce them with the exact translation from the German.

1. What is your impression regarding the behaviour of the British troops in the occupied territory?

The ex-Kaiser: "I have heard nothing but the best about them. They have borne themselves like the soldiers of a civilised state and of a well-disciplined army."

2. What do you think of the future relations between Germany and England?

"I hope that these two great peoples will live to see the day when, with a real understanding of each other, they will treat the common path of genuine friendship to the advantage and progress of all peoples."

3. What do you think of Mussolini?

"Mussolini has brought order into his country—a real, disciplined order. Italy to-day has become a land of peace and of work under united concentration of all the forces of the nation. That is Mussolini's achievement. A real man!"

4. Whom do you regard as the best democratic brain in Europe?

"Bernard Shaw (on account of his 'Apple Cart')."

5. In England your preface to the Empress Frederick's letters created great interest. Has any echo of this interest come to your Majesty's ears?

"I have received many letters on this subject from England. They made a great impression on me. The approval they expressed of the preface and the point of view they defended that, even in the case of an exiled monarch, there should be some limit imposed on family disclosures were proofs of the greatest chivalry."

6. Both in Germany and in England the description given by the historian Karl Nowak in his book "The Third German Empire" of the methods employed by Prince Bismarck has created a great sensation. Can you confirm the authenticity of Nowak's account? (This question refers to Nowak's statement that Bismarck bribed his own Ministers, notably the Emperor's chef de cabinet Lucanus, and that during a period of industrial unrest he had suggested to the Kaiser that the way to deal with the trouble was to shoot the workers down.)

The ex-Kaiser: "Nowak's account of the dismissal of Prince Bismarck is in every detail authentic. The incident between Bismarck and His Excellency von Lucanus described by Nowak corresponds word for word with the account given to me by my former chef de cabinet. The proposal which Bismarck made to me for dealing with a revolt is literally correct."

7. It is said that you exercised great influence over the writing of Nowak's book. In what form?

"It is not true. First, I had no inclination. Secondly, you seem to have little knowledge of how Nowak works. He writes only what he has proved to be authentic; that is, what he really knows and what he can defend by conviction. He does this with a polite, but nevertheless amazing, lack of consideration which must command every one's respect. He has made no exception in my case."

8. If I may ask a personal question, do you miss your shooting and other sporting activities, more especially yachting?

"An exiled monarch can neither shoot nor do many other things. That I have to live far from my dearly-loved country and my people to whom my whole being was dedicated is a trial imposed by God to which obediently and unresistingly I submit.

"Where my beautiful yacht is I do not know. The movement on the open sea, which I love above everything else, which is necessary to my health and which, above all, gives that feeling of largeness and of infinity, is indeed that which I miss most bitterly. For a love that is both deep and unchangeable binds me to the blue depths of the ocean. But this, too, is only a secondary thought. Important only is the future of my Fatherland and of the German and all other peoples and that one day one must face one's Maker and the world to come. And that, I am firmly persuaded, I shall do."

9. Do you believe that religion plays a larger or a smaller part in man's life since the war?

"Religion is for all peoples and for all mankind God's lawbook for all eternity. Individual peoples or persons can from time to time overstep these laws, but God remains the eternal foundation, without which mankind must perish."

As I left Doorn, the skies cleared and in the pale sunlight I strove to crystallise my impressions. In my student days in Berlin more than twenty years before I had seen the ex-Kaiser, reviewing his troops on the Tempelhofer Feld, riding down Unter den

Linden with the King of Spain, and on one or two other occasions which I have forgotten. Then he was and looked the Great War Lord. But I had not known him. To-day, he was an old bearded man who in the declining years of his life had found resignation as few men have found it.

I could react only to his own actions towards me. Of his charm and personal magnetism there could be no doubt. I was not and am not prejudiced in favour of absolute monarchs. Condemned to live in Doorn, I should have cut my throat. The ex-Kaiser's cheerfulness made a lasting impression on me. I doubt if any deposed monarch has ever borne his fate with greater equanimity. Partly it is to be explained by the intense religious feeling which to-day dominates his whole life. He regards his exile as a trial imposed by God, and to God's will he submits himself with the cheerful fearlessness of a man who is not afraid to face the Last Judgment. Partly, too, it can be accounted for by his extraordinary energy and by the amazing interest which he takes in every task, however trivial, to which he puts his hand. That he believes himself innocent of any blame for the war I am certain. That night when I reached my hotel in Utrecht I wrote an account of my visit. I submitted it to him the next day and it was returned to me approved and slightly amended the same evening. The corrections, written again in his own handwriting, were revealing. In one place I had written "I think that the statement that 'the ex-Kaiser is a very sad man, feeling terribly hurt by the one country that he loved—England' is a true estimate of the ex-Kaiser's attitude, that he still regards England as his second fatherland, that he did his personal best to keep peace, and that he regrets the English point of view which attributes to him the responsibility for the war." When my manuscript came back, the "still regards England" was stroked out and replaced by "regarded England"; the "regrets the English point of view" had been altered to "deeply wounded by the English point of view." There was one other very typical correction. In my article I had referred to his dog Arno as a "magnificent Alsatian." The word "Alsatian" was deleted and "German sheep-dog" written in its place!

Doubtless, the ex-Kaiser of 1929 was a very different person from the War Lord of 1909. The boisterous exuberance of the early years had been chastened. Nevertheless, I am convinced that we have not yet had the true picture of the ex-Kaiser. Nor can I believe that he is either the mountebank or the monster which the post-war historians have tried to make him. The extraordinary many-sidedness of his own character makes the drawing of a correct balance between his faults and his virtues almost impossible. If I wished to make an aphorism about him, I should say that he was too gifted intellectually to make a successful monarch. For that many-sided energy, that amazing intellectual vitality, which, perhaps because sex has played little or no part in his life, found and still finds its outlet in a thousand different directions, is not the attribute to a trivial or commonplace character. It may explain his failure as a monarch. It may be the reason why he has never grown up, never entirely put away childish things. But it makes him psychologically one of the most complex and interesting figures that history has ever known.

To-day, there is no villager in Doorn who does not speak highly of his generosity. He gives freely to the poor both in kind and in cash. He helps many, if indeed not most, of those Germans who have remained loyal to him. Of his gratitude to those who have tried to write impartially of him without having recourse to the usual mud-slinging I myself have had many proofs. From time to time he sends me books—generally about religion or the yellow peril. When in 1933 his favourite grandson came to England, he was put more or less under my tutelage. At the end of his visit I received from the ex-Kaiser a spontaneous and characteristic letter of thanks.

To-day, the ex-Kaiser belongs to a world which is past. But as an individual he has been more harshly treated than he deserves, and to lay on his shoulders the whole blame for the Great War is to misread its lesson and to make its repetition inevitable. As an individual, too, he is probably more human than was, say, Clemenceau, to take only one of the one-track-minded patriots, whose power to hate exalts them to eminence during the uncivilising process of war, and to do him justice I doubt if the ex-Kaiser would have made as foolish a peace as the obstinate Frenchman made. Certainly, he can challenge comparison, both as regards moral rectitude and ability, with many monarchs who figure in the school text-books as heroes; and ordinary decency, which has too long been silent in Europe, will one day compel history to revise its estimate of his character.

CHAPTER EIGHT

THE last chapter of this book falls chronologically into the journalistic period of my career. Its associations, however, are entirely Central European, and I have therefore included it in the place to which it belongs.

In the spring of 1929 I received a telegram from Nowak. He wished to see me urgently. He was interested in the translation rights of two English books: Mr. Lloyd George's "Slings and Arrows" and Lord Beaverbrook's "Politicians and the War." Using his telegram as a pretext, I arranged with my editor for ten days' leave of absence to be spent on the Continent, partly on business and partly as a holiday. The Beaverbrook Press had not yet turned its back on Europe, and my knowledge of Germany was still of some service to my newspaper. As to myself I had various reasons for wishing to go abroad. Six months in Fleet Street had brought back my innate Wanderlust with increased intensity. I wanted to see my boy who was in Switzerland. Moura, too, was returning to Berlin, after having acted for a long time as secretary and translator to Gorki at Sorrento. Jenia, too, was there and wished to consult me about the possibilities of a film contract in England. In addition to these sentimental considerations there was the desire to see Stresemann, who, alone of post-war politicians, had aroused my capacity for hero-worship. He was ill. A sound instinct told me that, if I did not go at once, I should never see him again. Nowak was at Baden-Baden. I took a circular ticket for Montreux, Baden-Baden, and Berlin.

At Montreux I spent three restful days with my wife and son, revisiting Geneva and looking up my friends at the League of Nations, rowing on the Lake and feeding the gulls. Are there any gulls in the world so tame and so clever at catching pellets of bread as the gulls of Lake Leman? I had twenty-four hours with Nowak at Baden-Baden, the charming little Kurort on the edge of the Black Forest. As it was deserted, its attractiveness was increased a thousandfold in my eyes.

The only other guests in the Hotel Stephanie were Sir Horace Rumbold, the British Ambassador, and his wife. I told him of my desire to see Stresemann. He shook his head. The German Foreign Minister still held his office, but he was a doomed man. The doctors wished him to resign. Stresemann, it is true, told them to go to hell, but special measures were taken to prevent him doing more than the minimum of essential work. The Ambassador himself had not seen him for several weeks. If to see Stresemann were the sole object of my journey to Berlin, I might as well go home.

This information depressed me, but I did not give up all hope. Before I left London, a prominent member of the German Embassy had told me a revealing story of the precautions taken by the Foreign Office to guard their chief from unnecessary interviews. Stresemann, who was suffering from an incurable kidney disease, was a most difficult patient. He knew that he was dying. Strict dieting and complete rest might have prolonged his life for a year or two. With a fine abandon he had made up his mind to renounce this self-denying ordinance and to live as he had always lived—fully and generously—to the last. Some time before he had been compelled to undergo a long cure at Wiesbaden, and in despair of inducing their patient to observe even the simplest dietary precautions the doctors had requested the German Foreign Office to attach a special private secretary to him, nominally to enable him to keep in touch with the Wilhelmstrasse, but actually to prevent the Minister from indulging in the sausages and beer, the beefsteaks and the Moselles, which he loved. For several weeks the secretary had watched over his chief with the attention and devotion of a hero-worshipper.

Finally, Stresemann grew weary of the restraint. He met guile with guile. One day, while he was walking on the outskirts of Wiesbaden with the faithful secretary, he stopped suddenly beside a telephone booth and puts his hand to his forehead. "Mein Gott," he exclaimed, "I've forgotten to telephone to Schubert about Neurath's transfer from Rome. See if you can get through to the Wilhelmstrasse from this booth. We'll just catch him before luncheon." The unsuspecting secretary entered the booth. While he was trying to obtain the long-distance connection with Berlin, Stresemann turned on his heel, hailed a passing taxi, and drove back to his hotel. When the secretary finally tracked him down, he found him in the restaurant with a broad grin on his face and the remains of a beefsteak and an empty bottle of choice Moselle before him.

In view of Stresemann's attitude towards life I felt that my chances of seeing him were not entirely hopeless. I had two claims on a favourable reception. I had written several articles supporting his policy, and he had liked them. I spoke German, and Stresemann, who was no linguist, was always glad to find an Englishman who spoke his language. If I could circumvent his watch-dogs, there was a sporting chance that he would receive me.

Having completed my business with Nowak, I spent the afternoon in exploring Baden-Baden. I strolled through the central park and regretted that I had brought no trout-rod. A stream ran through it, and in the warm April sunshine the trout were rising. I solemnly inspected the sanatorium of Dr. Dengler, where every year in the season the rich of England and America come to correct the ailments of self-indulgence. Among other qualities Dr. Dengler owes his success to the possession of a strong will. He has succeeded in imposing a firm discipline on a degenerate and over-sheltered aristocracy incapable of imposing it on itself. I foraged about in the antique shops and bought some worthless but attractive prints. And the same evening I left for Berlin.

The Berlin of April, 1929, was very different from the Berlin which I had visited so often in previous years. More poverty was visible in the streets, and in the absence of the American tourists the hotels were nearly empty. Prices were higher. The spate of bankruptcies was beginning. The great slump had not yet struck the capital with its full force, but its shadows were already projected. They lay most heavily on the faces of the citizens.

Recklessness and extravagance were still reflected on a sordid and unattractive night-life, but it was the recklessness and extravagance of despair. The population had abandoned faith in the Republic and in the future. Even the hard-working Prussian official seemed to have lost his former energy. There was, too, one of the usual government crises. The Socialists were making trouble over the payment of the instalments for the new German cruiser, "Ersatz-Pommern," and the government coalition seemed in some danger. It was not a very favourable moment for my interview with a sick and harassed Stresemann.

Immediately after my arrival I laid my plans. I had a letter from Nowak to Herr Eschenberg, a young protégé of Stresemann. I set in motion all the influence that I had in the German Foreign Office. I wrote a private letter to Stresemann himself. I enlisted the services of Harold Nicolson, who, in Sir Horace Rumbold's absence, was in temporary charge of the Embassy. Then, having done all that man could do, I made up my mind to extract the best I could from my visit in other directions. I called again on my old friend, General Seekt, and found him preoccupied with plans for the reform of the constitution. He was no fire-eater, but like many other moderate Germans he was in favour of putting an end to the interminable succession of interparty squabbles which were wrecking Parliamentary Government in Germany. I had two hours' interview with Dr. Hilferding, a former Austrian professor and then the Socialist Finance Minister of Germany. He looked tired and worn-out. He was frankly pessimistic—worried by the psychological effect of France's intransigence on reparations and by the attitude of the new generation in Germany, full of forebodings regarding the future of his own Party. The rich Germans, he told me, were leaving the country in order to avoid taxation. But taxation fell most heavily on the poor. Every German with an income of 1200 marks (£60) and over now paid income-tax.

I dined with Moura at Foerster's and asked her about Gorki. He had definitely left the Western world in order to devote the remainder of his life to the education and development of a new Russia. Since his return to the Bolshevik fold he had sold over

3,000,000 copies of his works in Russia alone. By the Russian people he was worshipped like a god.

As I listened, a feeling akin to remorse came over me. There was something impressive in the self-reliance of this man, a profound humanitarian, who at the age of sixty-two had convinced himself that all the things which he had once opposed so resolutely: tyranny, the use of force, the suppression of individual opinion, were justified if by their use a new and better order could be created. Was the new light to come from Russia? Like most men of my generation I was assailed by doubts. Vaguely I hoped for a new world which would be a selective compromise, combining the best features of capitalism and Bolshevism and avoiding the worst defects of both systems.

The next day Moura left for Baden in order to take her son to school. After seeing her off, I lunched with Frau von Siemens, the widow of the founder of the great Siemens electrical concern and a daughter of Helmholtz, the famous German physicist, who was the first man to investigate sound-waves and who paved the way for Herz, his pupil, and for Marconi. She was a charming old lady, very gentle and cultured and tolerant in all her views. She told me a poignant story of Chicherin, of whom she had been seeing a good deal. Chicherin was then in Berlin, undergoing a cure for advanced diabetes. He was being treated by Klemperer, the brilliant German specialist, who had been summoned to attend Lenin after his first stroke. Klemperer, moved by the utter loneliness of Chicherin's existence, had asked Frau von Siemens to take pity on him, and she had thrown open to him the beautiful grounds of her country-home at Wannsee. And there he sat all day reading French novels—a tired, nervous wreck of a man seeking to forget and to be forgotten.

One day she had given a small open-air musical party for the benefit of a well-known quartette. As the quartette played on her verandah, she saw Chicherin move his chair nearer and nearer. His book was discarded. He was listening rapturously, until finally she saw the tears course down his cheeks. After her guests had departed, she spoke to him. "You are fond of music?" she said. His bent shoulders shook, as he apologised to her for his emotion. Then he told her his story. He had not been out of doors or heard good music since he became a Bolshevik. As a young man of good family and fortune he had had to decide between music and Socialism. He had chosen Socialism and, knowing that he could not combine the one with the other, had deliberately put music out of his life. In his youth he had been a pupil of Anton Rubinstein. Now his diabetes was under control, but his nerves were shattered. The Bolsheviks wanted him to go back to the Crimea. He did not wish to go. This was a very different Chicherin from the Commissar for Foreign Affairs who in 1918 had stared at me with red-rimmed eyes, mistrusting my every word. Here, too, was a strange contrast: Gorki, who at first had doubted and who had spent his every winter in the warm sunshine of Italy, had at last convinced himself and was going back; Chicherin, who for twelve years had directed the foreign policy of Soviet Russia, now asked nothing more of life than to be left in peace.

Every day, too, I saw Jenia, dined or supped with her, and went to the theatre. She, at any rate, seemed happy and was doing well. She was still unmarried, with her whole life before her. She had mapped it out in her mind and with the confidence of youth was preparing to construct it according to plan. Her cheerful egotism banished all the gloom from my thoughts. There were, she thought, too many pessimistic people in the world, and both from politeness and from conviction I agreed with her.

My days passed pleasantly enough, but there was still no news of my Stresemann interview. Every day I went to the Wilhelmstrasse. I saw Eschenberg. I was put off with vague promises. I had to leave on Sunday morning at the latest. When Friday came without any message, I abandoned hope. I went to see Harold Nicolson at the Embassy. He was very kind, but in his condolences there was a faint but justifiable note of "I told you so." Then, on the Friday evening, I received an urgent message to telephone at once to Herr Kaufmann of the German Foreign Office. Stresemann would receive me to-morrow at 12.30. There were, however, a lot of "buts." I was to be at the Foreign Office five minutes before the appointed time. I was to stay not one second longer than fifteen minutes. Bernhard, his secretary, would come into the room at 12.45 and I was to go. The interview was to be absolutely private, and not even the fact that I had seen him must be published. Above all, I was not to excite the Minister in any way.

The same instructions were repeated to me when I arrived at the Foreign Office the next morning. I was received to the minute. As I entered the room, Stresemann came forward to meet me. There was a smile on his face. His handshake was vigorous enough. But the change in his appearance chilled me and the commonplace "How do you do" froze unuttered on my lips. The burly frame had shrunk so that his great bullet-head looked grotesquely large. The colour of the face was the pale yellow of faded paper relieved only by sinister black pouches under the eyes. His voice, always harsh, was now little more than a hoarse whisper.

The old energy, however, was still there. If his walk was laboured, his legs now unable to support the heavy stomach, his mind was as alert as ever. We sat down opposite each other at a small table. He lit a German cigar and plunged at once into politics. The internal situation was bad. There would have to be some curbing of the power of Parliament. But there was no necessity to reform the constitution. Under the present constitution the President and the Chancellor had power enough to put an end to the Parliamentary deadlock. The problem was one of personalities and of the method of approaching political problems. German Ministers had more expert knowledge than English Ministers, but they were more hide-bound and more conventional. "An illustration? Well, I'll give you two. During the war I begged Delbrück, who was then Minister of Food, to import all the stores he could, coffee, cocoa, maize, flour, anything and everything, from Italy before she entered the war. What did our conventional Delbrück do? His answer was: 'What will happen to my stores and to me if the war ends before I can use them?' I had the same experience with the Ministry of Marine. When I implored them to build more submarines, their answer was: 'What will happen after the war to the extra commanders and first lieutenants who will have to be created?' I had no influence then. I was only a member of a Reichstag Commission. But now, although I am a Minister, I still have the same difficulties."

Passing from the internal situation to foreign affairs he began to explain to me how closely the fate of the Republic was linked with a conciliatory Allied policy towards Germany. He had hardly begun to question me about the feeling in England: was public opinion in favour of Sir Austen Chamberlain's pro-French policy, did he think he could obtain anything from the French by flattery, when Bernhard came into the room and said that the Spanish Ambassador was waiting. I looked down discreetly at my wrist-watch. It was exactly 12.45. My heart sank. My interview seemed ended almost before it had begun. Stresemann nodded. "All right," he said, "I'll see him in one minute." When Bernhard had left, he took me by the arm. "We must talk this out," he said. "You know what Ambassadors are. They don't like being kept waiting. If you have time to stay, we can continue our conversation. I'll be through in seven minutes." Then he pushed me into an anteroom on the opposite side from that by which I had entered. When the seven minutes were up and the Ambassador had left, he came and fetched me himself. I felt rather like a guilty schoolboy.

The conversation which followed lasted for over an hour. Stresemann talked with complete frankness. He told me about his career, about his hopes and ambitions. During the war he had been a patriot. He had worked for Germany's victory to the last. To-day, he was still a patriot. Germany must have a place in the sun. But after the war had been lost and won, he had realised that the old order had vanished for ever and he had worked sincerely for peace and conciliation among the peoples of Europe. He had favoured an Anglo-Franco-German understanding. He had won eighty per cent of the German population for his policy. He had brought his country to the League of Nations. He had signed Locarno. He had given, given, given, until his countrymen had turned against him. He worked himself up into a nervous passion as he spoke of Poland. There were no Germans, he said, who would fight for the return of Alsace-Lorraine, but there was not a German from the ex-Kaiser to the poorest Communist who would ever accept the present German-Polish frontier. With a rectification of the Polish frontier Europe could have peace for a hundred years.

As he spoke, beads of sweat stood out under his eyes. His voice grew hoarser. "Locarno!" he said with increasing bitterness. "It is five years since we signed Locarno. If you had given me one concession, I could have carried my people. I could still do it to-day. But you have given nothing, and the trifling concessions which you have made have always come too late."

I told him that public opinion in England was changing, that there were many people who were in favour of a square deal for Germany. He was not appeased.

"I know, I know," he said impatiently. "In their private conversations your diplomatists, your Ministers, are friendly and full of promises. But in public, at Geneva, everywhere they fall into line with the French. And it is by their public actions that I must judge them. Patience, they say, and all will be well. But can they not see that the ground here is slipping away under my feet?"

He was bitter over England because he had expected too much from her. England, he knew, was not interested in foreign affairs. But there was a limit. He had sent his son to Cambridge. The boy had just come back astounded at the lack of knowledge of the English undergraduates. Their only question about Germany was: "When is the ex-Kaiser coming back?" Most bitter of all were his references to Sir Austen Chamberlain. He had never placed high hopes on the French. But Chamberlain was different. He had signed Locarno with him. With him, too, he had drunk the loving cup at the Guildhall. He had asked him for a concession about the date of ending the occupation—a concession which would have made the reparation's question and all his internal problems much easier. But even on this point there had been no concession. Did the man really believe that he could cajole the French into concessions? It was no use fencing with the French. They were clever. There was only one way to deal with them: to take a line and to stand rock-firm on it. Wittingly, or unwittingly, Sir Austen had played France's game all through. He had given him, Stresemann, not a single court card.

The sentences had been rapped out in a series of short, breathless jerks. Now he pulled up, as if realising that he had gone too far. He smiled wearily and shrugged his shoulders. "Sir Austen is a gentleman," he said. "I know he means well. But for the last ten years Europe has been suffering from gentlemen who mean well."

He rose from his chair and walked slowly towards the window. The fire had gone from his eyes. He was in a state of exhaustion. "Well," he said at last. "Nothing remains now except brute force. The future is in the hands of the new generation. And the youth of Germany, which we might have won for peace and for the new Europe, we both have lost. That is my tragedy and your crime."

As we shook hands, I knew that it was for the last time. The date was April 13th, 1929. Six months later Stresemann was dead.

I went out into the warm spring sunshine and walked to our Embassy to say goodbye to Harold Nicolson and to tell him what Stresemann had said. To Harold there was little that was new in it, and I imagine that he agreed with most of it. Then, missing my luncheon, for I was already late, I hurried to my hotel, where Jenia was waiting for me. I had promised to drive her out to Wannsee for tea.

All the way out I sat beside her in silence. I was still under the emotional influence of my interview. I had no illusions about Stresemann. I knew that he wanted what every German patriot wants—a strong and prosperous Germany. But I believed and still believe that he was prepared to build it on the foundations of the new European order for which, indeed, millions of men had given their lives. There was, too, profound truth in much that he had said. A policy based on fear and force could have only one end. It could not be justified even by expediency. Sooner or later it must lead to war. Nearly eleven years had passed since the war, and the smouldering fires of hate, instead of being quenched, were being fanned again into flames. Mr. Winston Churchill's dictum flashed again through my mind: "In war resolution, in defeat defiance, in victory magnanimity, in peace goodwill." In the post-war policy towards Germany there had been neither magnanimity nor goodwill.

One thing was certain. The new Europe, which we had hoped to build, was crumbling rapidly. The period of glory was ended. The armed peace of the victors had made a travesty of the League of Nations, had sown resentments deeper than the war had created. It was destroying the German Republic. In the Succession States millions of Slavs had been liberated from the yoke of Austria and Hungary. Freedom, education, and countless new benefits had been bestowed on the former down-trodden. But, in spite of enlightened statesmen like President Masaryk, they had not benefited by their own experience. Nearly everywhere they were repeating the same injustices and the same intolerance as their former oppressors had once shown towards them. Not a single one of the problems left by the Peace had been solved. Germany was a festering sore. Hungary, who had learnt least from the war, was, admittedly, a difficult problem. But Austria, whose favour and goodwill the little Entente could have won without difficulty in 1922, had been left in hopeless destitution. Bulgaria, whose people at any rate should not have been punished for the sins of their former King, was still without an outlet to the Ægean. The choicest fruits of man's intelligence, peace by enlightenment, fraternity, justice, and fair play, democracy, freedom of individual opinion, had been allowed to rot ungathered. Common sense had gone by the board. Idealism was dead, and everywhere the cynics and the armament firms were coming into their own.

Doubtless, the French would blame the Germans and, when the clash came, would flatter themselves that this policy of the strong hand had been fully justified. Doubtless, too, in future years historians would debate the question whether a different peace and a different policy would have stabilised democratic government in Germany. It was a question which would never be proved. But in my heart I knew that the Republic had never been given a chance.

Much as I tried to understand the point of view of the French, I could not appreciate the logic of their terrible consistency. I knew, as every one knew, that there were militarists in Germany —irreconcilable militarists who wished to re-establish rule by the sword. In 1919 they had been discredited. But ever since Versailles French policy had played into their hands. There could be no peace in Europe so long as any Frenchman who dared to suggest a policy of reconciliation with Germany was considered a traitor by other Frenchmen and so long as German militarists were allowed to proclaim that the German army had been defeated not by the arms of the Allies, but by the treachery of German Socialists and Republicans.

Yet by some fatality French fear and German aggression seemed to be working together in a tragic combination for evil. European diplomacy, including our own, had failed to check these currents. Its time, its energy, and its intelligence had been spent in elaborating finicky formulæ and in devising an endless series of patch-work agreements which, at the best, afforded only a temporary postponement of trouble and which were often out of date before they were concluded. They bore no relation to the first principles of European policy: a Franco-German understanding or inevitable war sooner or later. Their structure was as fragile as a cobweb. They would be swept away as easily.

Try as I might I was unable to rid myself of my forebodings. This was supposed to be the age of reason and scientific progress. Never before had the scientists and economists played so important a rôle in public affairs. But they had found no solution for the chaos which had been created. The financiers, the great business geniuses, stood the critical test no better. True, the absurd reparations claims had been fixed by the politicians and the bureaucrats. But the financiers must have foreseen the dislocations which would be caused to the world's exchanges and to international trade. At the time they had made no protest, or, if they did, it was not vocal. Hate had dominated their judgment, and the hate had been prolonged until international confidence had been destroyed. In the last war the moral factor had been as important as money and machine guns. On whose side would the moral factor be in the next war? Would the peoples of Europe march again if their governments drifted into war or would they turn against the muddlers?

My mood continued until we had almost reached Wannsee. Then, Jenia, who had been very understanding, pulled me up with a jerk.

"Roman Romanovitch," she said, "enough, enough, enough! Stop thinking about these fusty politicians. Who cares about politicians any way? You're getting old."

I laughed. We strolled over to a little restaurant with a verandah overlooking the lake. We were the only guests on the terrace. Although it was a Saturday, it was too early in the year for the trippers. The sun was setting, and one part of the lake was already in the shadows. There was almost no wind, and, spread out across the home bay, the few sailing boats that were out were trying rather helplessly to make harbour. The whole scene was extraordinarily peaceful.

As I was drinking my Russian tea and listening to Jenia's chatter, an old woman with a basket of flowers came on to the verandah. She was poorly clad and her face was pinched, but, like all the German lower classes, she was neat and clean and very polite. Recklessly I bought the whole basket and, heaping the flowers on Jenia's lap, I said to her: "Spring violets for youth! I, too, would be young again."

My banter was cut short by the sound of marching feet. I leant over the balustrade. Down the path below us came a band of forty or fifty young men. They were dressed in breeches and khaki shirts. Their faces were bronzed. Their legs were sturdy. Their physique compared very favourably with that of English youth. But for the fact that they marched in military order, they might have been hikers or Boy Scouts.

"Who are these lads?" I asked Jenia.

She gave a cursory glance. "National Socialists, I expect," she answered without any show of interest. "Young fools playing at soldiers. Nobody takes them seriously."

Involuntarily my mind went back to my interview. I saw again the yellow face of the stricken Stresemann. I heard again the harsh, disillusioned whisper: "And the youth of Germany, which we might have won for peace, we both have lost."

In that moment my depression returned. When I looked back on my ten years in Central Europe, I felt a sense of futility and shame. I had seen the fire, but, like so many others during those frivolous post-war years, I had not helped, as even the most insignificant could have helped, to quench it. And my own ideals had perished in the flames.

Were the Mussolinis and the biologists right who said that war was a physical necessity of man and that alternating periods of war and peace were a natural sequence in man's history? Or was it merely that I belonged to a lost generation? I could find no satisfactory answer. In my doubts I was conscious only of one fact. My generation was tired.

Involuntarily, my mind went back to the last words of one of my wild Macgregor ancestors spoken to his son on his deathbed nearly three hundred years before: "Keep thou unsoiled the freedom which I leave thee as a birthright. Barter it neither for the rich garment, nor for the stone-roof, nor for the coveted board. Son of the Mist! be free as thy forefathers. Own no lord, receive no law, take no hire...."

In twenty years I had changed my profession five times. I had been unable to adjust my life to this business of living. Now, at the age of forty-one, I was going into popular journalism in Fleet Street, still prepared to gamble with Fate, thankful, when so many of my generation were without work, that I was able to carry on, to earn my bread and butter, and to provide the means to educate my son.

INDEX

Akers-Douglas, 185, 189
Aleander, King, of Yugoslavia, 289
Allen, Colonel, 206
Alsace-Lorraine, 338
Anglo-Oesterreichische Bank, 154, 156-7, 170, 187
Anne of Bohemia, 47
Anti-Bolshevik intervention, 30
Armistice Day in Sarajevo, 281
Aronowitz, 304, 305
Astor, Lady, 19, 20
Austrian and Hungarian Reparation Loans, 215
Austrian Reconstruction Loan, 187
Aveling, Frank, 117, 239, 240

Baldwin, Mrs., 185
Balfour, 11, 13-15, 32
Barclay, Sir Colville, 259
Bark, M. Peter, 165-67, 187, 191, 215, 219, 256, 304, 306-7
Barry, Gerald, 310
Beaverbrook, Lord, 27-29, 90, 306-8, 331
Begbie, Harold, 19
Bela Kun, 60, 64
Belgrade, 36, 37
Beneš, Dr., 62, 67, 72-6, 82, 132, 146, 151-54, 187-89, 190-92, 219, 228, 243-44, 255, 276
Bergen, 10
Bethel, Lord, 252
Bexhill, 25-27
Birch, John Henry Stopford, 85-89
Birley, Dr. J. L., 210, 213-14
Blair, Colonel James, 272
Blaške, Pan, 135, 158
Blumenfeld, R. D., 30
Bogretsoff, Colonel, 147
Bohemia, 48

Bolsheviks, 3, 4, 7, 12, 15, 19, 20, 26, 304
Boyle, Irene, 65, 124
Brade, Sir Reginald, 30
Bridgeman, Reginald, 174
British Military Mission, The, 174
Brittain, Sir Harry, 9
Bubela, Ctibor, 216
Bud, Dr., 259
Bureš, 135

Capuchins, Convent of the, 182
Carnegie, Andrew, 31
Carnock, Lord, 21
Casanova, 145
Cecil, John, 117, 121, 141, 146-48, 215
Ceruojeveč, Ivan, 288
Chamberlain, Sir Austen, 338, 339
Cheka, The, 5, 6
Chicherin, 4, 335
Churchill, Winston, 15, 30, 31, 55, 58, 78, 340
Clark, Sir William, 36
Clerk, Sir George, 37, 49, 50, 52, 60-66, 86-91, 99, 114, 115, 121, 136, 153, 159, 161, 167, 189, 215-16, 219, 228-233, 236-41, 245, 256
Cobb, Mr., 252
Coulson, Basil, 50, 65, 247
Crane, Richard, 117
Cromie, Captain, 8, 9
Curie, M. and Mme., 120
Currency Bill, The new, 310
Curzon, Lord, 73
Czech Land Reform Law, 188
Czechs, 49-57, 67, 74-76

D'Abernon, Lord, 89, 90, 280
Dalmatian Islands, 302, 303

345

Darton, T. H., 217
Deeping, Warwick, 323
De Forest, Baron, 239-245
Degoutte, General, 202, 204-5
Delbrück, 337
Delibes, 180
Dengler, Dr., 333
Denikin, General, 30, 36
De Valera, 314
Dickson, A. S. M., 160, 286-88, 291-92
Die Meistersinger, 302
Diocletian, Palace of, 289
Dorten, Dr., 202
Douglas, 233
Drummond, Sir Eric, 11
Dunsany, Lord, 91

East Lothian, 30
Einstein, Mr. Lewis, 236, 238
Engliš, 255

Faringdon, Lord, 160
Feldkirchen, 45
Ferdinand, Tsar, 106
Fettes, 37, 38
Foreign Office, 5, 6, 11
Franz Ferdinand, Archduke, 116, 282
Franz Josef, Emperor, 183, 184, 257
Freeman, Victor E., 291-95

Geduldiger, 218, 220
George V, King, 17
Gilroy, Charlie, 213
Goldwyn, Samuel, 309
Goode, Sir William, 188, 238, 260, 262-63, 296
Goodwillie, 259
Gordon, John, 219
Gorki, 222-23, 334, 336
Gosling, Cecil, 49
Graham, Sir Ronald, 11, 299

Hailsham, Lord, 305
Hambling, Sir Henry, 252
Hamlyn, Ralph, 177-81, 184, 187, 194, 217
Hanbury-Williams, General Sir John, 179
Hardinge, Lord, 11
Harris, Admiral Sir E. H. J., 324

Harvey, Sir Ernest, 165, 252
Helmholtz, 335
Henderson, Mr. Arthur, 21-23, 180
Hermine, The Princess, 324
Herz, 335
Hicks, Will, 26, 220-25
Hilferding, Dr., 334
Hitler, Herr, 129
Hoare, Sir Samuel and Lady Maude, 19, 89
Hohler, Sir Thomas, 189
Holden, Sir Edward, 179
Hooper, Bernard, 179-181
Hoover, Herbert, 260
Hotowetz, Dr., 153, 255
Hutchison, Lord, 253

Jan Hus, Statue of, 47
Jenia, 254-55, 273-74, 317, 331, 336, 340, 343
John, Augustus, 28

Kaplan, "Dora," 3, 8
Karachen, 4
Karl, Emperor, 104-106
Karolyi, Count, 174
Kaufmann, Herr, 336
Kennard, Sir Howard, 279
Kenworthy, Commander, 253
Kerensky, 94, 180
Keynes, J. Maynard, 16
Kilmarnock, Lord, 200
Kitchener, Lord, 86
Kleinwort, Sir Alexander, 252
Klemferer, 335
Konopišt, 116, 117
Kramař, Dr. Karel, 67, 77-79
Kremlin, The, 11
Kropotkin, Princess, 321

Lacroma, 302, 303, 304
Latter, John, 46, 50
Lawrence, General Sir Herbert, 165, 181, 252, 291-93
League of Nations, 225, 238
Leefe, Walter Scott, 241
Leeper, Rex, 11, 26-7
Lenin, 4, 5, 11, 12, 22, 224
Lenz, Dr., 235
Leverhulme, Lord, 313
Lindley, Sir Francis, 174, 180
Liška, Pan, 126, 127

346

Litvinoff, 3, 10, 26-7
Lloyd George, 13, 14, 77, 331
Lobkowitz, Princess, 65
Locrano, 338, 339
Loeffelholz, Herr, 135
"Luna," 266, 267

MacDonald, Ramsay, 247, 248
Macgregor, 33-35, 344
Macmillan, Sir Frederick, 319
Madonna of the Rock, 285, 286
Maid Lilliard, 211
Mallet, Sir Bernard, 22
Malmesbury, Lord, 324
Manzi Fé, M., 252
Marconi, 335
Marinkovitch, Voya, 280
Masaryk, T. G., 63, 67-72, 74-76, 85, 146, 189-91, 192, 212, 233, 243, 341
Matthews, Theo, 318
Maximilian of Mexico, Emperor, 283
Mažuranič, 270
McCardie, Justice, 305
McKechnie, 233, 234
McNab, Father Vincent, 213
Metternich, 57
Meyrick, Mrs., 171
Michiels, 133
Milner, Lord, 17-19, 29
Morand, Paul, 144
Moscow, 3-8, 11, 14, 28, 40, 70
Moscow Art Theater, 95
Moura, 5, 40, 147, 209, 220-24, 226, 231, 334-35
Mozart, 59, 143-45, 180
Mussolini, 102, 293, 303, 326-27

Neilson, 247
Nicolson, Harold, 15, 21, 334, 340
Norman, Montagu, 150, 152, 165, 179, 180, 247, 310
Northcliffe, Lord, 210
Nowak, Karl Friedrich, 318-34

Page, Philip, 91
Paget-Thurston, 206
Parr, Raymond, 259
Peace Conference, The, 13, 192
Pearson, Fred, 220
Pearson, Sir Arthur, 260
Peel, Lord, 30
Peterson, Maurice, 215, 228, 233, 235-36
Poliakova, Nastia, 147

Ponsonby, Sir Frederick, 318
Pontnik, Marshal, 280
Porters, R. H., 179-80
Prague, 36-40, 45-52, 54, 58, 59-67, 84, 94, 110
Prince of Wales, The, 275
Prince Rupert, 47
Prinkipo, 15

Račič, Puniča, 311
Rada, Vladika, 289
Radek, 4
Radič, Stepan, 269, 312
Rašin, Dr., 67, 76, 149-51
Raubritter or robber barons, 198
Red Terror, The, 8
Reel of Tulloch, 36
Reimer, Karl, 59
Rhineland Separatist Movement, 202
Richard II, 47
Rigby, 239, 240, 241, 243
Riihimäki, 4
Ringhoffer, Baron, 132
Rob Roy, 32, 35
Robson, Fred, 26
Rolland, M. Romain, 316
Rosenberg, 154-57, 172, 187
Rosslyn, Lord and Lady, 167, 275, 309
Rubinstein, Anton, 336
Ruggieri, 140
Ruhr, The, 202, 204-5, 207
Rumbold, Sir Horace, 317, 332, 334
Russia, 4, 12, 28, 30, 36, 39-40, 71

Sacher, Madame, 174-75, 184
Salm, Count, 174
Sarajevo, 281
Savinkoff, Boris, 94
Schratt, Frau, 183, 184
Scott, Sir Leslie, 305
Seekt, General, 334
Seipel, Monsignor, 101, 185
Seymour, Cynthia, 65, 124
Sharp, Clifford, 91
Shaw, Bernard, 315, 322
Siepmann, Harry, 260, 262, 263
Simon, Dr., 154, 187, 188, 208
Smith, Babington, 160
Snowden, Lady, 185
Sonntag, Kuneš, 216, 255
Soviet Government, 4
Spencer-Smith, 150-59, 170, 172, 180, 209-10, 219, 241, 254

Speyside, 32, 33
St. Joachimsthal, 120-21
Stanislavsky, 95
Steed, Wickham, 40
Steel-Maitland, Sir Arthur, 29, 40
Sternberg, Count Adalbert, 58
Stevenson, Sir James, 310
Strakosch, Sir Henry, 165
Strauss, Richard, 195
Stresemann, Gustav, 273, 317, 331-340, 343
Stuart, Prince Charles Edward, 7, 313
Švehla, Dr., 67, 76, 191
Sverljuga, Stanko, 270, 271, 278-9, 282

Thelwall, Colonel, 273
Thirty Years' War, 47, 48
Thomas, J. H., 20, 21
Thornhill, 273
Tilly, William, 274, 275
Tirard, M., 201
Trotsky, 4, 81
Turnbull, Malcolm, 301
Tusar, Vlastimil, 79, 80

Versailles, 19, 25, 130, 232, 342
Vojnovič, 276-81, 284-86, 290, 294-95

Von Kuehlmann, 318
Von Siemans, Frau, 335
Voženilek, 243, 245

Wagner, 59, 180
Walko, Dr., 259
Warsaw, 29
Waters, General Hely-Hutchinson, 321
Watson, Seton, 40
Waverley novels, 211, 212
Webb, Mr. and Mrs. Sidney, 20
Wells, H. G., 70, 91-95
Whitehall, 30
Wilhelm II, Ex-Kaiser, 317-29, 338-39
Wilson, President, 191
Winslow, Alan, 87, 247
Wolff, 135-39
Wood, Sir Henry, 91
World Economic Conference, 10
Worsley, Sir Arthur, 252

Young, George, 217
Young, Sir Alban, 37

Žižka, 125